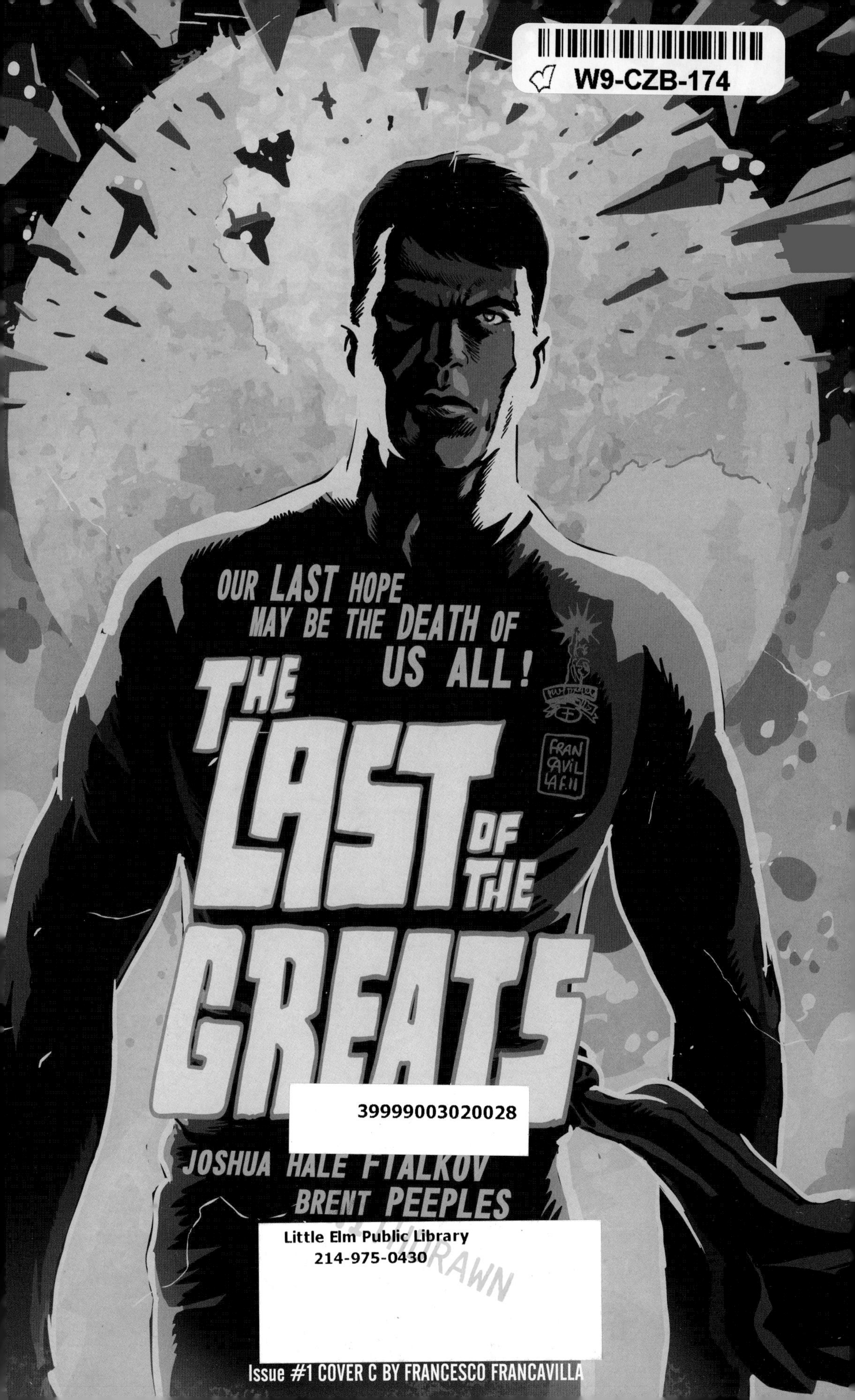
OUR LAST HOPE
MAY BE THE DEATH OF
US ALL!
THE LAST OF THE GREATS
JOSHUA HALE FIALKOV
BRENT PEEPLES
Issue #1 COVER C BY FRANCESCO FRANCAVILLA

THE LAST OF THE GREATS

Created by **JOSHUA HALE FIALKOV** and **BRENT PEEPLES**

Meet mankind's last hope for survival. He's called The Last, and he hates our guts.

Writer JOSHUA HALE FIALKOV
Penciller BRENT PEEPLES

Inker MATTHEW WAITE (chapter 1-2), NICK NIX (chapter 3-5)
Colorist MIRKA ANDOLFO (chapter 1-2), EDDY SWAN (chapter 3-5)

MAT LOPES (chapter 3), BRIAN BUCCELLATO (chapter 3), BLOND (chapter 3)

Letterer TROY PETERI
Logo KODY CHAMBERLAIN
Editor ROB LEVIN

Special thanks to TONY FLEECS **and** PHIL SMITH

IMAGE COMICS, INC.
Robert Kirkman - chief operating officer
Erik Larsen - chief financial officer
Todd McFarlane - president
Marc Silvestri - chief executive officer
Jim Valentino - vice-president

Eric Stephenson - publisher
Todd Martinez - sales & licensing coordinator
Jennifer de Guzman - pr & marketing director
Branwyn Bigglestone - accounts manager
Emily Miller - administrative assistant
Jamie Parreno - marketing assistant
Sarah deLaine - events coordinator
Kevin Yuen - digital rights coordinator
Tyler Shainline - production manager
Drew Gill - art director
Jonathan Chan - senior production artist
Monica Garcia - production artist
Vincent Kukua - production artist
Jana Cook - production artist
www.imagecomics.com

For more visit www.thelastofthegreats.com
Cover BRENT PEEPLES and IMAGINARY FRIENDS STUDIOS

TABLE OF CONTENTS

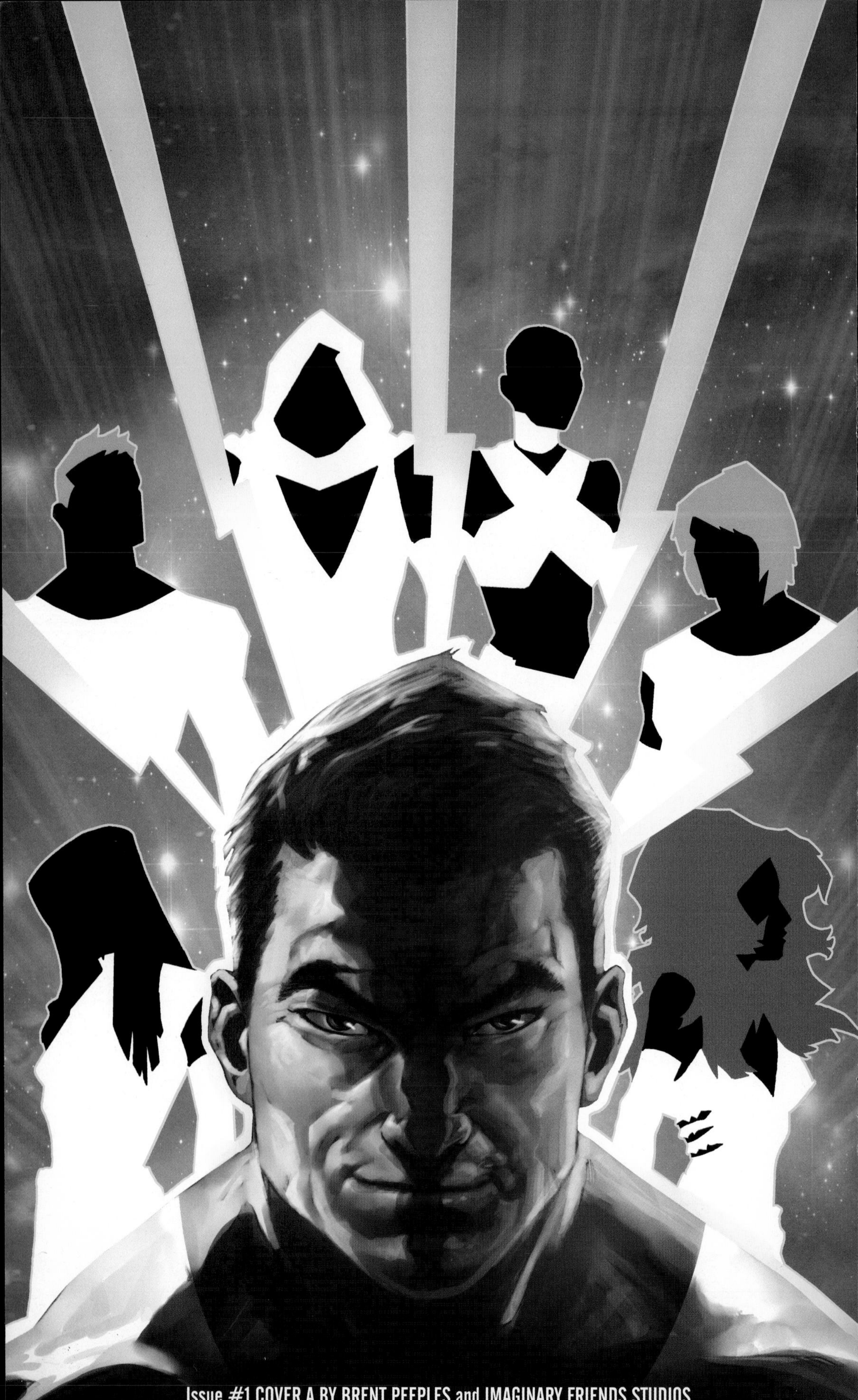

Issue #1 COVER A BY BRENT PEEPLES and IMAGINARY FRIENDS STUDIOS

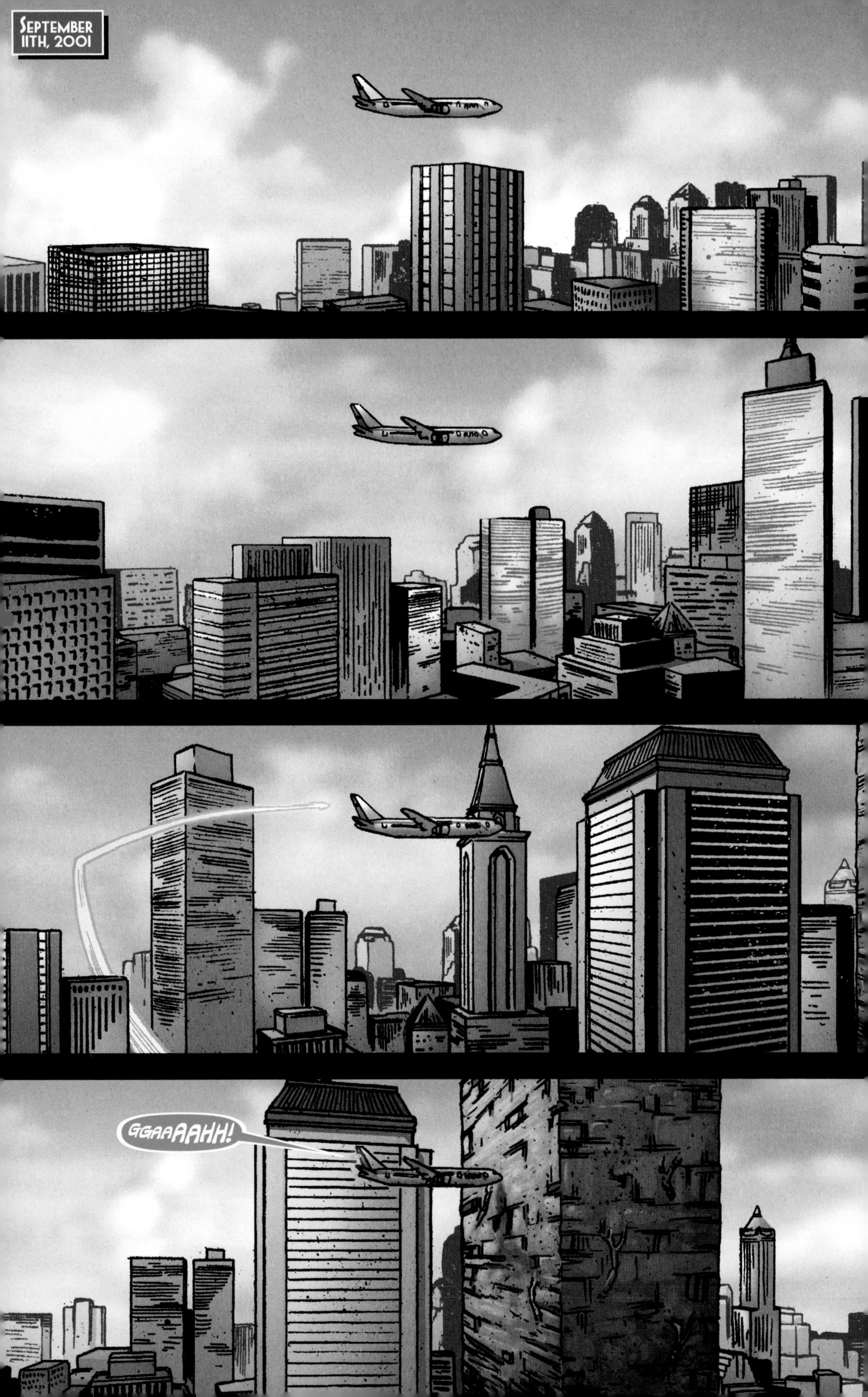
SEPTEMBER 11TH, 2001
GGAAAAHH!

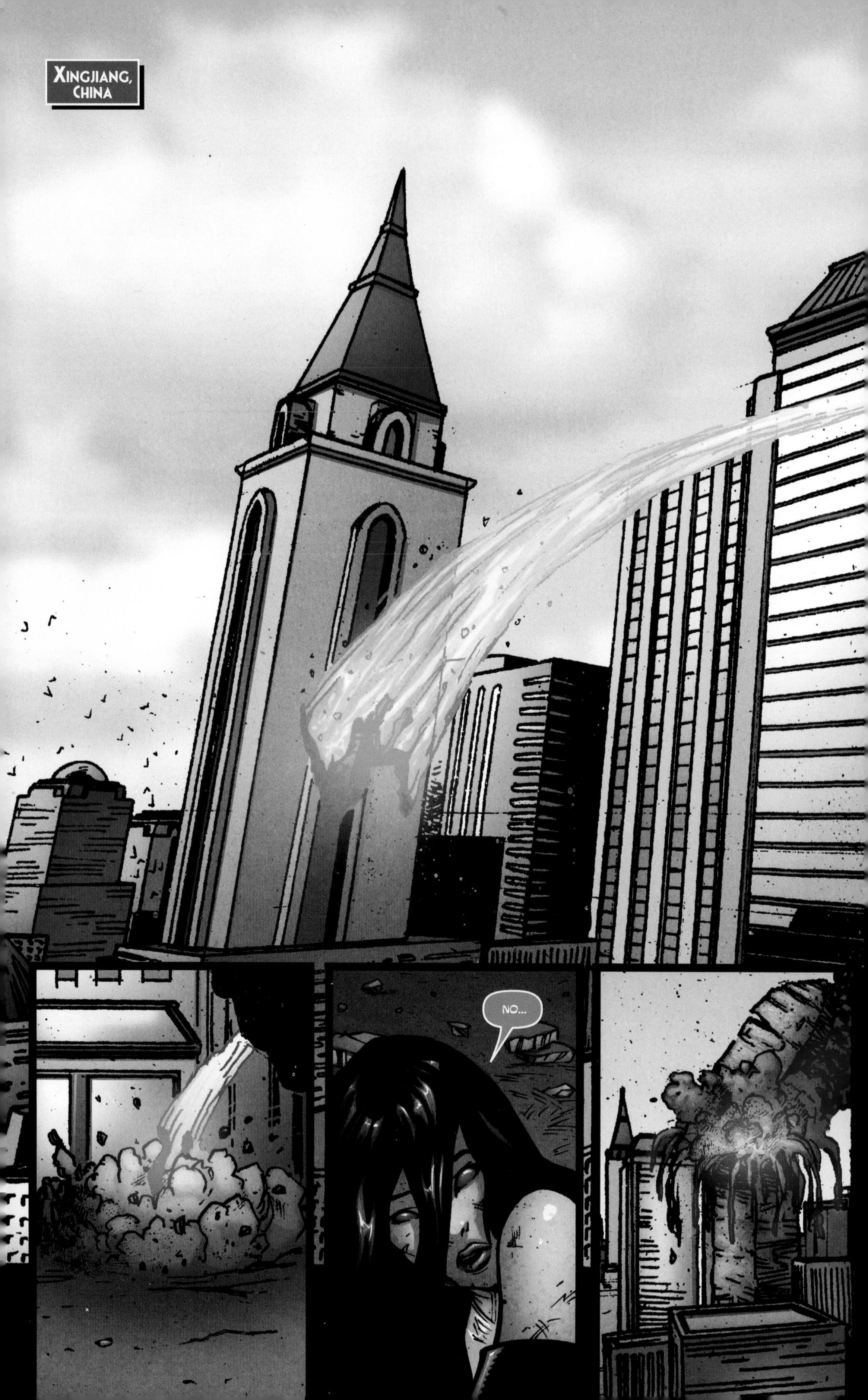
XINGJIANG, CHINA
NO...

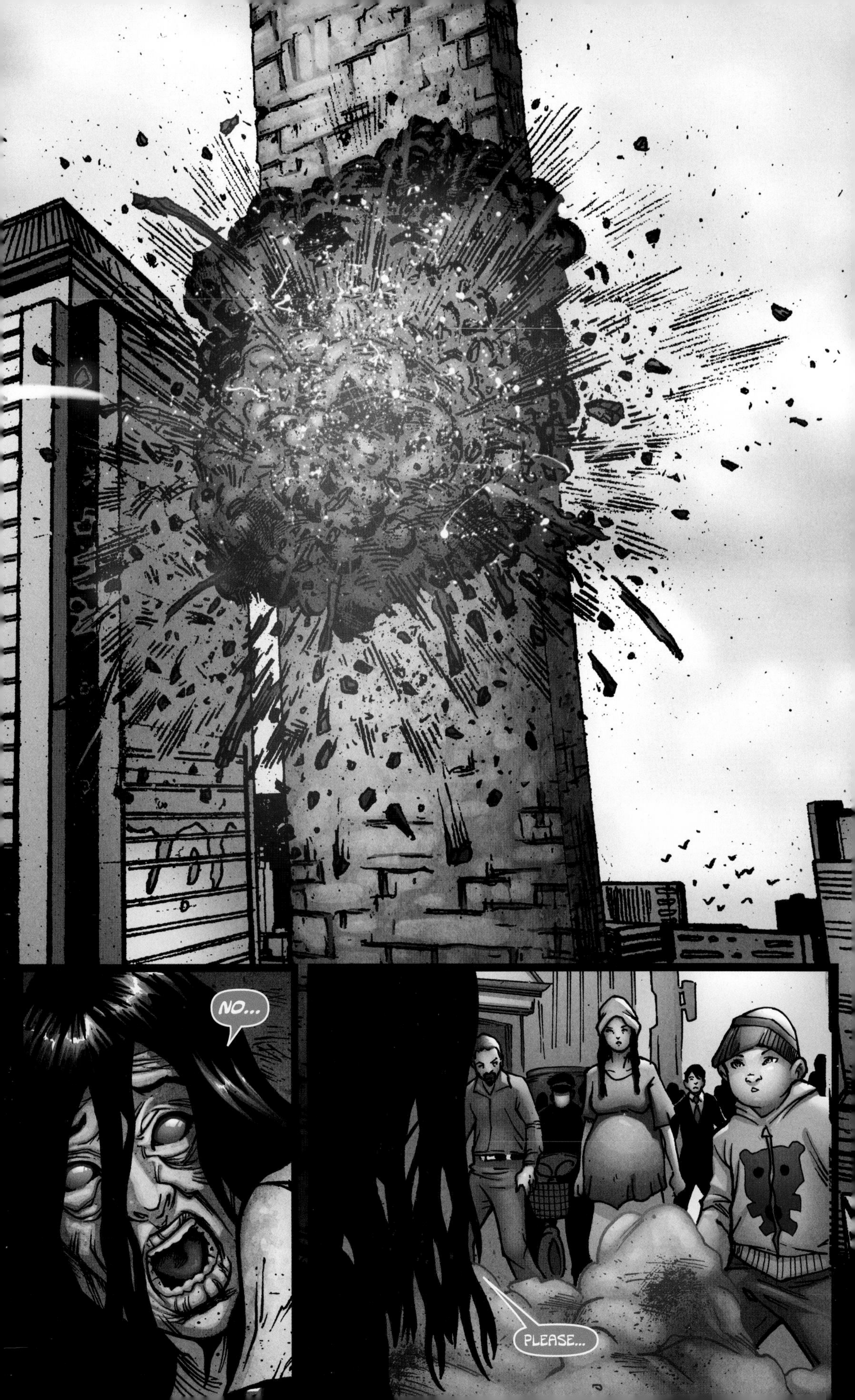
NO...
PLEASE...

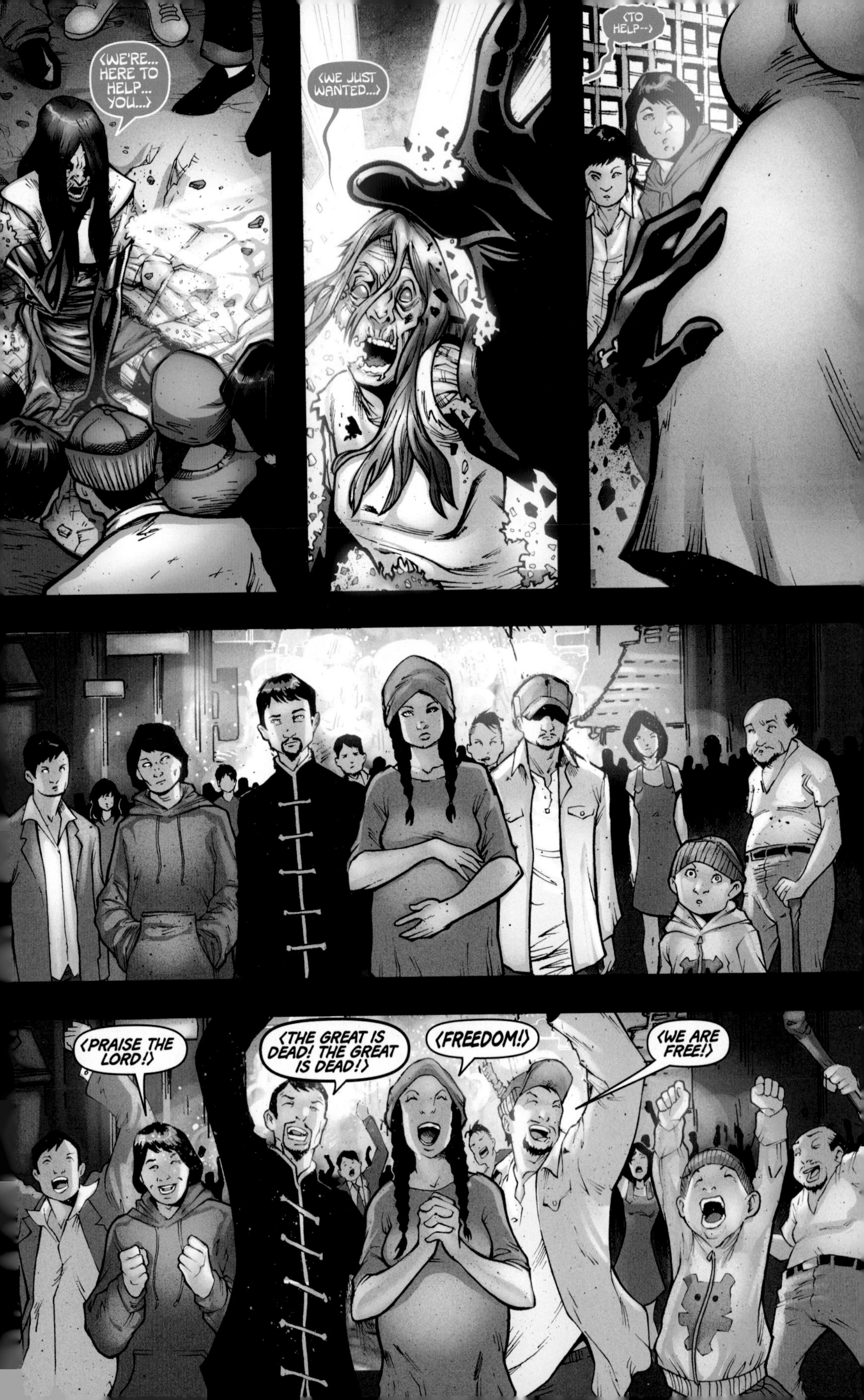

<WE'RE... HERE TO HELP... YOU...>
<WE JUST WANTED...>
<TO HELP-->
<PRAISE THE LORD!>
<THE GREAT IS DEAD! THE GREAT IS DEAD!>
<FREEDOM!>
<WE ARE FREE!>

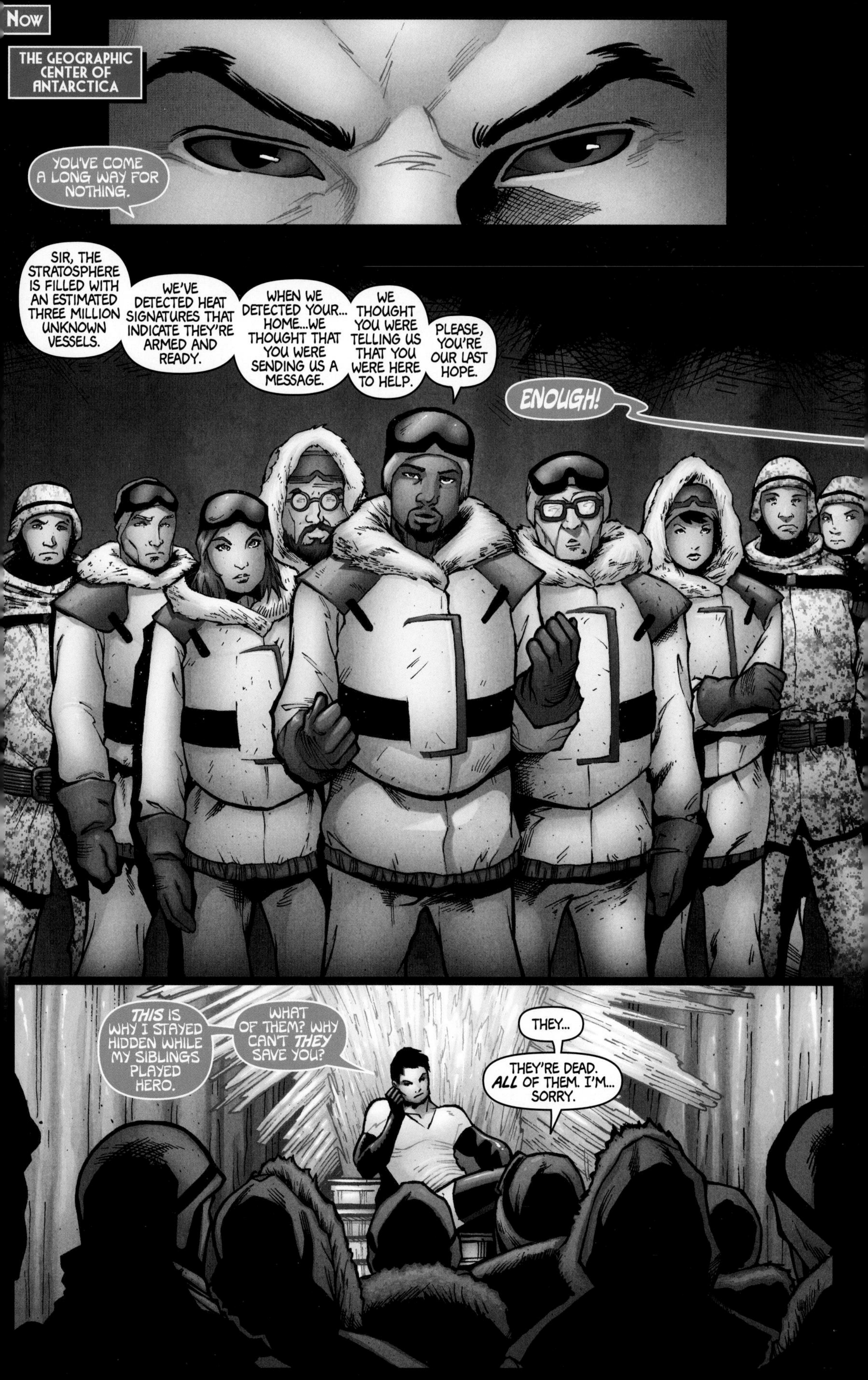
Now
THE GEOGRAPHIC CENTER OF ANTARCTICA
YOU'VE COME A LONG WAY FOR NOTHING.
SIR, THE STRATOSPHERE IS FILLED WITH AN ESTIMATED THREE MILLION UNKNOWN VESSELS.
WE'VE DETECTED HEAT SIGNATURES THAT INDICATE THEY'RE ARMED AND READY.
WHEN WE DETECTED YOUR... HOME...WE THOUGHT THAT YOU WERE SENDING US A MESSAGE.
WE THOUGHT YOU WERE TELLING US THAT YOU WERE HERE TO HELP.
PLEASE, YOU'RE OUR LAST HOPE.
ENOUGH!
THIS IS WHY I STAYED HIDDEN WHILE MY SIBLINGS PLAYED HERO.
WHAT OF THEM? WHY CAN'T THEY SAVE YOU?
THEY...
THEY'RE DEAD. ALL OF THEM. I'M... SORRY.

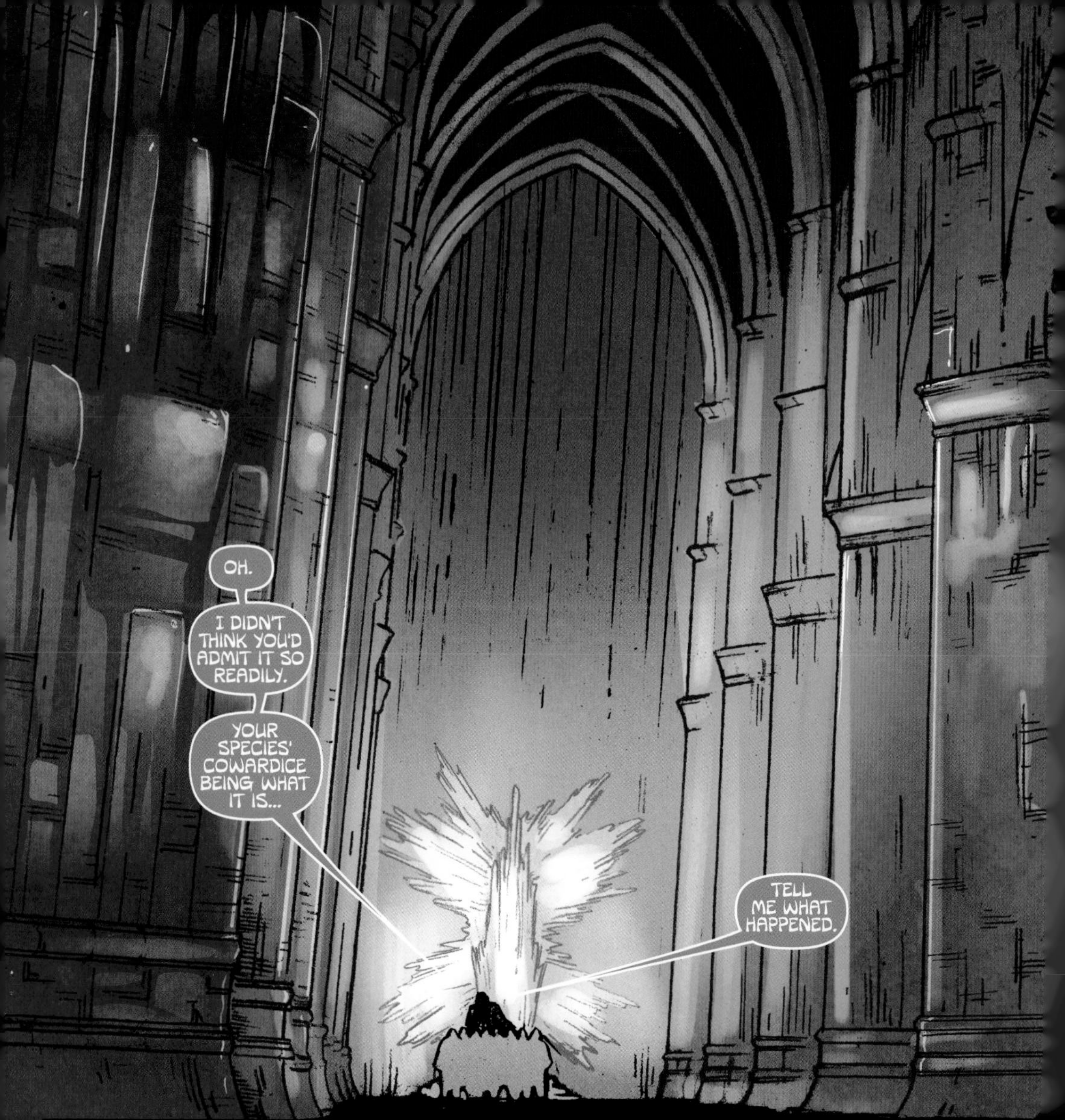
OH.
I DIDN'T THINK YOU'D ADMIT IT SO READILY.
YOUR SPECIES' COWARDICE BEING WHAT IT IS...
TELL ME WHAT HAPPENED.

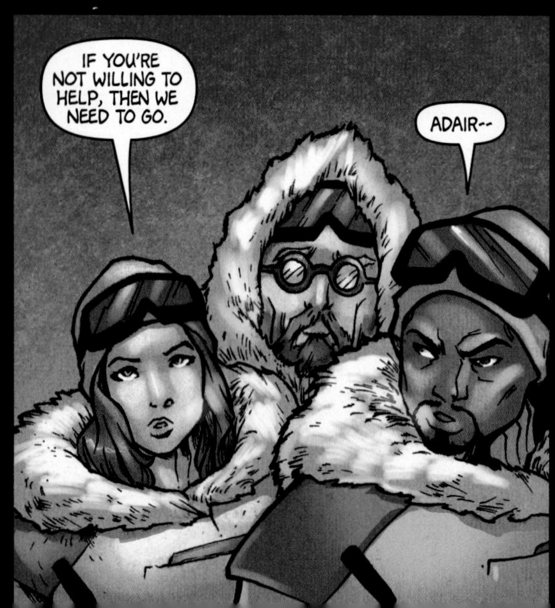
IF YOU'RE NOT WILLING TO HELP, THEN WE NEED TO GO.
ADAIR--

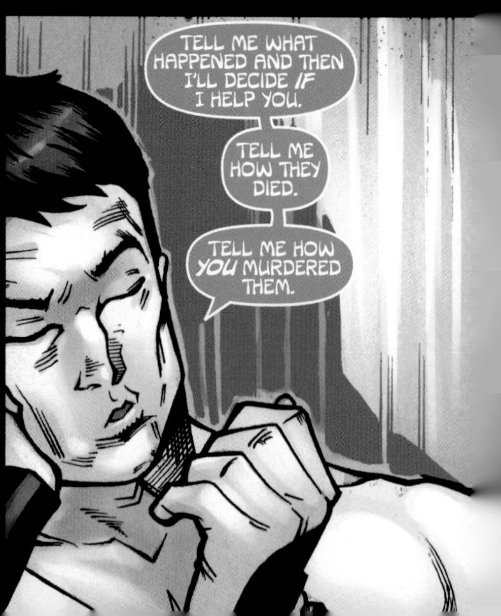
TELL ME WHAT HAPPENED AND THEN I'LL DECIDE *IF* I HELP YOU.
TELL ME HOW THEY DIED.
TELL ME HOW *YOU* MURDERED THEM.

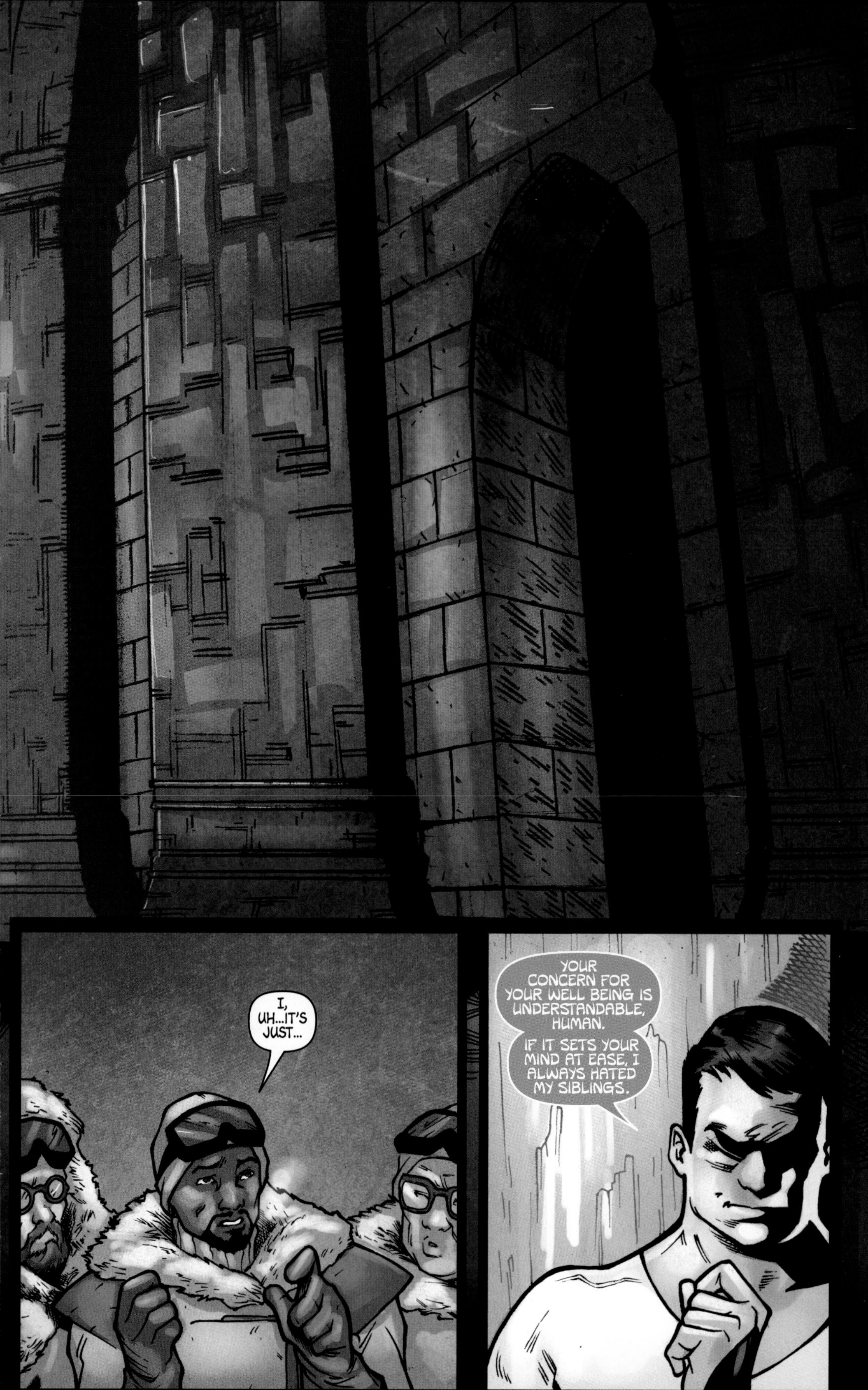
I, UH...IT'S JUST...
YOUR CONCERN FOR YOUR WELL BEING IS UNDERSTANDABLE, HUMAN.
IF IT SETS YOUR MIND AT EASE, I ALWAYS HATED MY SIBLINGS.

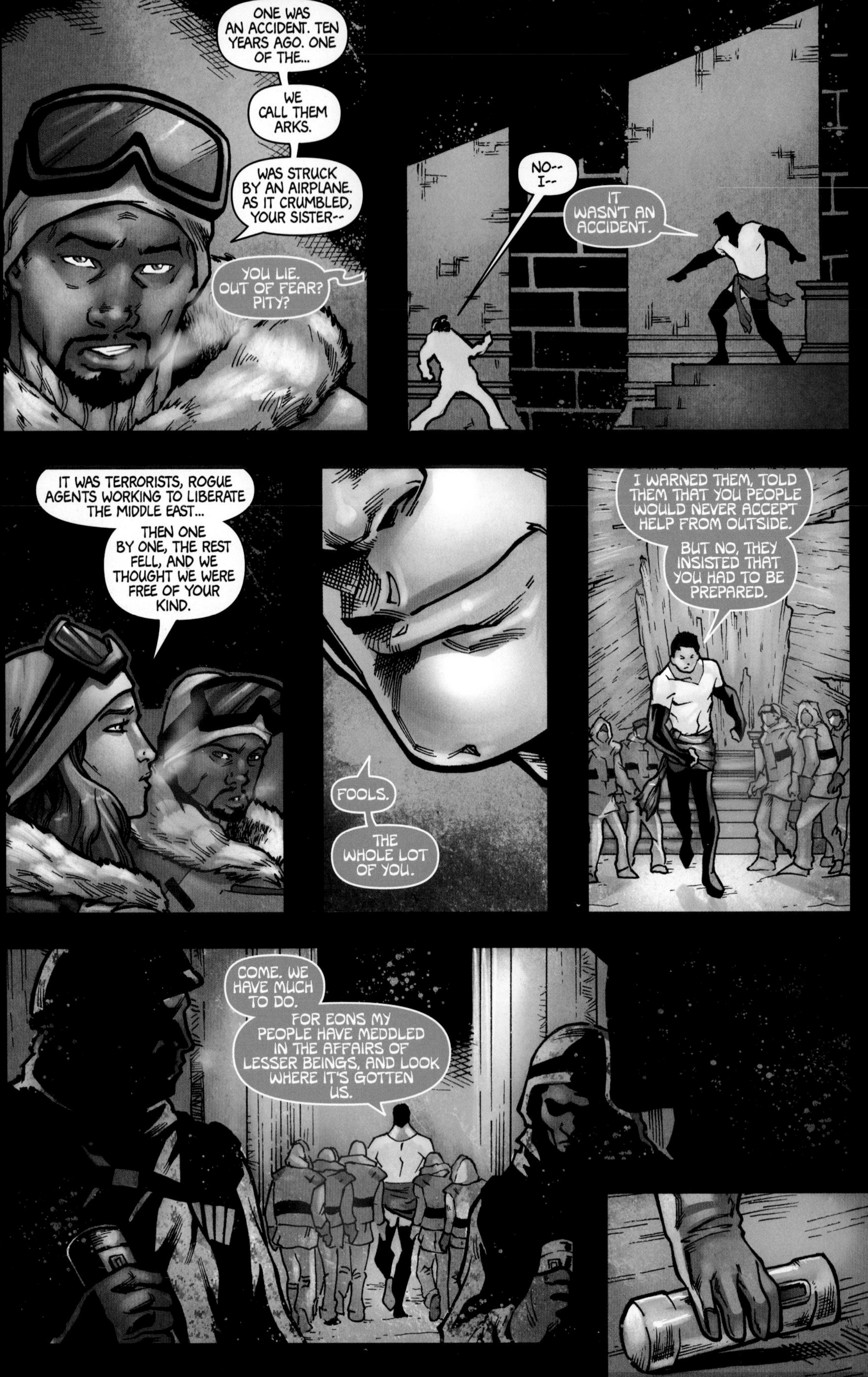
ONE WAS AN ACCIDENT. TEN YEARS AGO. ONE OF THE...
WE CALL THEM ARKS.
WAS STRUCK BY AN AIRPLANE. AS IT CRUMBLED, YOUR SISTER--
YOU LIE. OUT OF FEAR? PITY?
NO-- I--
IT WASN'T AN ACCIDENT.
IT WAS TERRORISTS, ROGUE AGENTS WORKING TO LIBERATE THE MIDDLE EAST...
THEN ONE BY ONE, THE REST FELL, AND WE THOUGHT WE WERE FREE OF YOUR KIND.
FOOLS.
THE WHOLE LOT OF YOU.
I WARNED THEM, TOLD THEM THAT YOU PEOPLE WOULD NEVER ACCEPT HELP FROM OUTSIDE.
BUT NO, THEY INSISTED THAT YOU HAD TO BE PREPARED.
COME. WE HAVE MUCH TO DO.
FOR EONS MY PEOPLE HAVE MEDDLED IN THE AFFAIRS OF LESSER BEINGS, AND LOOK WHERE IT'S GOTTEN US.

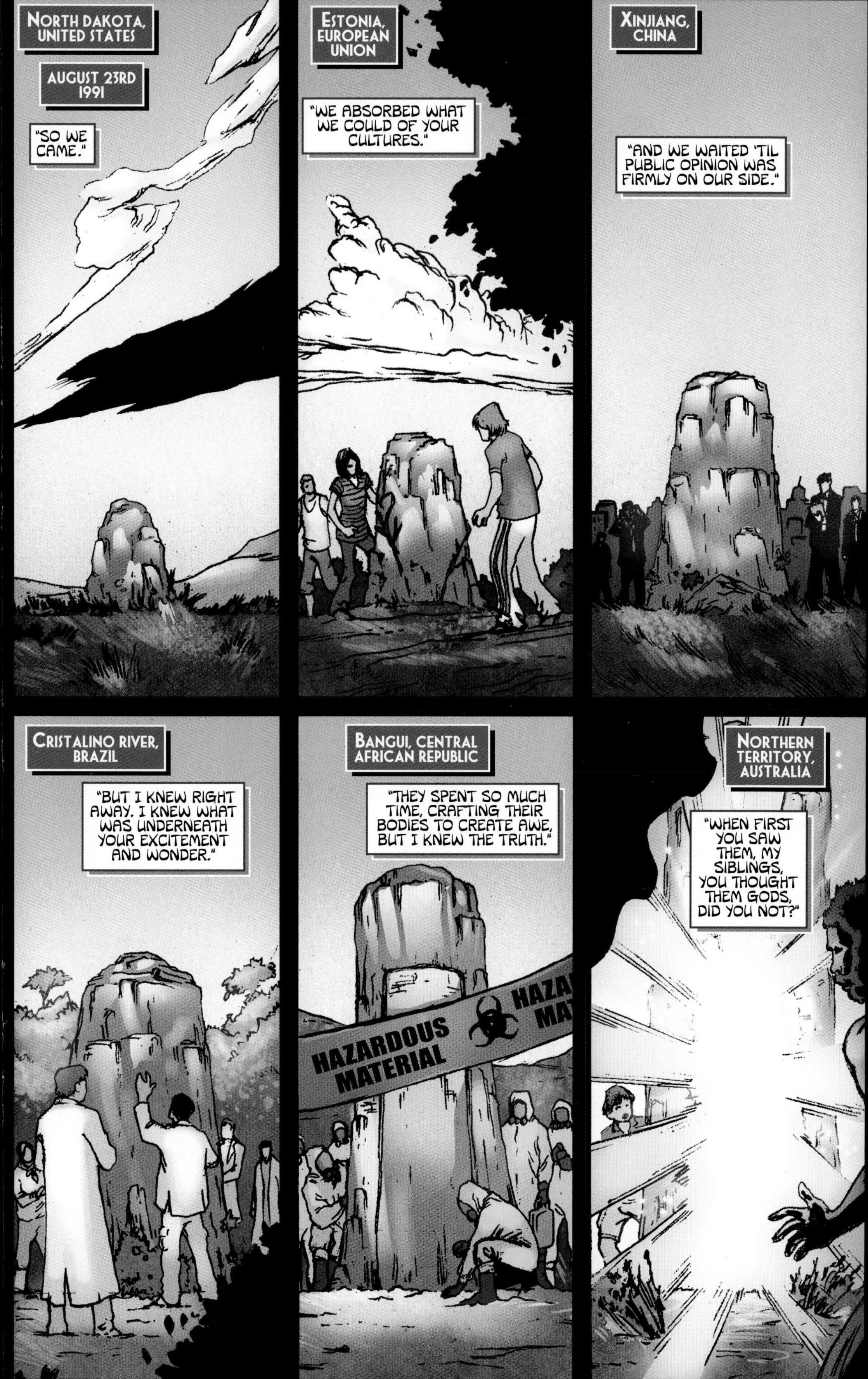
North Dakota, United States
August 23rd 1991
"So we came."
Estonia, European Union
"We absorbed what we could of your cultures."
Xinjiang, China
"And we waited 'til public opinion was firmly on our side."
Cristalino River, Brazil
"But I knew right away. I knew what was underneath your excitement and wonder."
Bangui, Central African Republic
"They spent so much time, crafting their bodies to create awe, but I knew the truth."
HAZARDOUS MATERIAL
Northern Territory, Australia
"When first you saw them, my siblings, you thought them gods, did you not?"

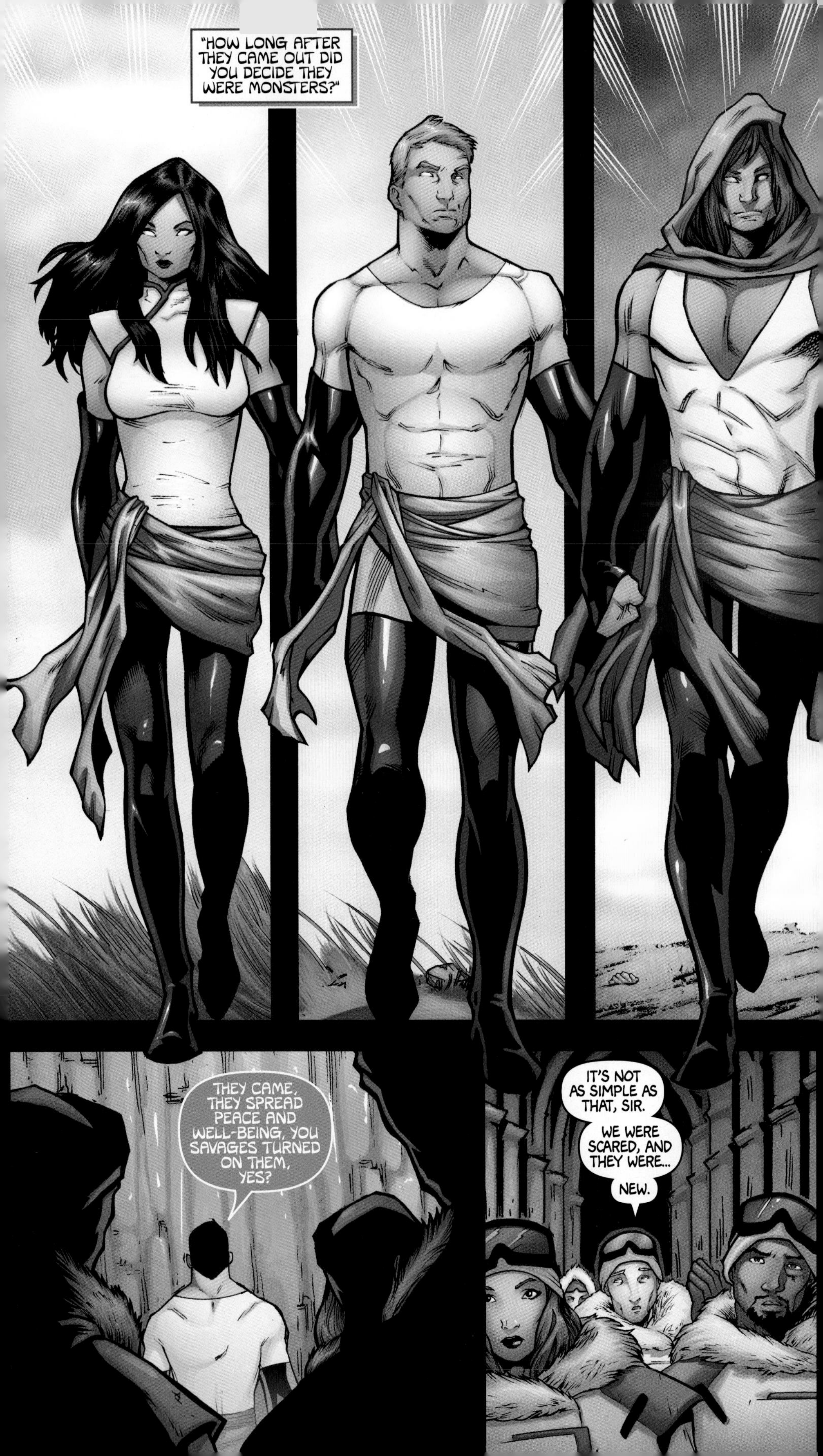
"HOW LONG AFTER THEY CAME OUT DID YOU DECIDE THEY WERE MONSTERS?"
THEY CAME, THEY SPREAD PEACE AND WELL-BEING, YOU SAVAGES TURNED ON THEM, YES?
IT'S NOT AS SIMPLE AS THAT, SIR.
WE WERE SCARED, AND THEY WERE...
NEW.

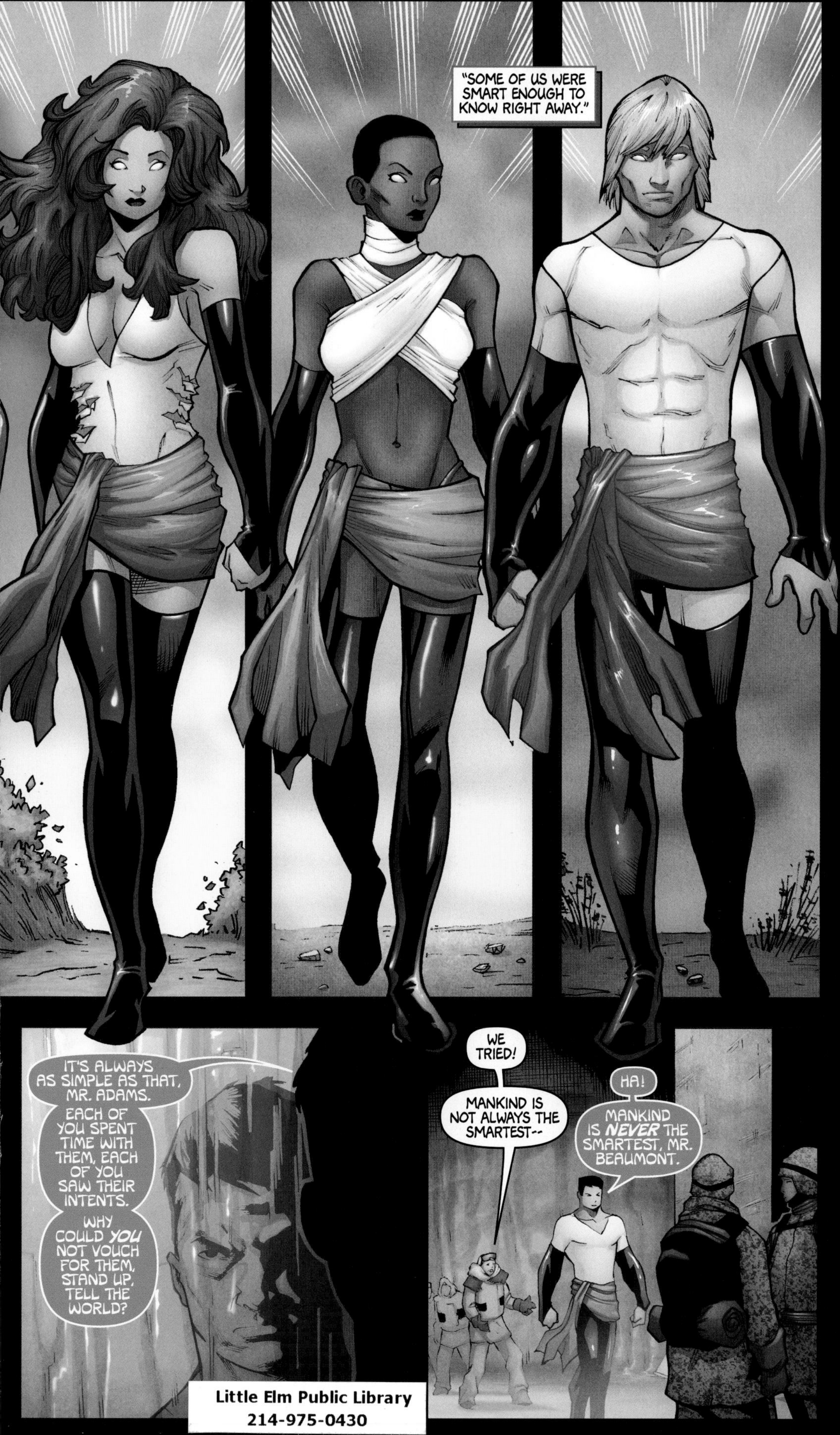
"SOME OF US WERE SMART ENOUGH TO KNOW RIGHT AWAY."
IT'S ALWAYS AS SIMPLE AS THAT, MR. ADAMS.
EACH OF YOU SPENT TIME WITH THEM, EACH OF YOU SAW THEIR INTENTS.
WHY COULD *YOU* NOT VOUCH FOR THEM, STAND UP, TELL THE WORLD?
WE TRIED!
MANKIND IS NOT ALWAYS THE SMARTEST--
HA!
MANKIND IS ***NEVER*** THE SMARTEST, MR. BEAUMONT.

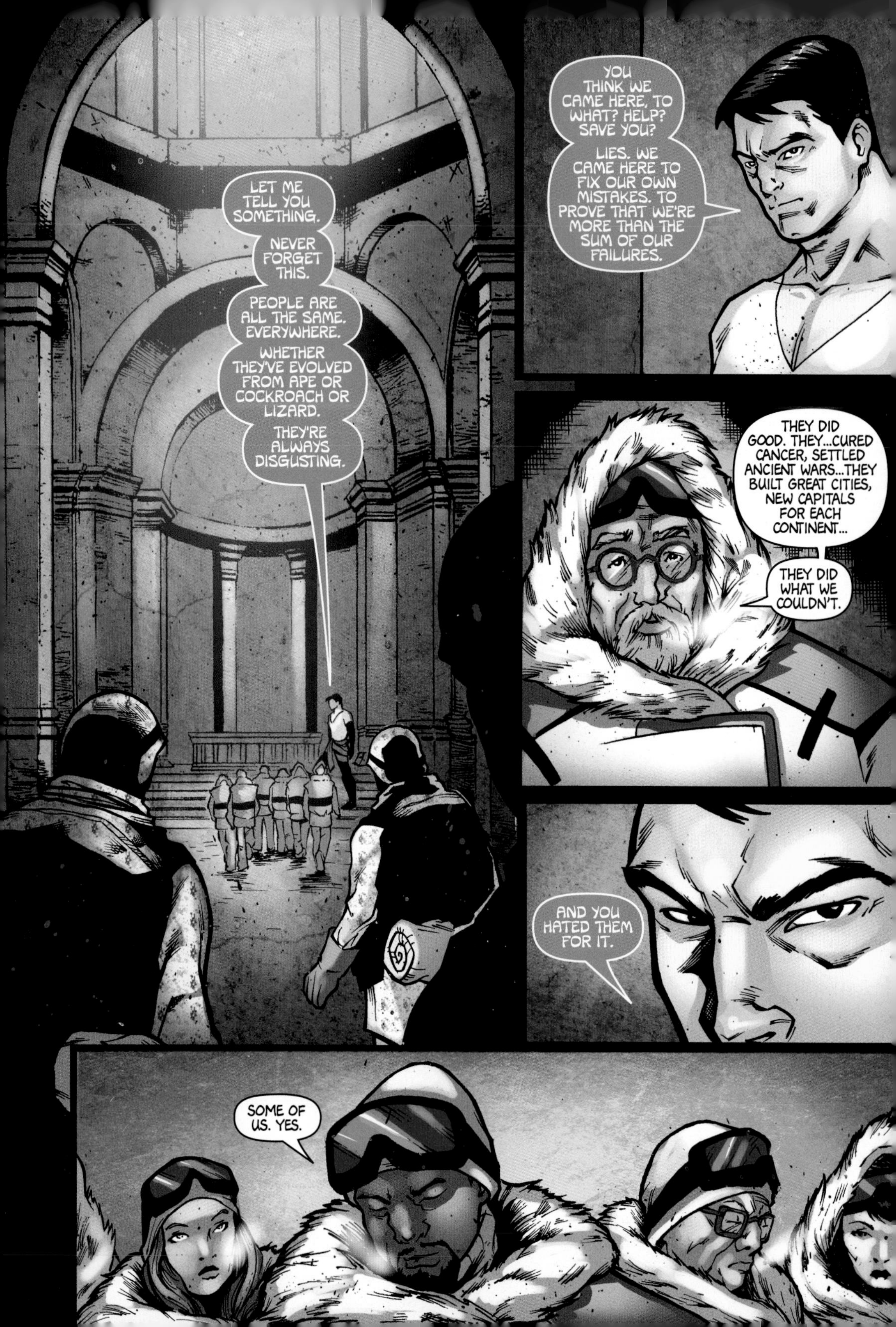
LET ME TELL YOU SOMETHING.
NEVER FORGET THIS.
PEOPLE ARE ALL THE SAME. EVERYWHERE.
WHETHER THEY'VE EVOLVED FROM APE OR COCKROACH OR LIZARD.
THEY'RE ALWAYS DISGUSTING.
YOU THINK WE CAME HERE, TO WHAT? HELP? SAVE YOU?
LIES. WE CAME HERE TO FIX OUR OWN MISTAKES. TO PROVE THAT WE'RE MORE THAN THE SUM OF OUR FAILURES.
THEY DID GOOD. THEY...CURED CANCER, SETTLED ANCIENT WARS...THEY BUILT GREAT CITIES, NEW CAPITALS FOR EACH CONTINENT...
THEY DID WHAT WE COULDN'T.
AND YOU HATED THEM FOR IT.
SOME OF US. YES.

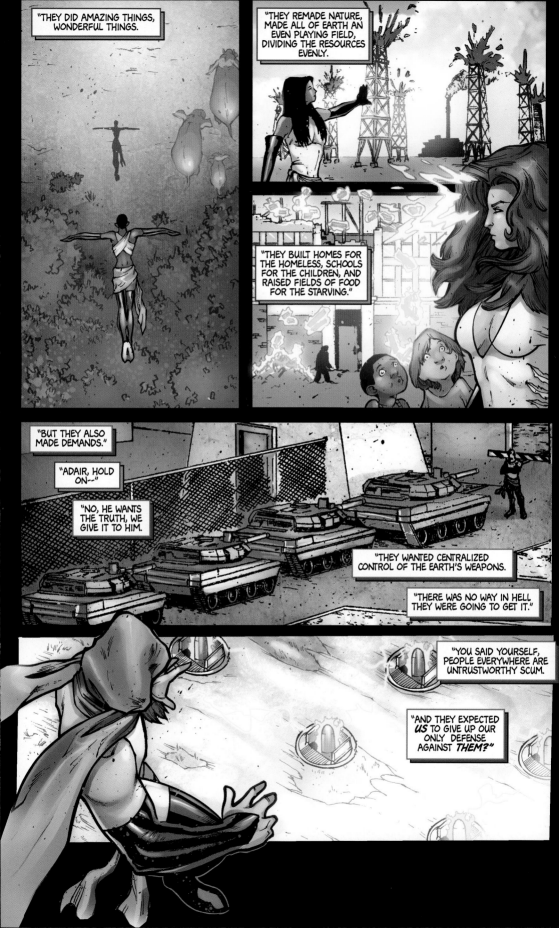

"THEY DID AMAZING THINGS, WONDERFUL THINGS.

"THEY REMADE NATURE, MADE ALL OF EARTH AN EVEN PLAYING FIELD, DIVIDING THE RESOURCES EVENLY."

"THEY BUILT HOMES FOR THE HOMELESS, SCHOOLS FOR THE CHILDREN, AND RAISED FIELDS OF FOOD FOR THE STARVING."

"BUT THEY ALSO MADE DEMANDS."

"ADAIR, HOLD ON--"

"NO, HE WANTS THE TRUTH, WE GIVE IT TO HIM.

"THEY WANTED CENTRALIZED CONTROL OF THE EARTH'S WEAPONS.

"THERE WAS NO WAY IN HELL THEY WERE GOING TO GET IT."

"YOU SAID YOURSELF, PEOPLE EVERYWHERE ARE UNTRUSTWORTHY SCUM.

"AND THEY EXPECTED *US* TO GIVE UP OUR ONLY DEFENSE AGAINST *THEM?*"

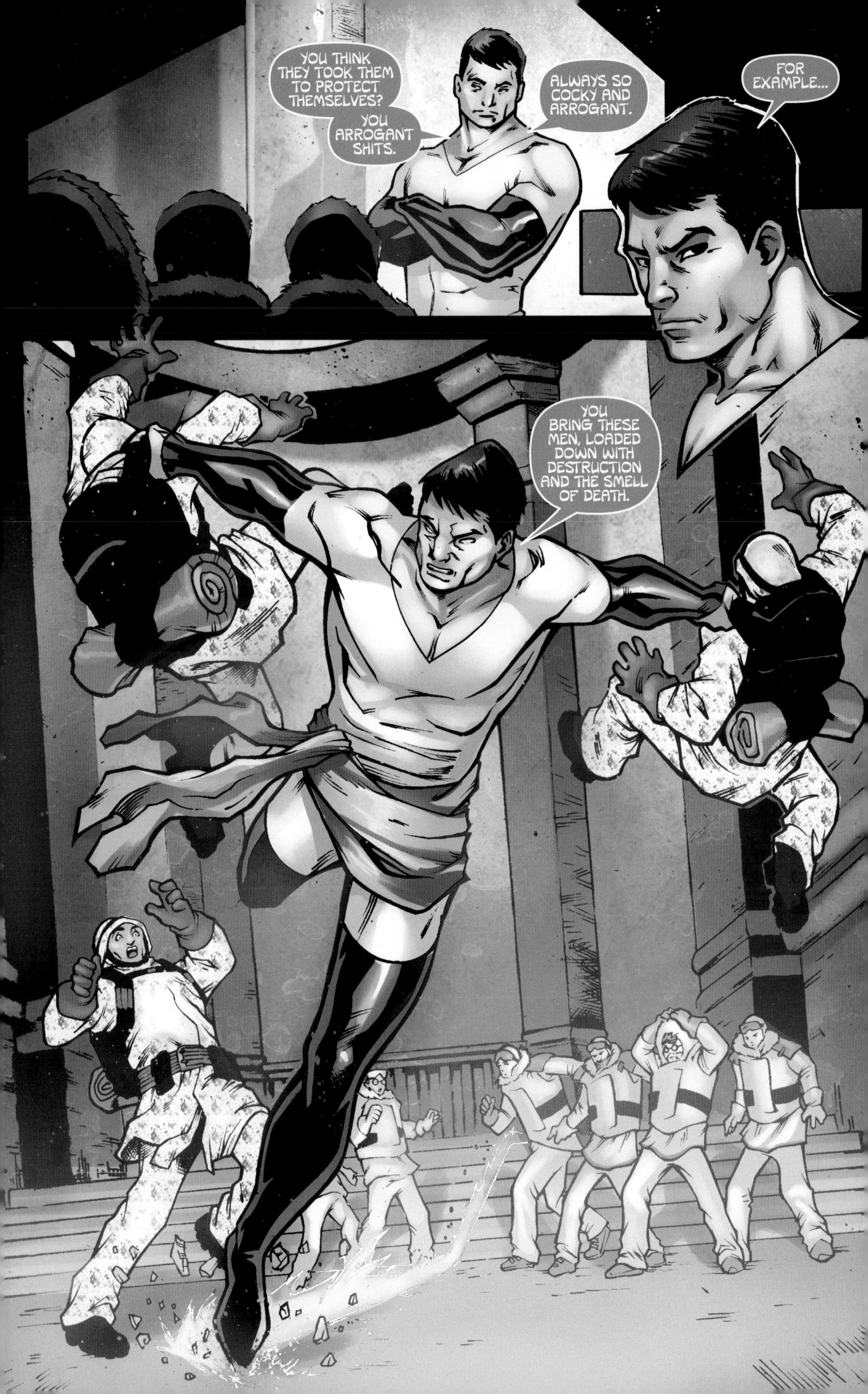
YOU THINK THEY TOOK THEM TO PROTECT THEMSELVES?
YOU ARROGANT SHITS.
ALWAYS SO COCKY AND ARROGANT.
FOR EXAMPLE...
YOU BRING THESE MEN, LOADED DOWN WITH DESTRUCTION AND THE SMELL OF DEATH.

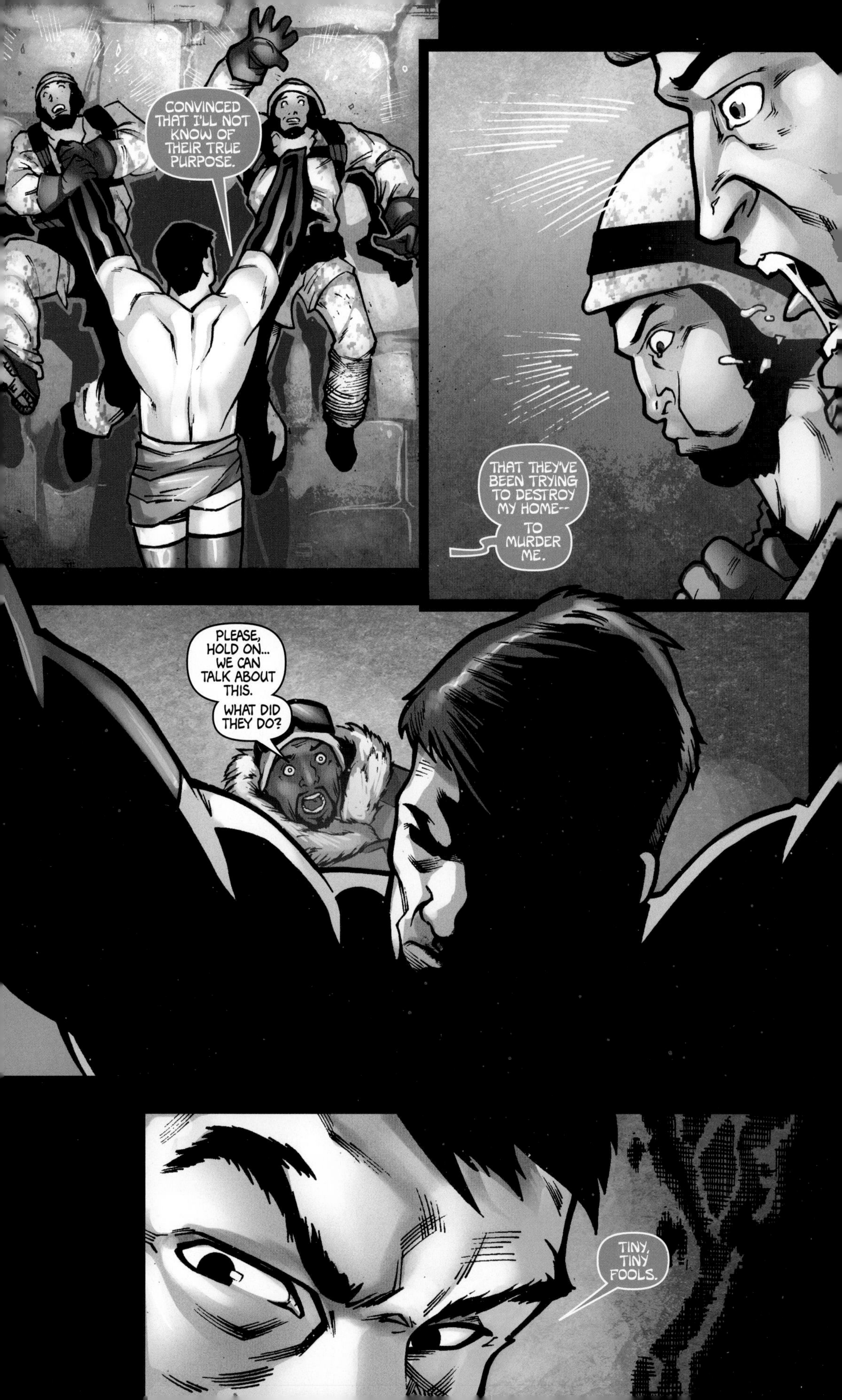
CONVINCED THAT I'LL NOT KNOW OF THEIR TRUE PURPOSE.
THAT THEY'VE BEEN TRYING TO DESTROY MY HOME--
TO MURDER ME.
PLEASE, HOLD ON... WE CAN TALK ABOUT THIS.
WHAT DID THEY DO?
TINY, TINY FOOLS.

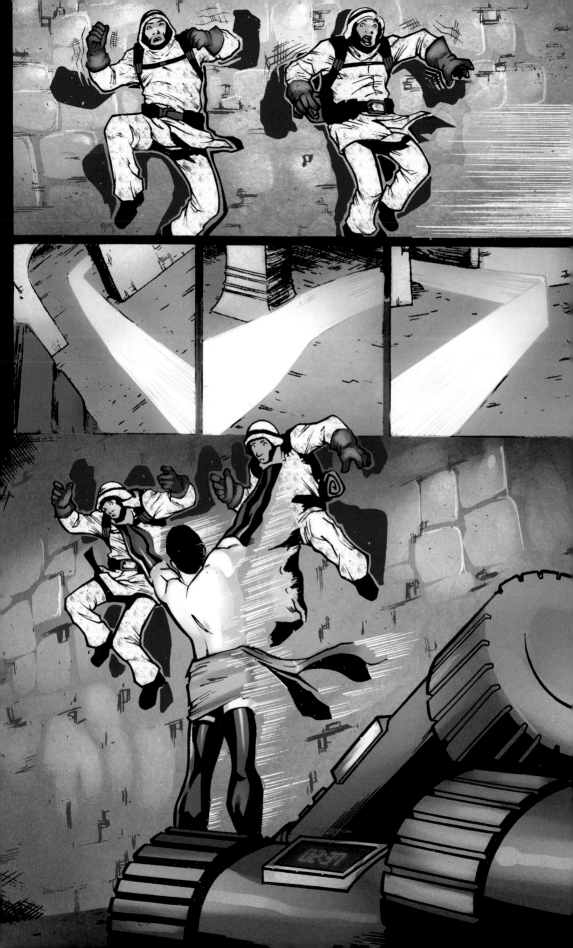

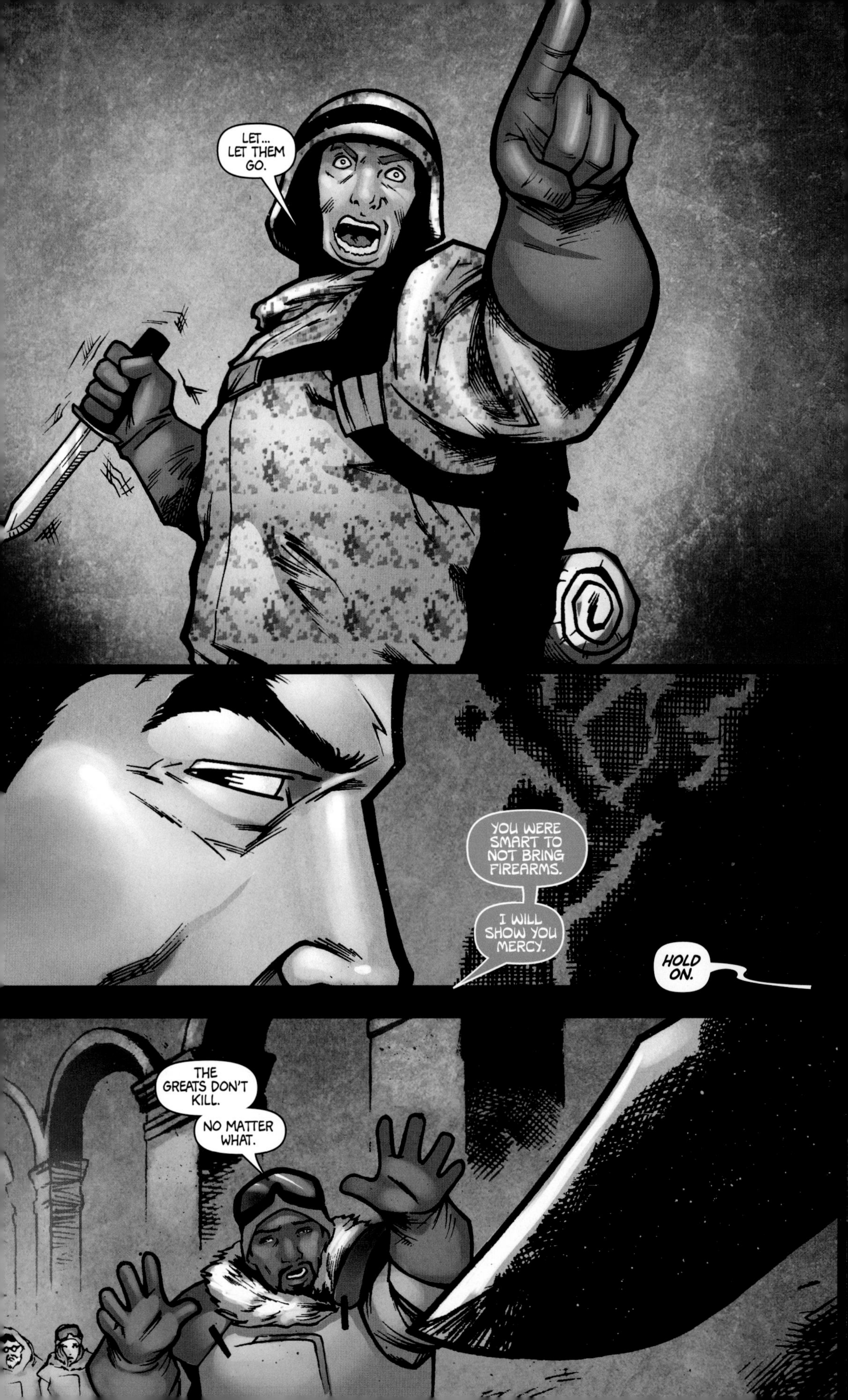
LET... LET THEM GO.
YOU WERE SMART TO NOT BRING FIREARMS.
I WILL SHOW YOU MERCY.
HOLD ON.
THE GREATS DON'T KILL.
NO MATTER WHAT.

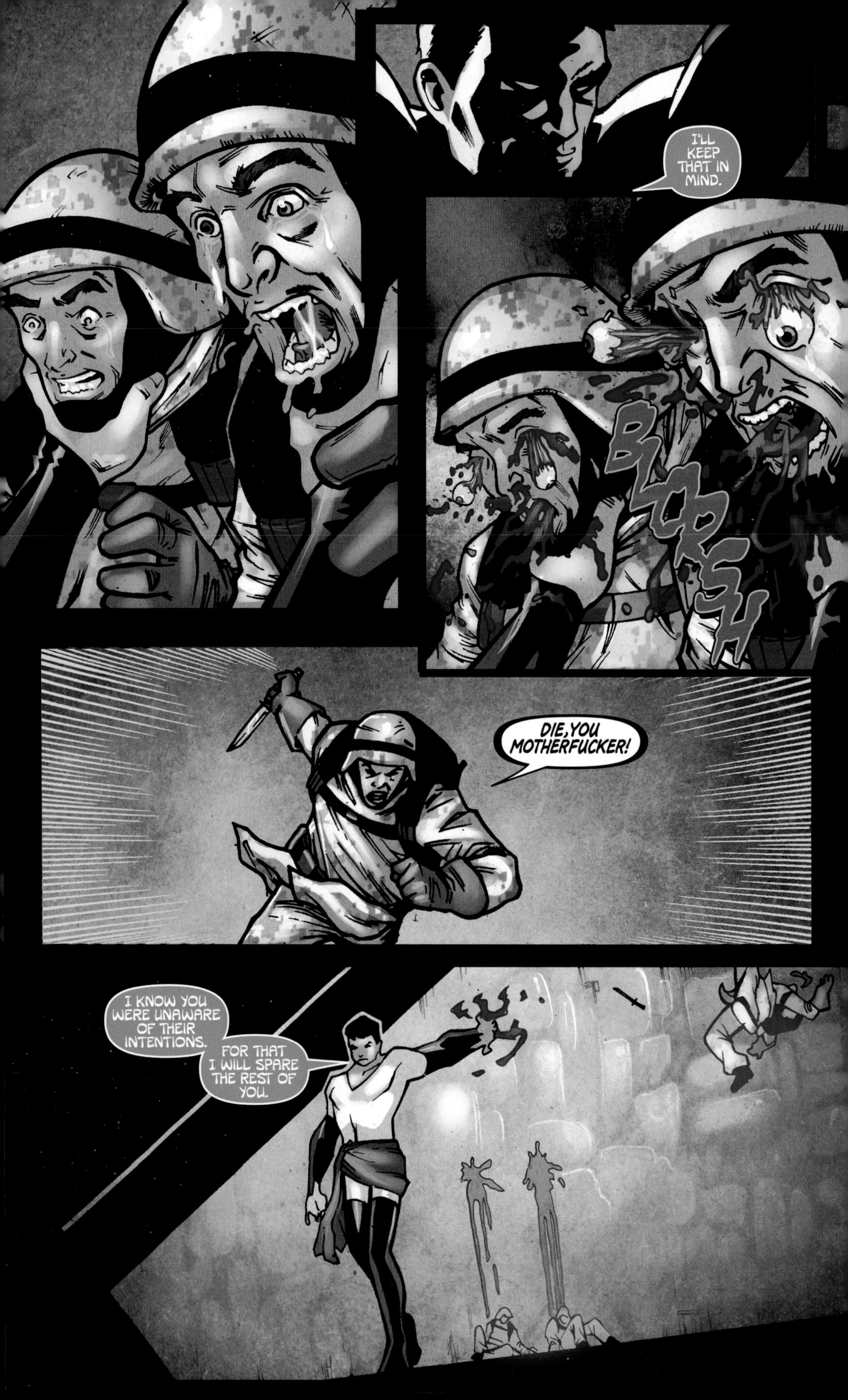

I'LL KEEP THAT IN MIND.
BLORSH
DIE, YOU MOTHERFUCKER!
I KNOW YOU WERE UNAWARE OF THEIR INTENTIONS.
FOR THAT I WILL SPARE THE REST OF YOU.

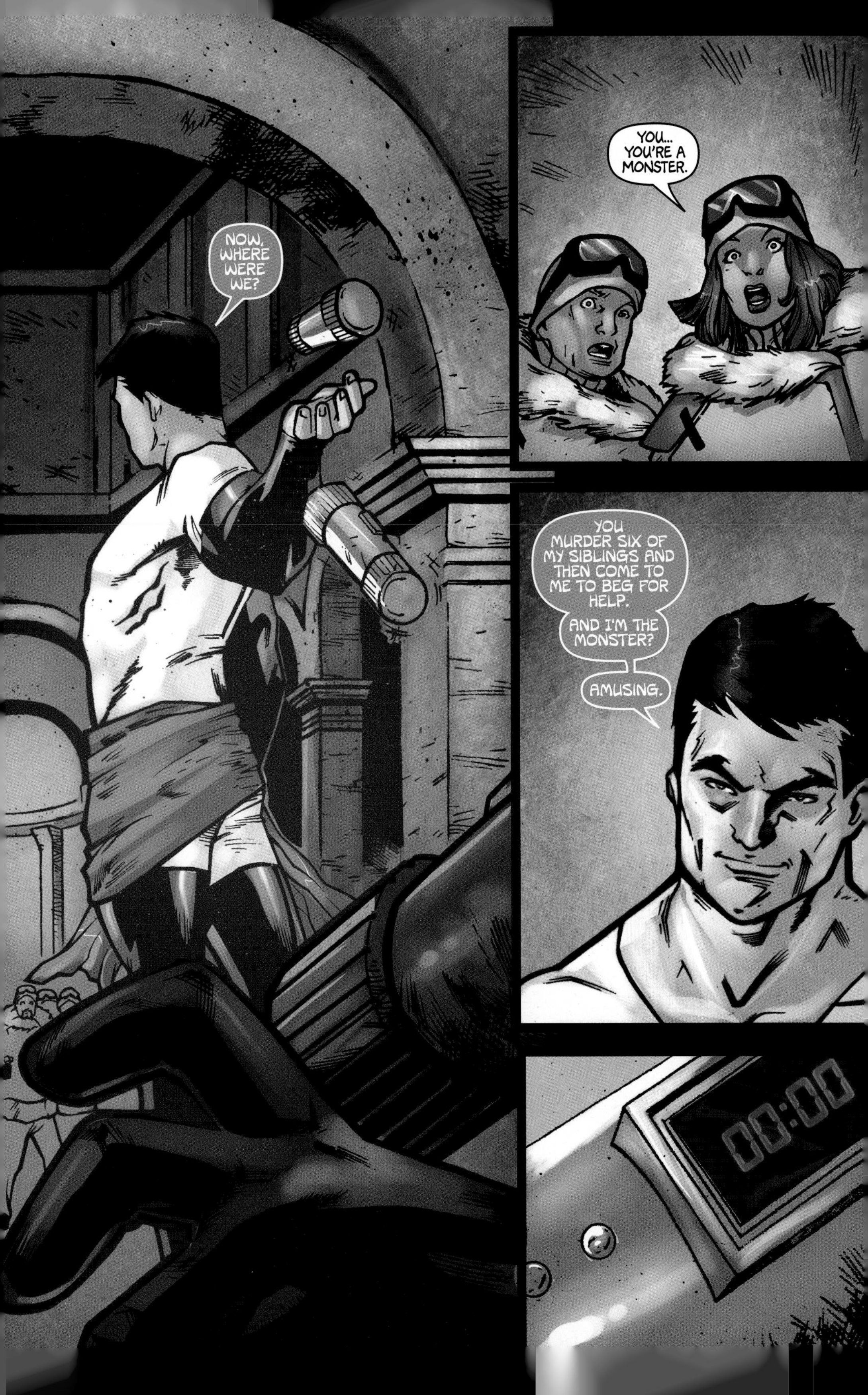
NOW, WHERE WERE WE?
YOU... YOU'RE A MONSTER.
YOU MURDER SIX OF MY SIBLINGS AND THEN COME TO ME TO BEG FOR HELP.
AND I'M THE MONSTER?
AMUSING.
00:00

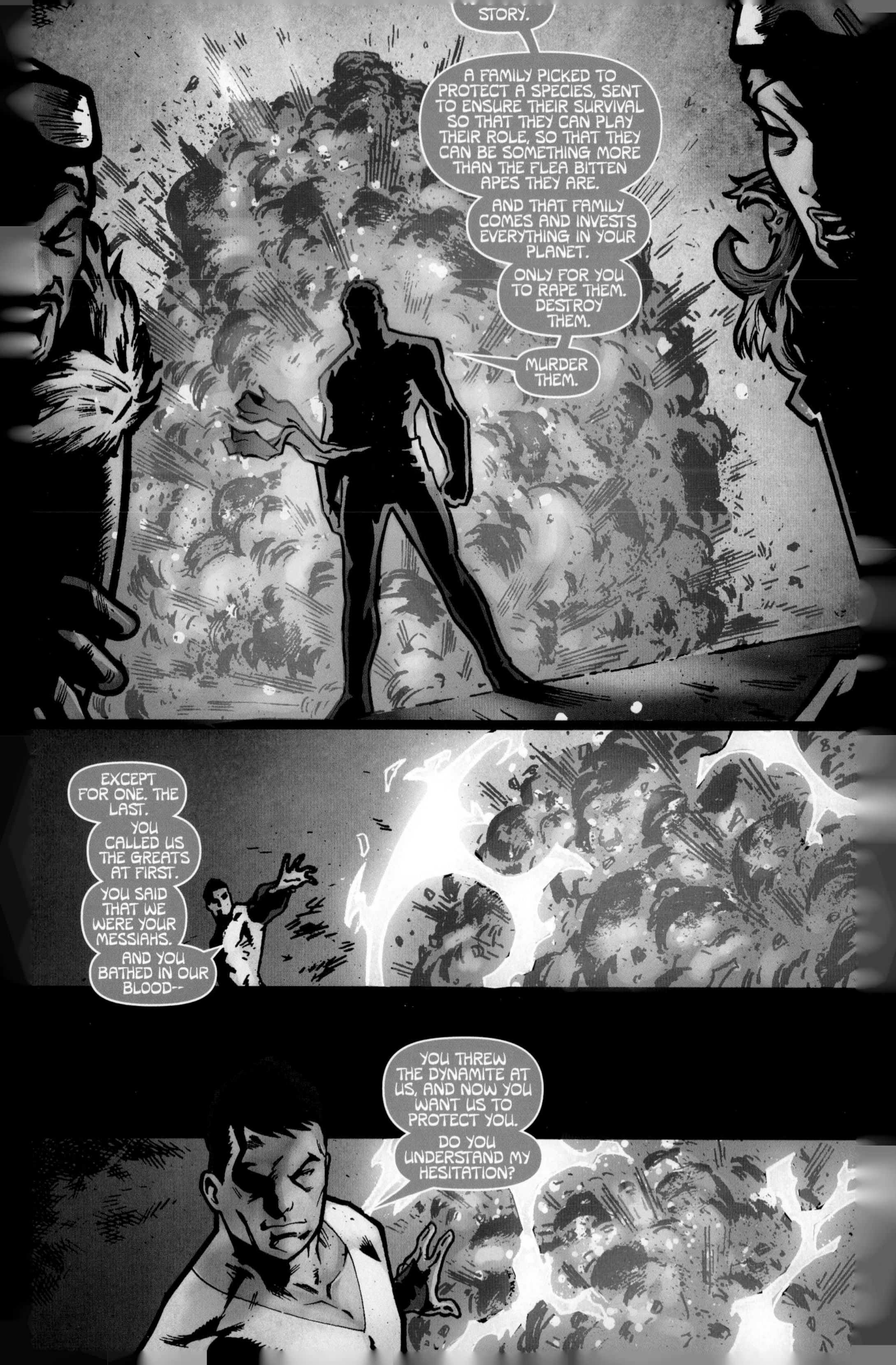
STORY.
A FAMILY PICKED TO PROTECT A SPECIES, SENT TO ENSURE THEIR SURVIVAL SO THAT THEY CAN PLAY THEIR ROLE, SO THAT THEY CAN BE SOMETHING MORE THAN THE FLEA BITTEN APES THEY ARE.
AND THAT FAMILY COMES AND INVESTS EVERYTHING IN YOUR PLANET.
ONLY FOR YOU TO RAPE THEM. DESTROY THEM.
MURDER THEM.
EXCEPT FOR ONE. THE LAST.
YOU CALLED US THE GREATS AT FIRST.
YOU SAID THAT WE WERE YOUR MESSIAHS.
AND YOU BATHED IN OUR BLOOD--
YOU THREW THE DYNAMITE AT US, AND NOW YOU WANT US TO PROTECT YOU.
DO YOU UNDERSTAND MY HESITATION?

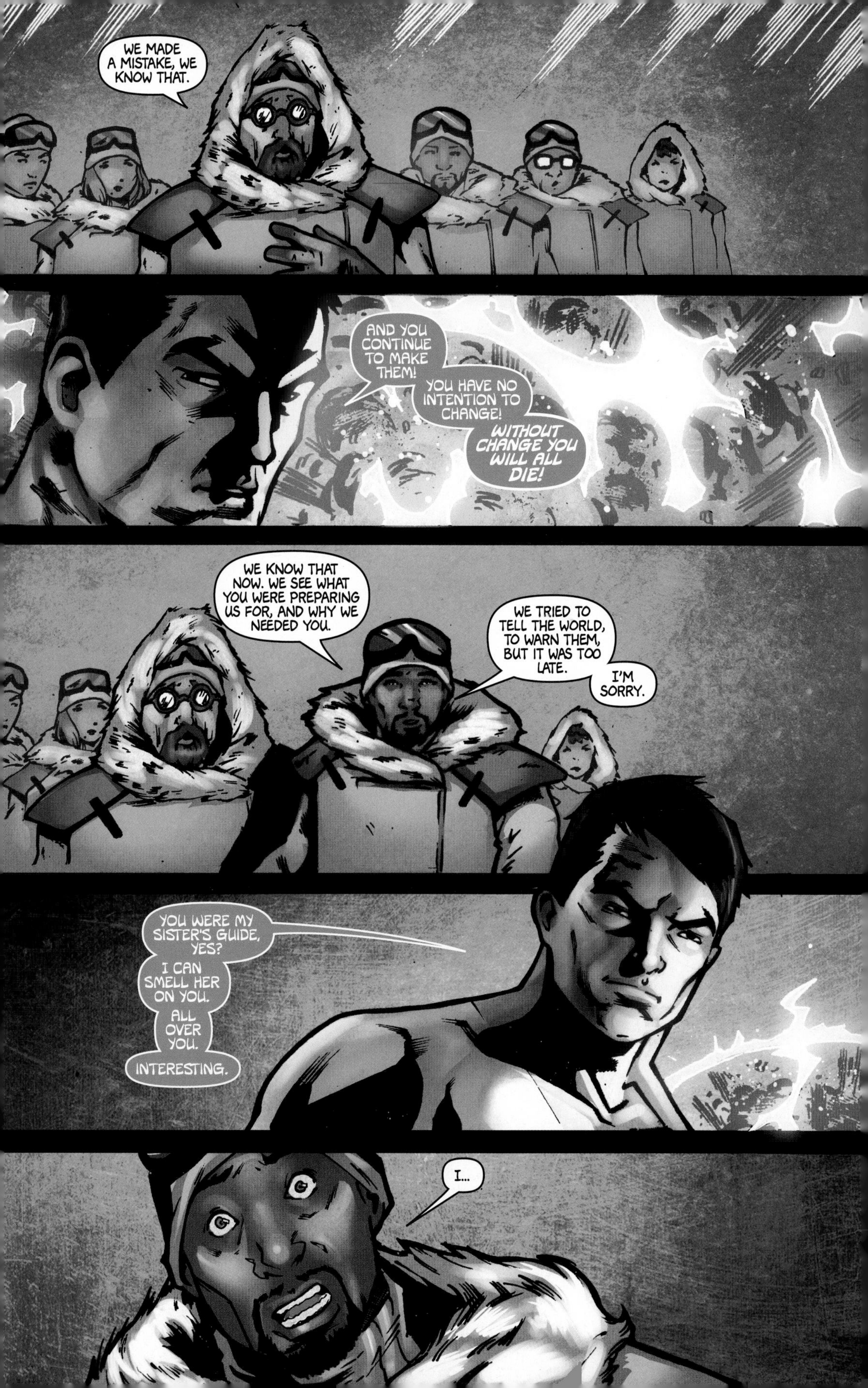
WE MADE A MISTAKE, WE KNOW THAT.
AND YOU CONTINUE TO MAKE THEM!
YOU HAVE NO INTENTION TO CHANGE!
WITHOUT CHANGE YOU WILL ALL DIE!
WE KNOW THAT NOW. WE SEE WHAT YOU WERE PREPARING US FOR, AND WHY WE NEEDED YOU.
WE TRIED TO TELL THE WORLD, TO WARN THEM, BUT IT WAS TOO LATE.
I'M SORRY.
YOU WERE MY SISTER'S GUIDE, YES?
I CAN SMELL HER ON YOU.
ALL OVER YOU.
INTERESTING.
I...

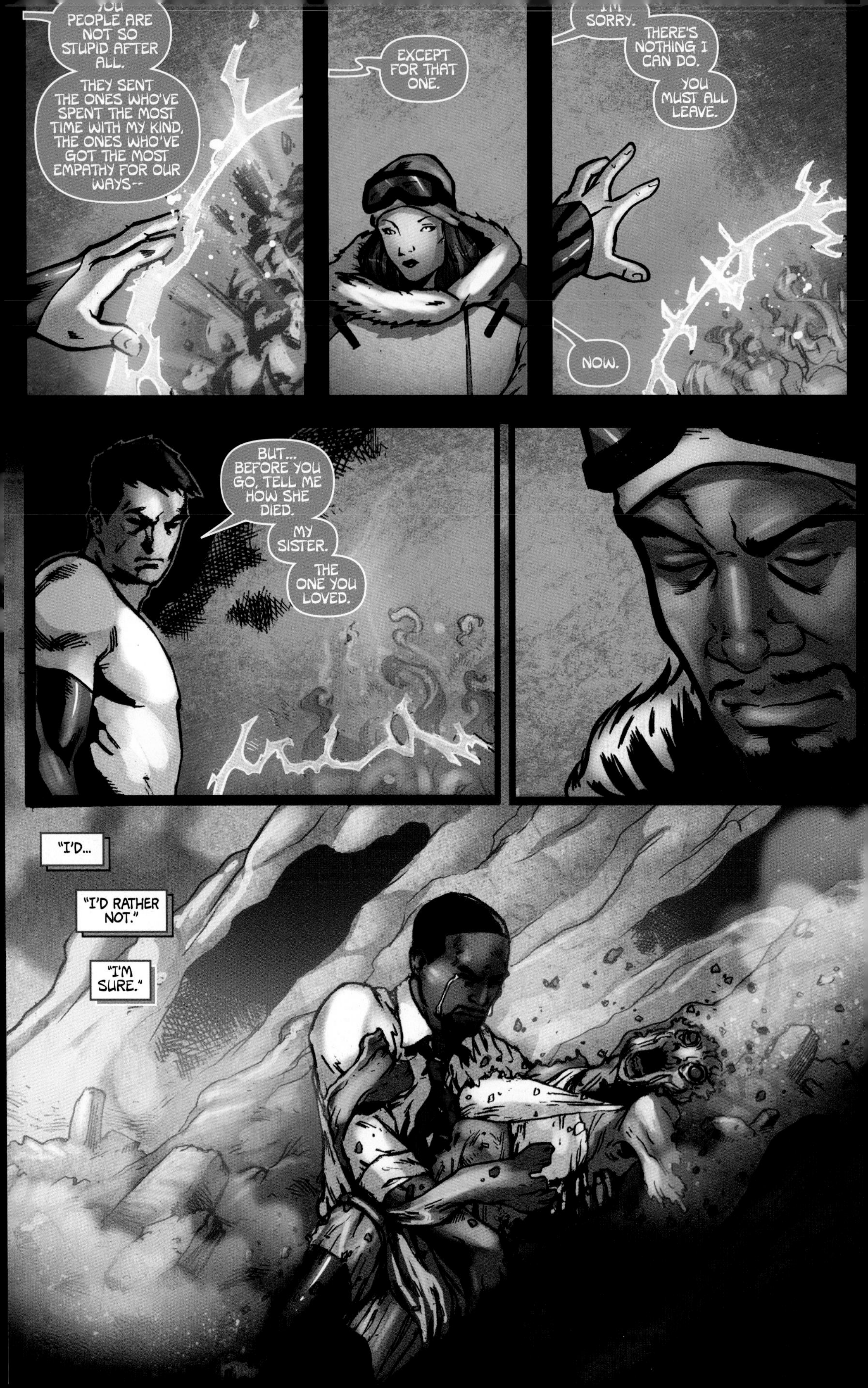
YOU PEOPLE ARE NOT SO STUPID AFTER ALL.
THEY SENT THE ONES WHO'VE SPENT THE MOST TIME WITH MY KIND, THE ONES WHO'VE GOT THE MOST EMPATHY FOR OUR WAYS--
EXCEPT FOR THAT ONE.
I'M SORRY.
THERE'S NOTHING I CAN DO.
YOU MUST ALL LEAVE.
NOW.
BUT... BEFORE YOU GO, TELL ME HOW SHE DIED.
MY SISTER.
THE ONE YOU LOVED.
"I'D...
"I'D RATHER NOT."
"I'M SURE."

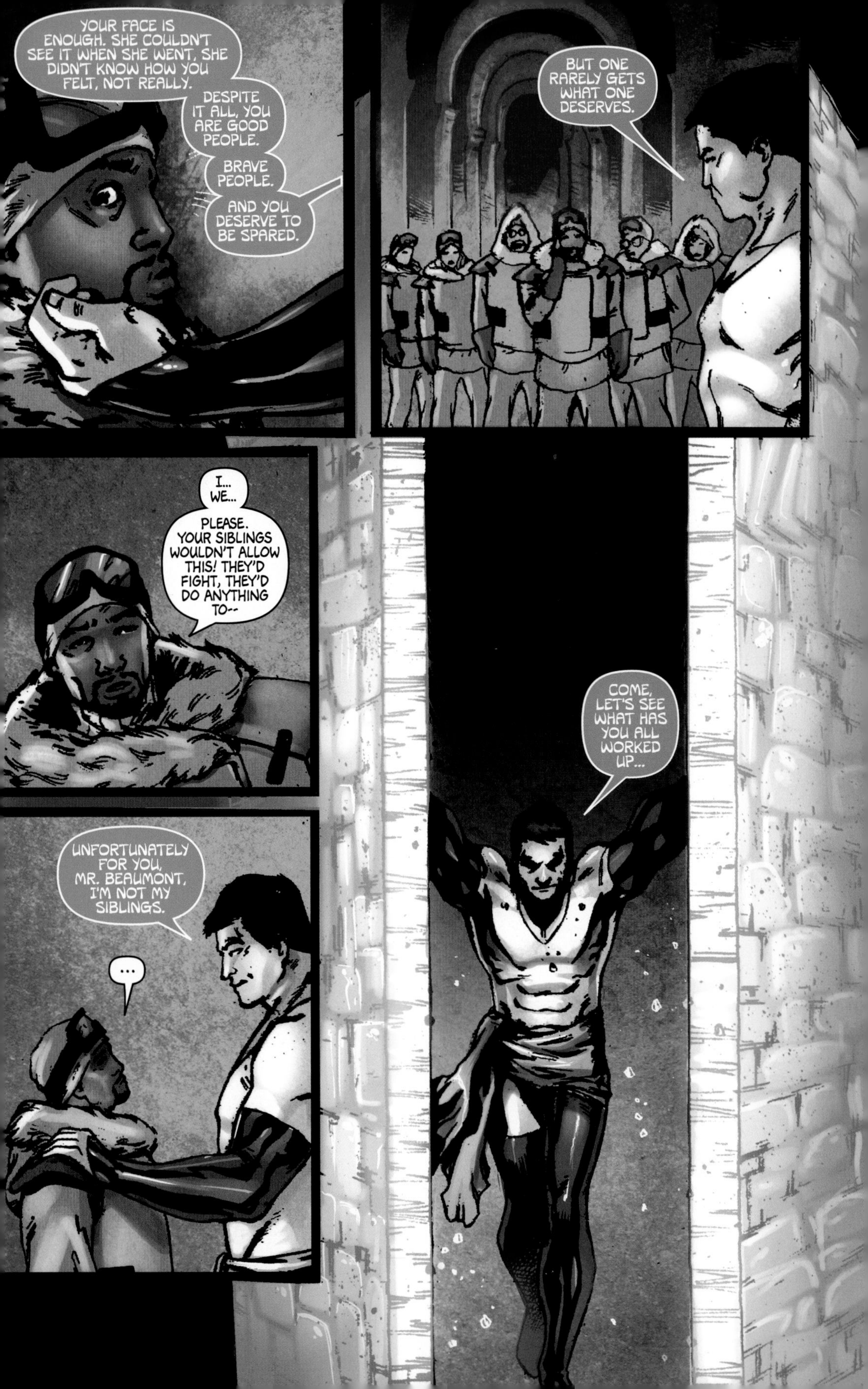

YOUR FACE IS ENOUGH. SHE COULDN'T SEE IT WHEN SHE WENT, SHE DIDN'T KNOW HOW YOU FELT, NOT REALLY.
DESPITE IT ALL, YOU ARE GOOD PEOPLE.
BRAVE PEOPLE.
AND YOU DESERVE TO BE SPARED.
BUT ONE RARELY GETS WHAT ONE DESERVES.
I... WE...
PLEASE. YOUR SIBLINGS WOULDN'T ALLOW THIS! THEY'D FIGHT, THEY'D DO ANYTHING TO--
UNFORTUNATELY FOR YOU, MR. BEAUMONT, I'M NOT MY SIBLINGS.
...
COME, LET'S SEE WHAT HAS YOU ALL WORKED UP...

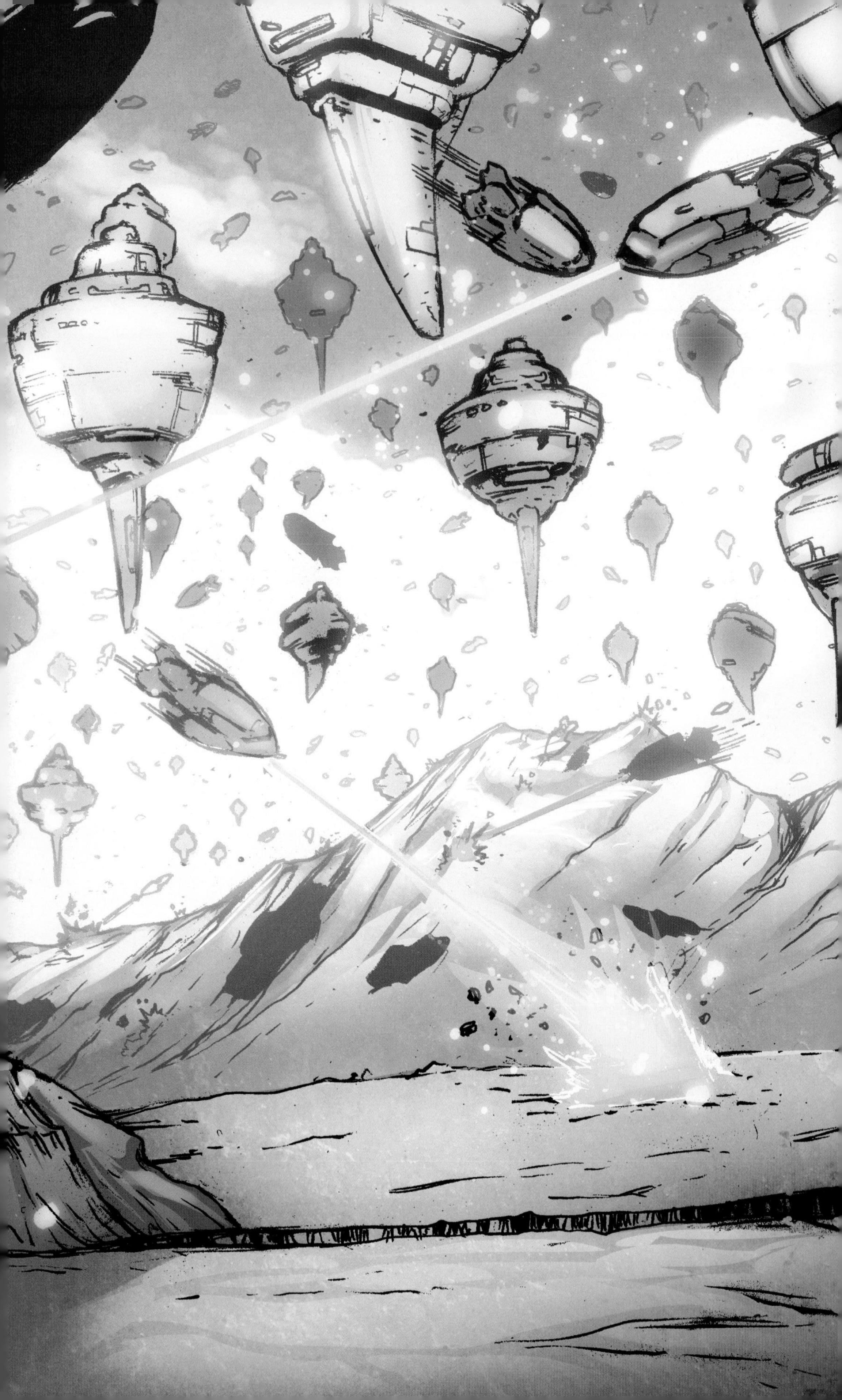

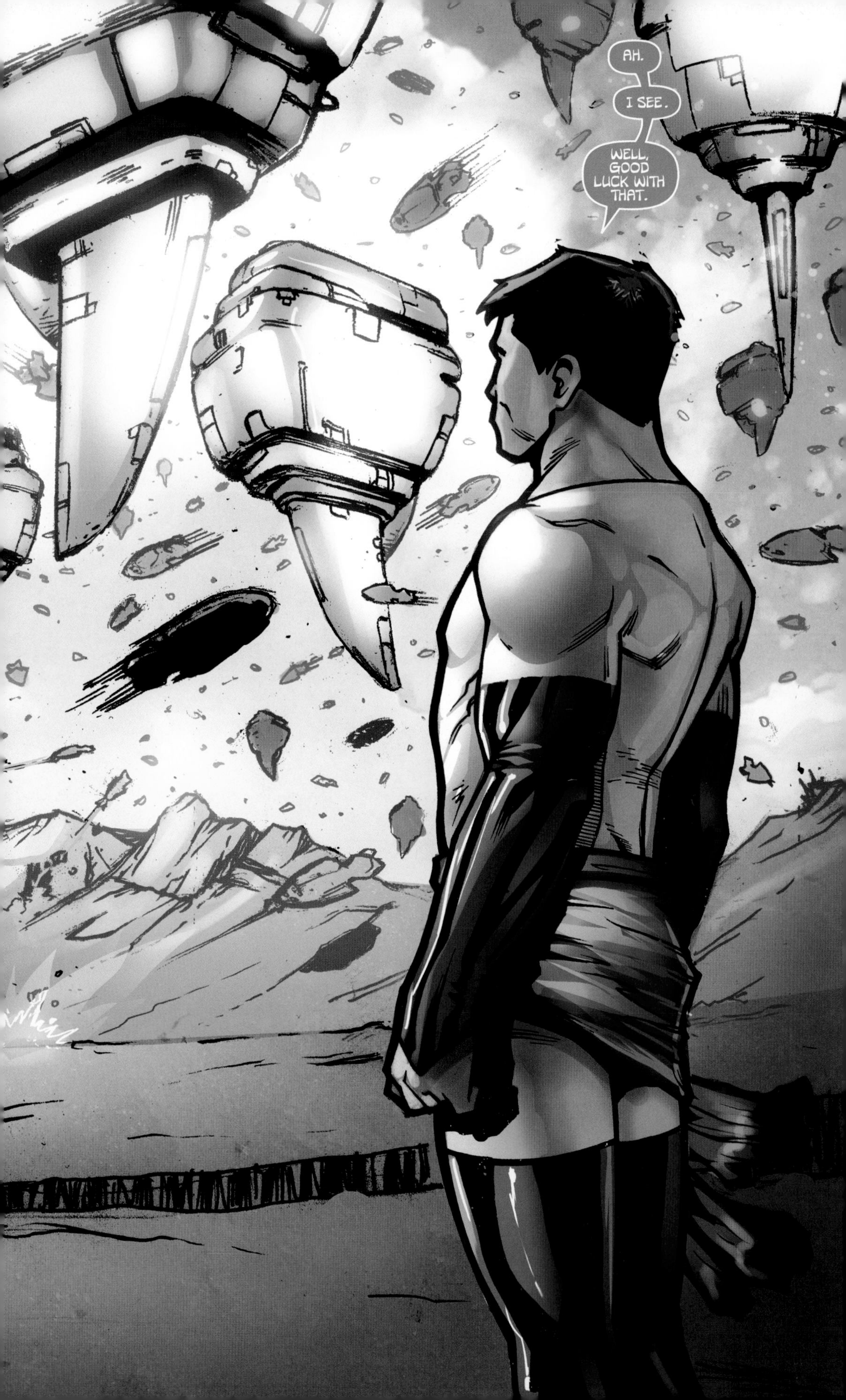
AH.
I SEE.
WELL, GOOD LUCK WITH THAT.

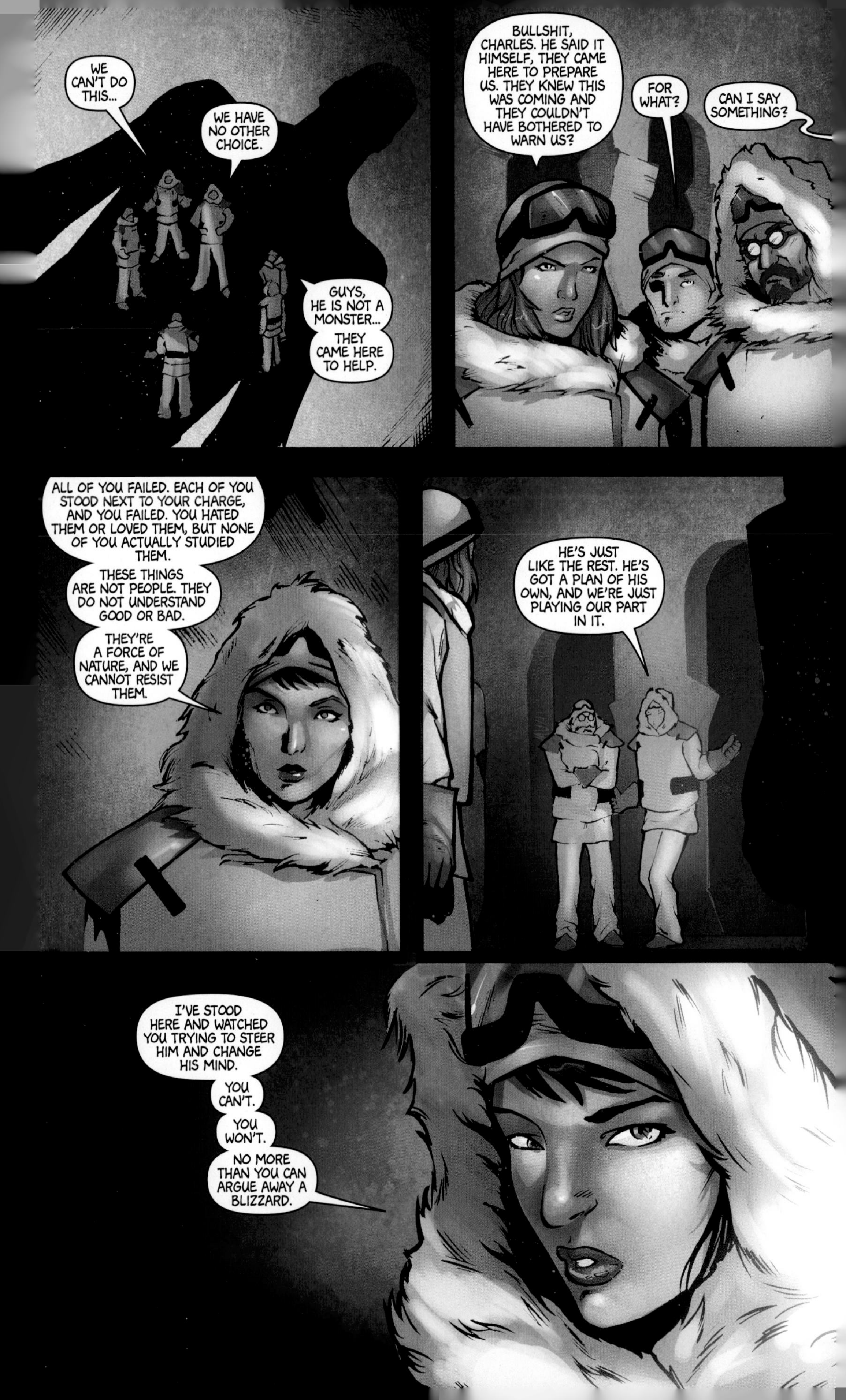
WE CAN'T DO THIS...
WE HAVE NO OTHER CHOICE.
GUYS, HE IS NOT A MONSTER...
THEY CAME HERE TO HELP.
BULLSHIT, CHARLES. HE SAID IT HIMSELF, THEY CAME HERE TO PREPARE US. THEY KNEW THIS WAS COMING AND THEY COULDN'T HAVE BOTHERED TO WARN US?
FOR WHAT?
CAN I SAY SOMETHING?
ALL OF YOU FAILED. EACH OF YOU STOOD NEXT TO YOUR CHARGE, AND YOU FAILED. YOU HATED THEM OR LOVED THEM, BUT NONE OF YOU ACTUALLY STUDIED THEM.
THESE THINGS ARE NOT PEOPLE. THEY DO NOT UNDERSTAND GOOD OR BAD.
THEY'RE A FORCE OF NATURE, AND WE CANNOT RESIST THEM.
HE'S JUST LIKE THE REST. HE'S GOT A PLAN OF HIS OWN, AND WE'RE JUST PLAYING OUR PART IN IT.
I'VE STOOD HERE AND WATCHED YOU TRYING TO STEER HIM AND CHANGE HIS MIND.
YOU CAN'T.
YOU WON'T.
NO MORE THAN YOU CAN ARGUE AWAY A BLIZZARD.

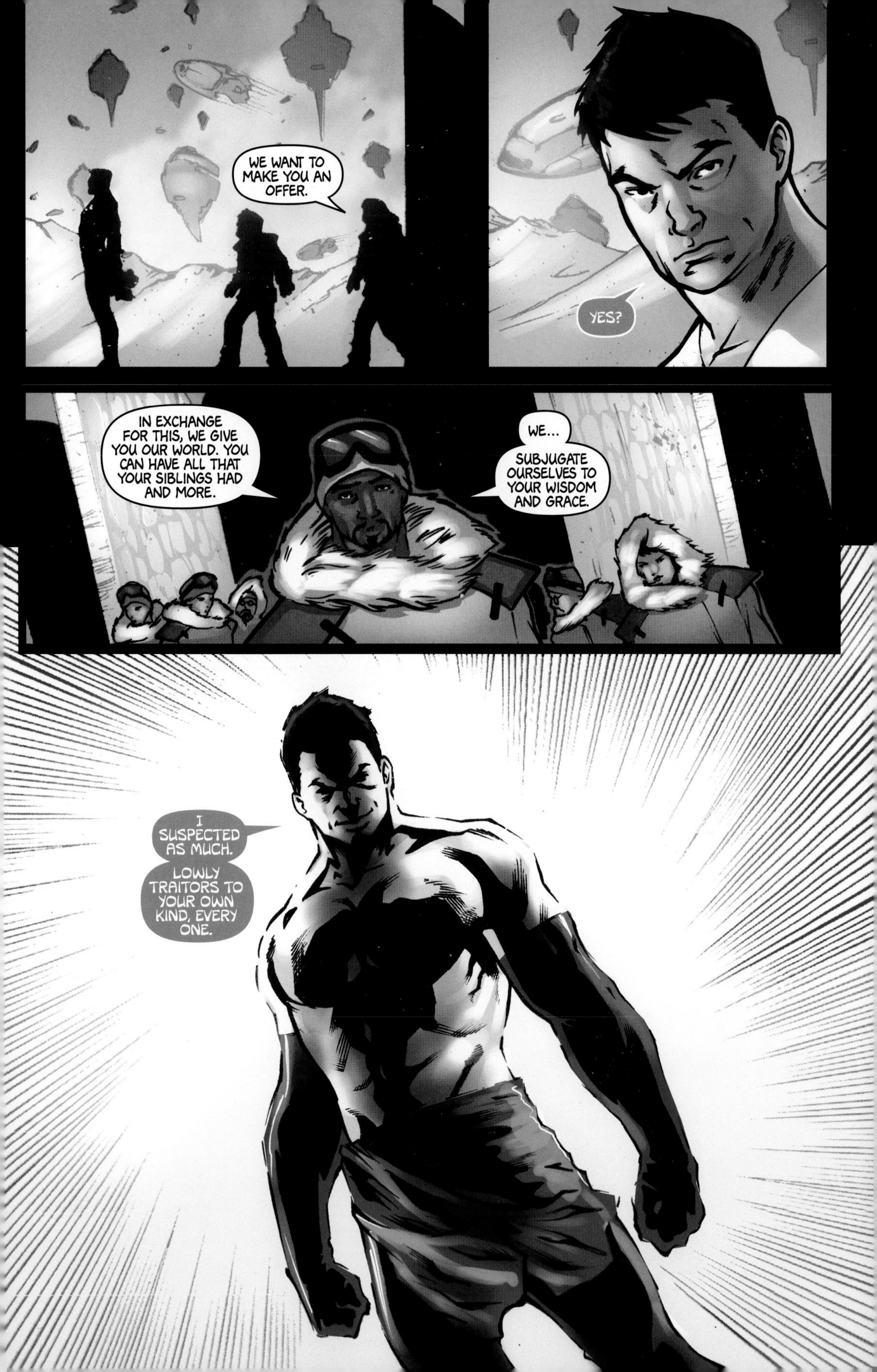
WE WANT TO MAKE YOU AN OFFER.
YES?
IN EXCHANGE FOR THIS, WE GIVE YOU OUR WORLD. YOU CAN HAVE ALL THAT YOUR SIBLINGS HAD AND MORE.
WE...
SUBJUGATE OURSELVES TO YOUR WISDOM AND GRACE.
I SUSPECTED AS MUCH.
LOWLY TRAITORS TO YOUR OWN KIND, EVERY ONE.

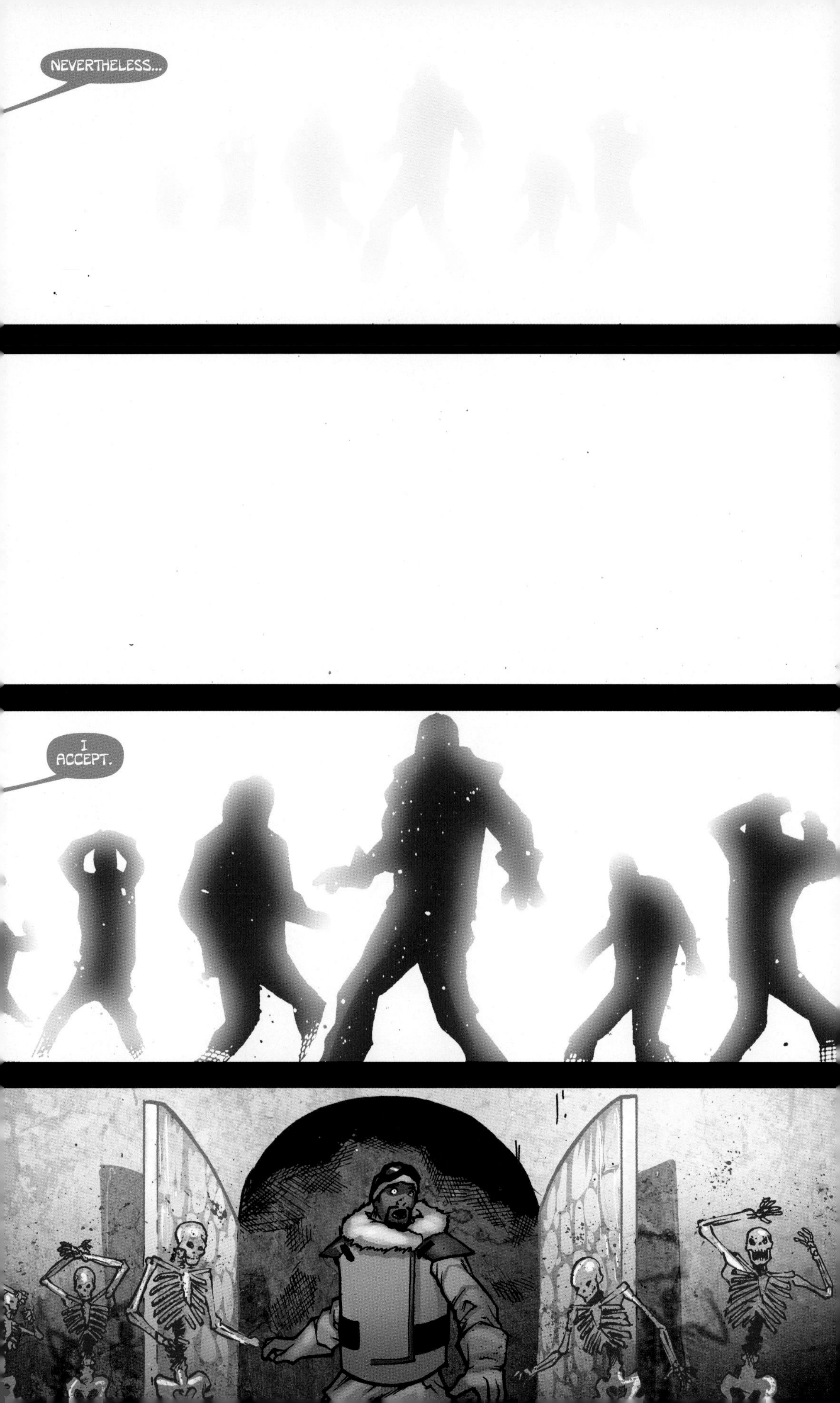
NEVERTHELESS...
I ACCEPT.

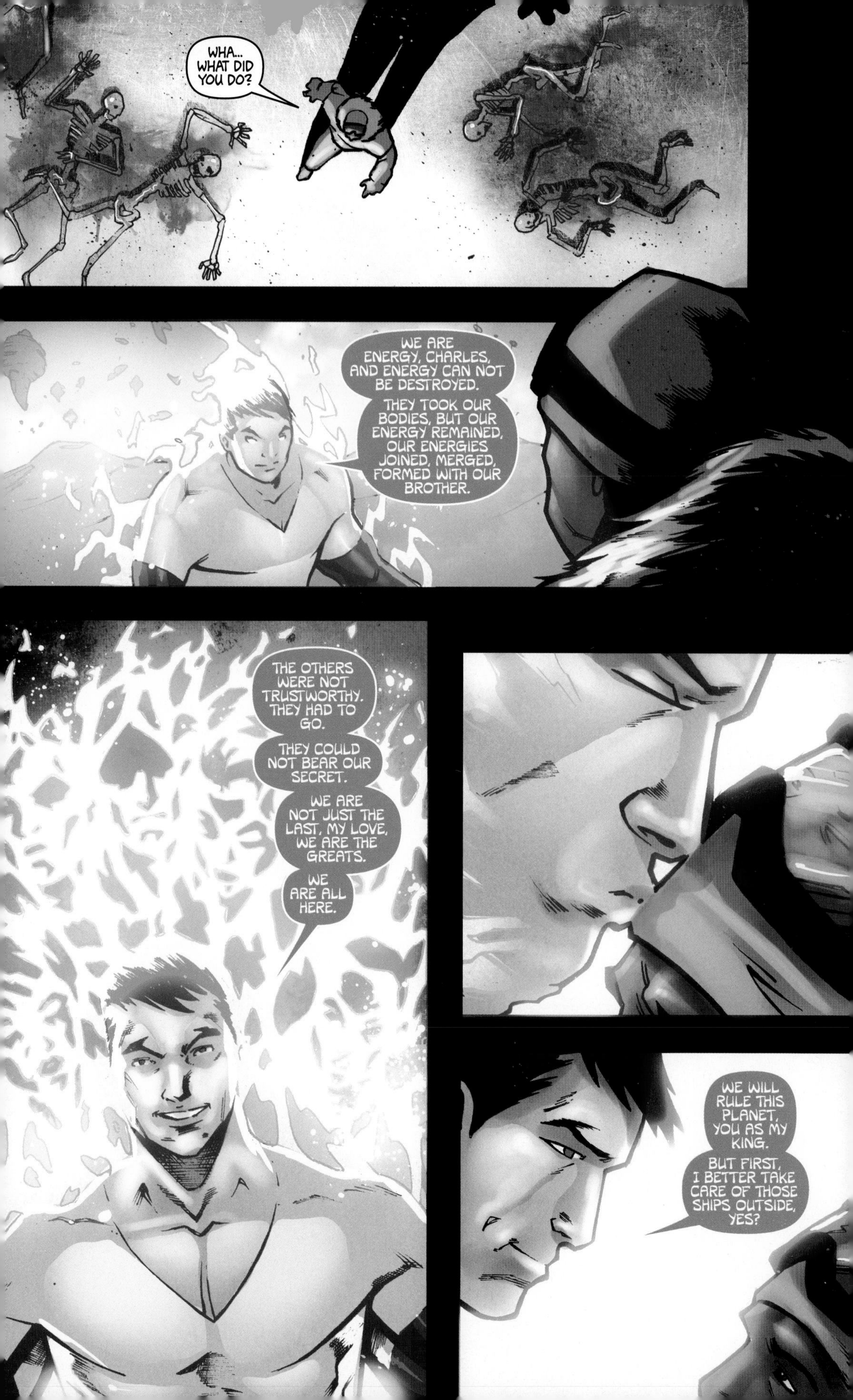
WHA... WHAT DID YOU DO?
WE ARE ENERGY, CHARLES, AND ENERGY CAN NOT BE DESTROYED.
THEY TOOK OUR BODIES, BUT OUR ENERGY REMAINED, OUR ENERGIES JOINED, MERGED, FORMED WITH OUR BROTHER.
THE OTHERS WERE NOT TRUSTWORTHY. THEY HAD TO GO.
THEY COULD NOT BEAR OUR SECRET.
WE ARE NOT JUST THE LAST, MY LOVE, WE ARE THE GREATS.
WE ARE ALL HERE.
WE WILL RULE THIS PLANET, YOU AS MY KING.
BUT FIRST, I BETTER TAKE CARE OF THOSE SHIPS OUTSIDE, YES?

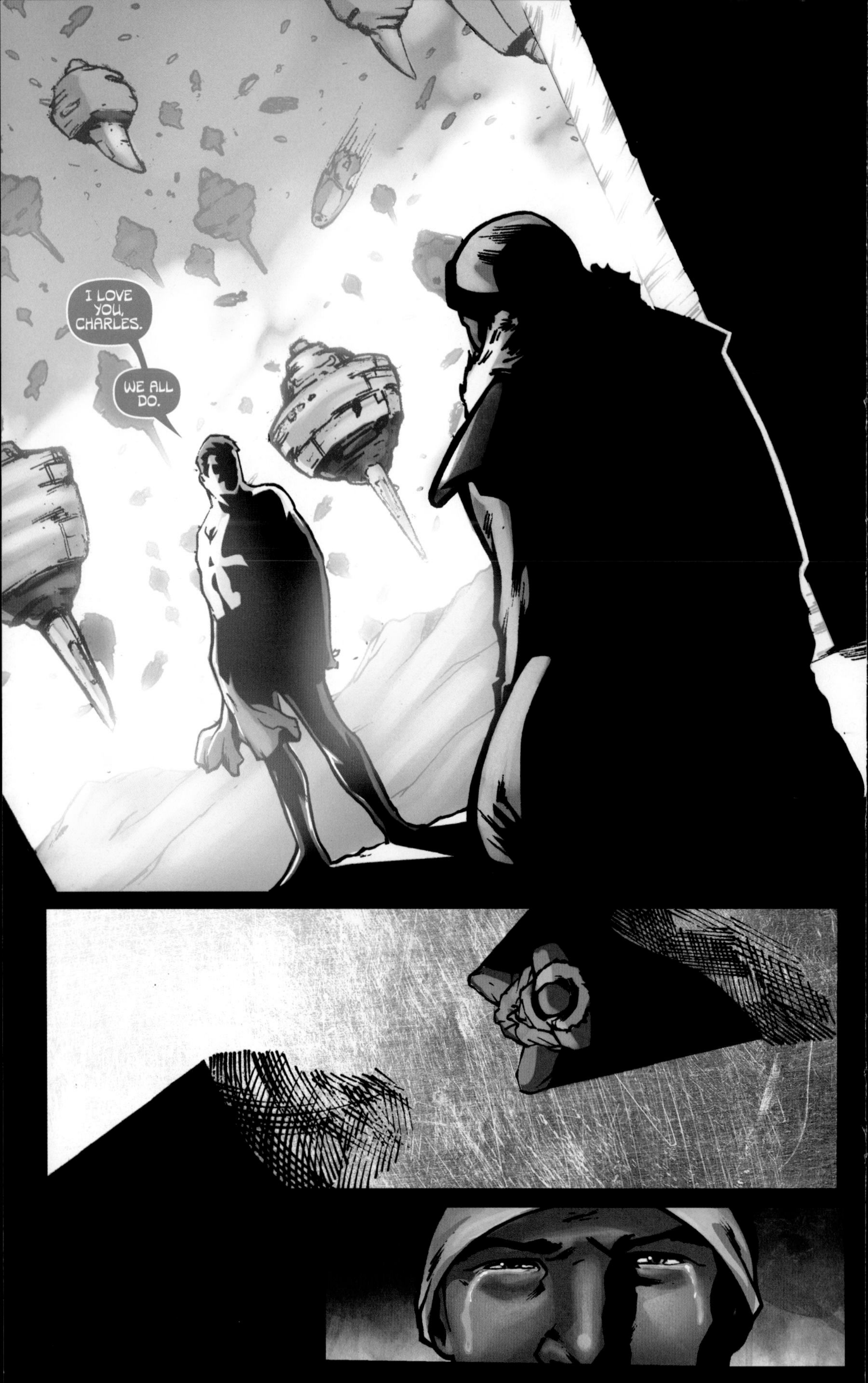
I LOVE YOU, CHARLES.
WE ALL DO.

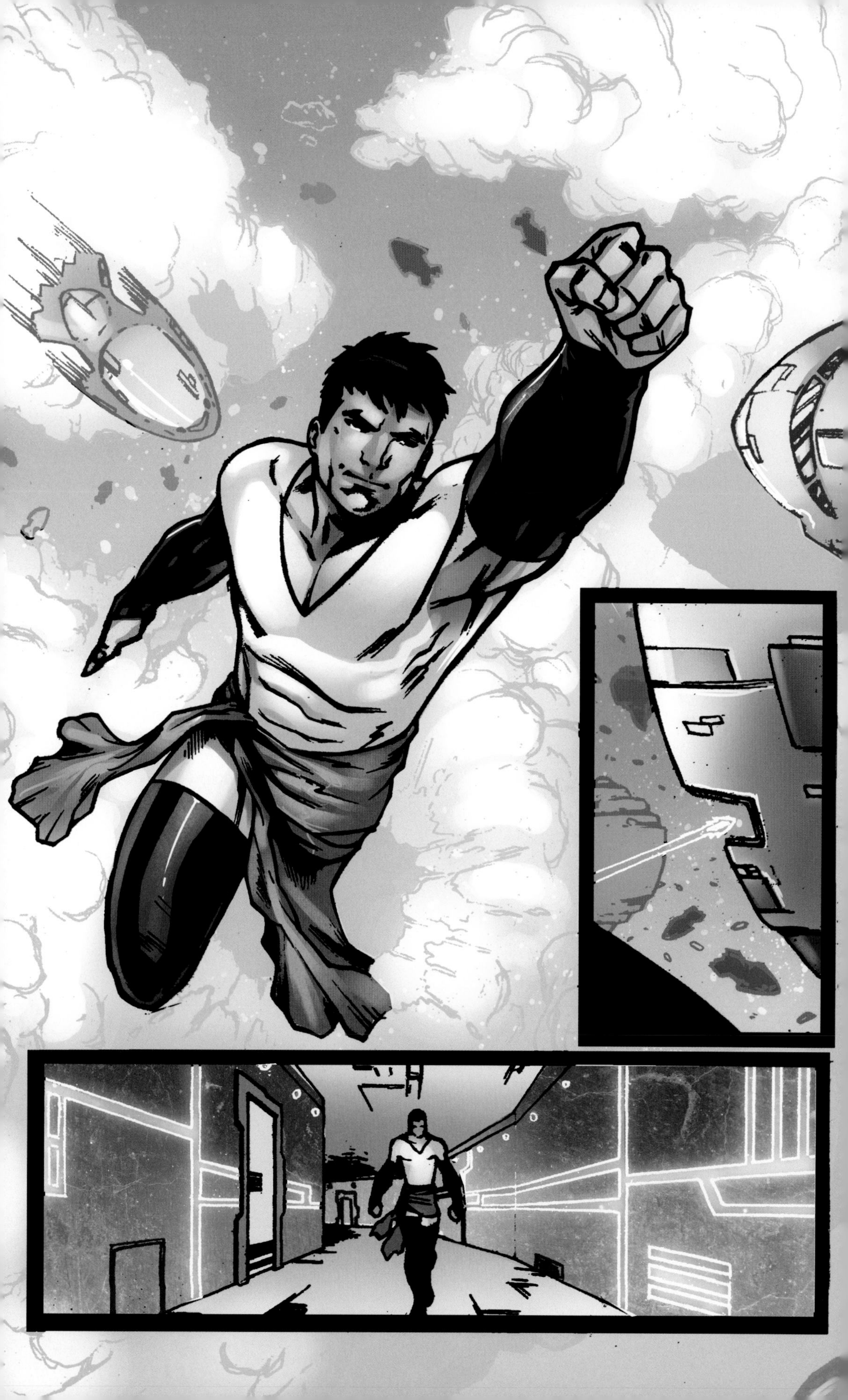

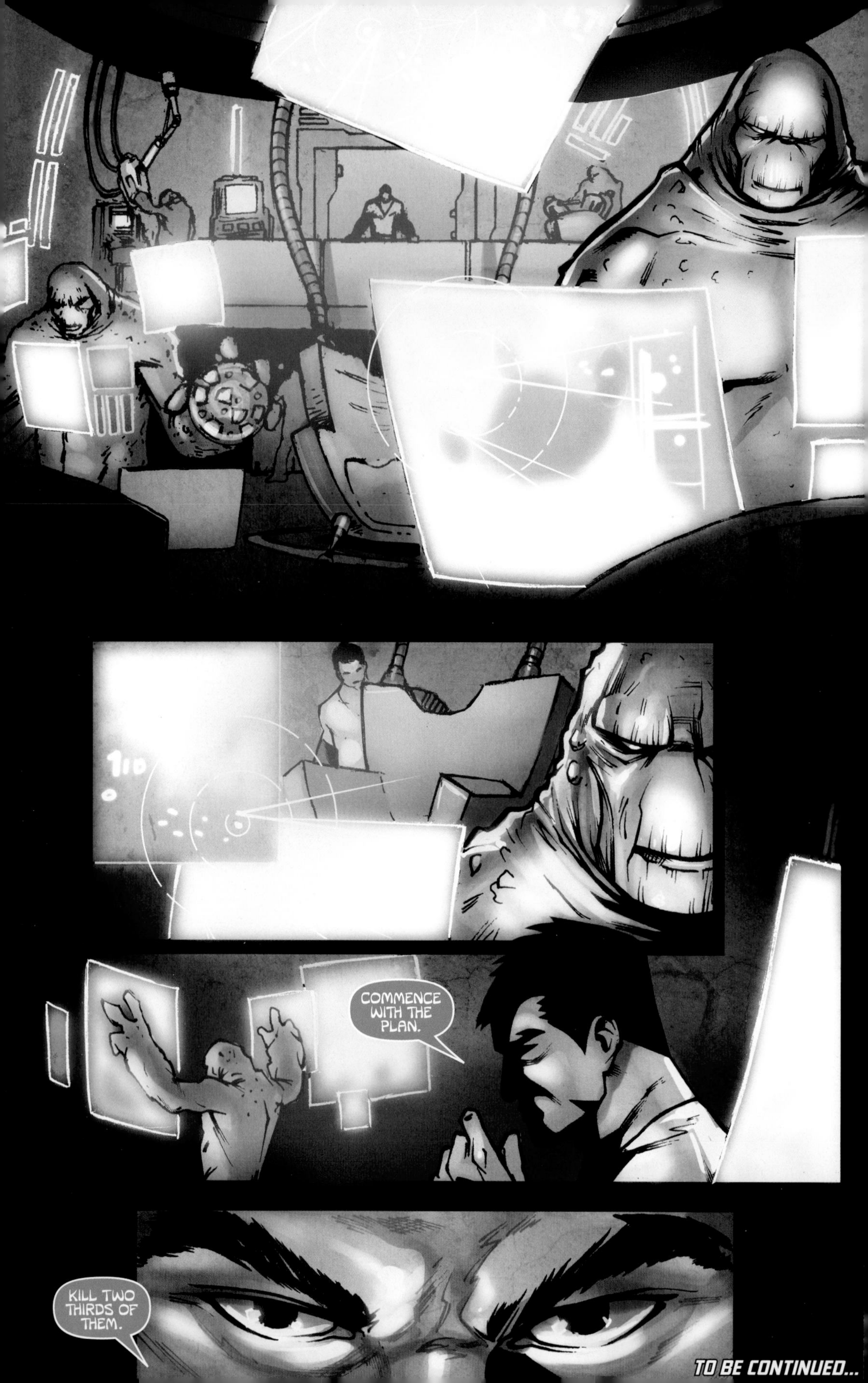
COMMENCE WITH THE PLAN.
KILL TWO THIRDS OF THEM.
TO BE CONTINUED...

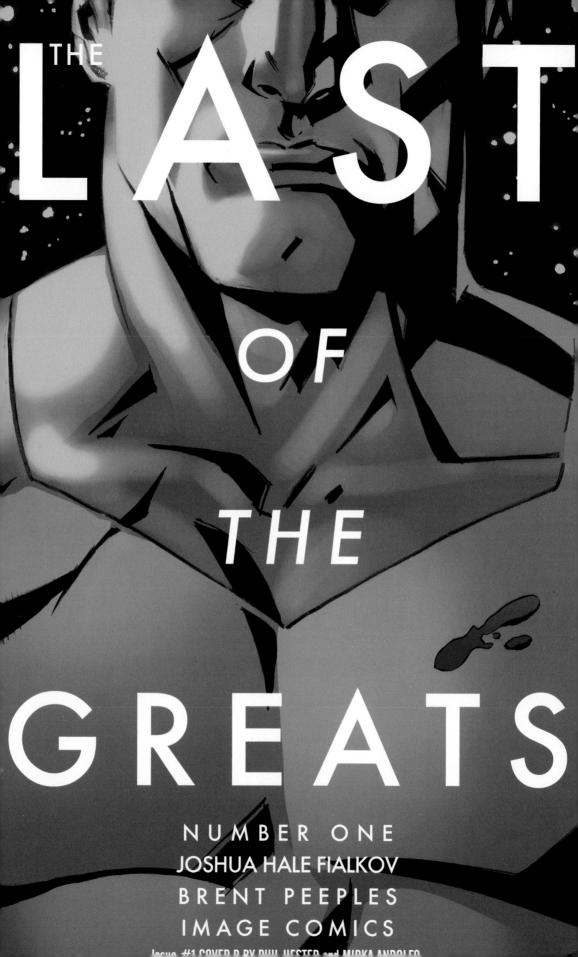

THE LAST OF THE GREATS

NUMBER ONE
JOSHUA HALE FIALKOV
BRENT PEEPLES
IMAGE COMICS

Issue #1 COVER B BY PHIL HESTER and MIRKA ANDOLFO

Issue #2 COVER A BY BRENT PEEPLES, MATTHEW WAITE and MIRKA ANDOLFO

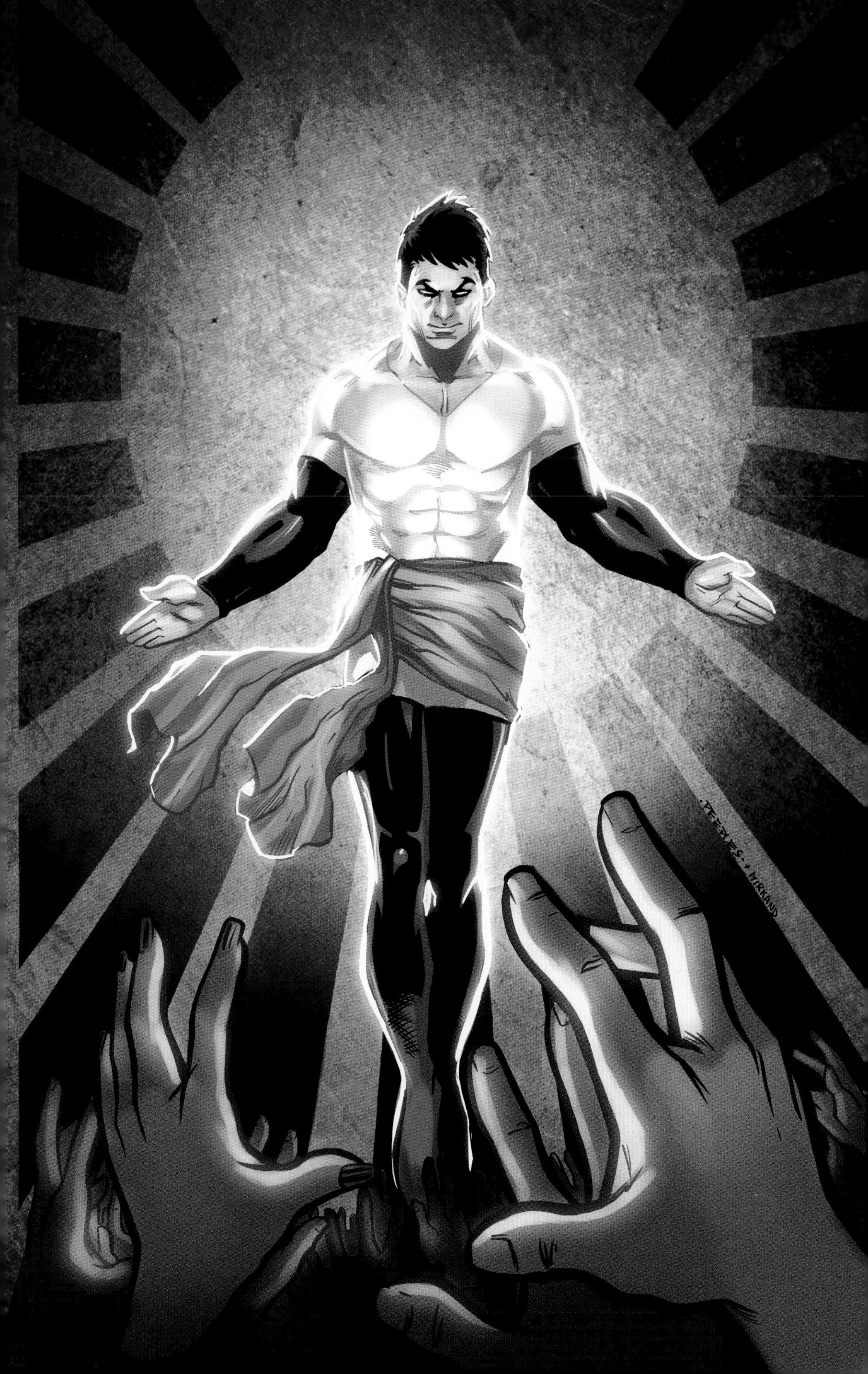

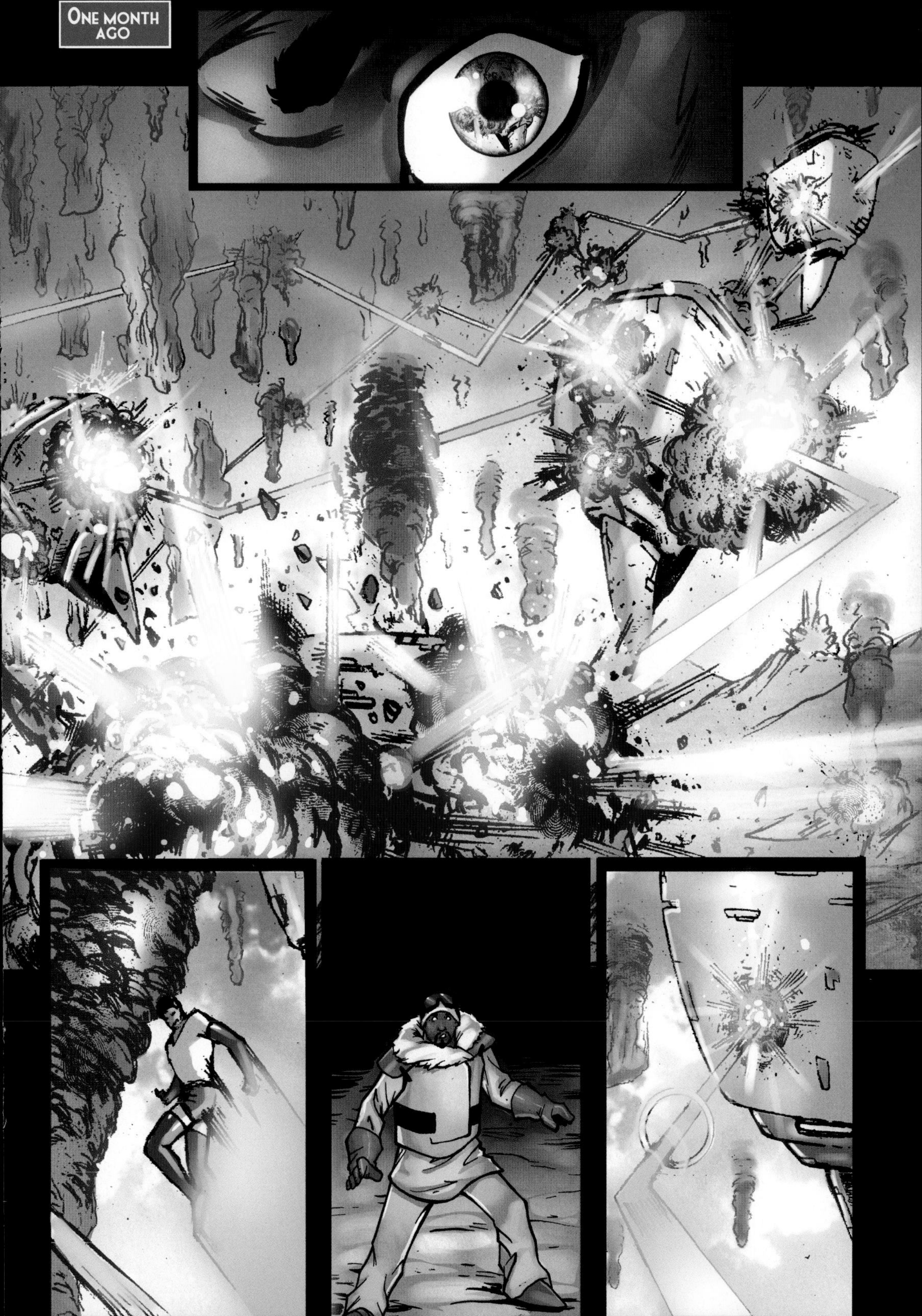
ONE MONTH AGO

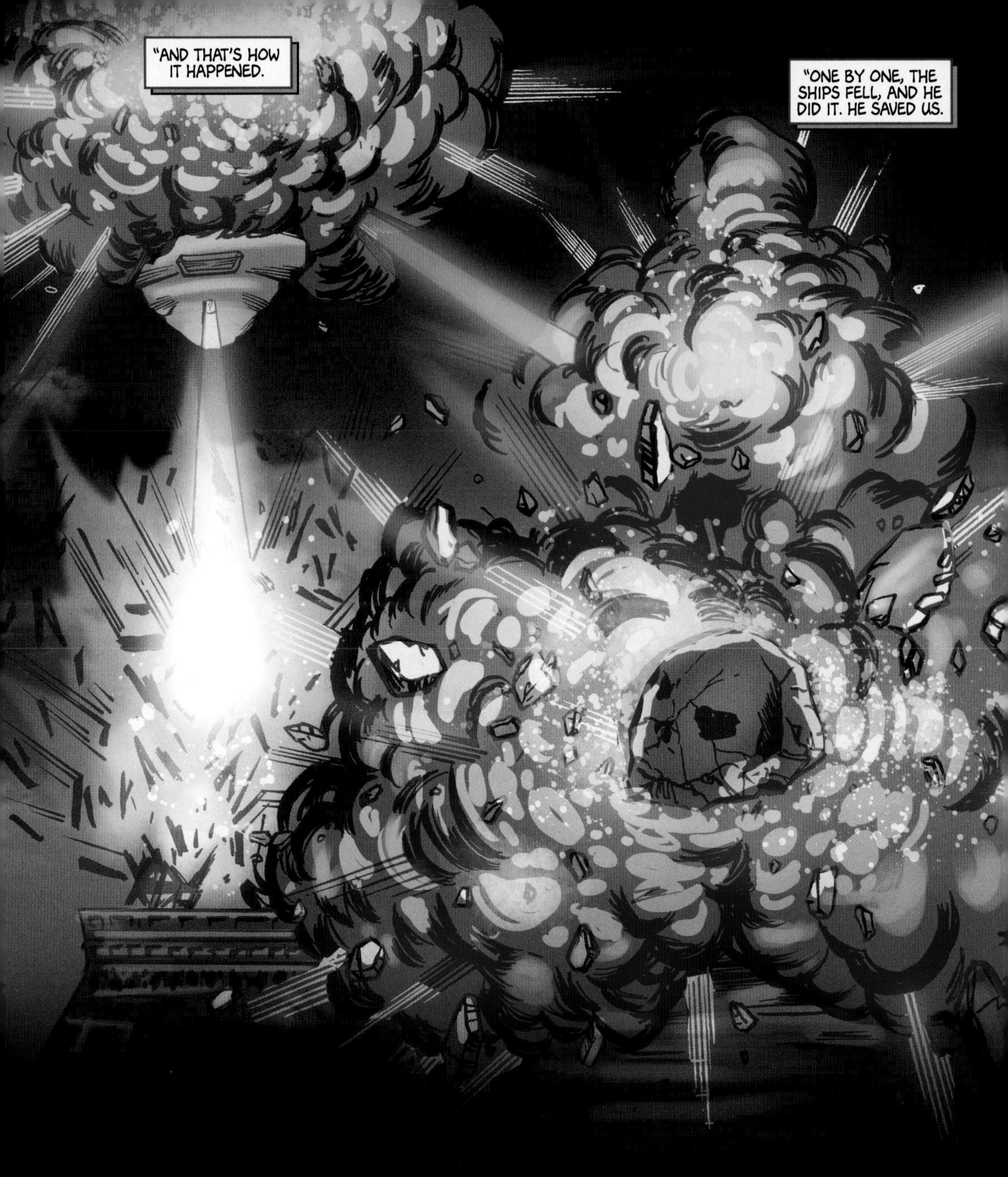
"AND THAT'S HOW IT HAPPENED.
"ONE BY ONE, THE SHIPS FELL, AND HE DID IT. HE SAVED US.

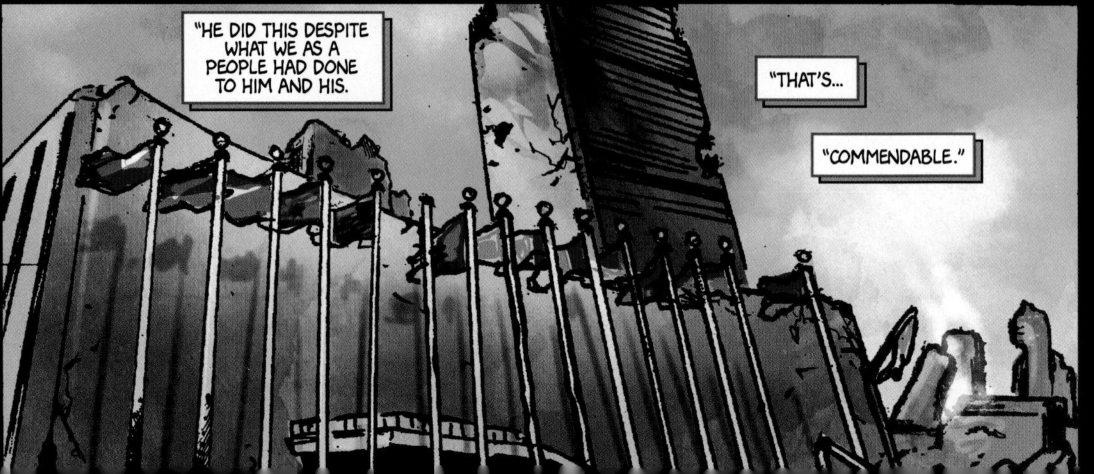
"HE DID THIS DESPITE WHAT WE AS A PEOPLE HAD DONE TO HIM AND HIS.
"THAT'S...
"COMMENDABLE."

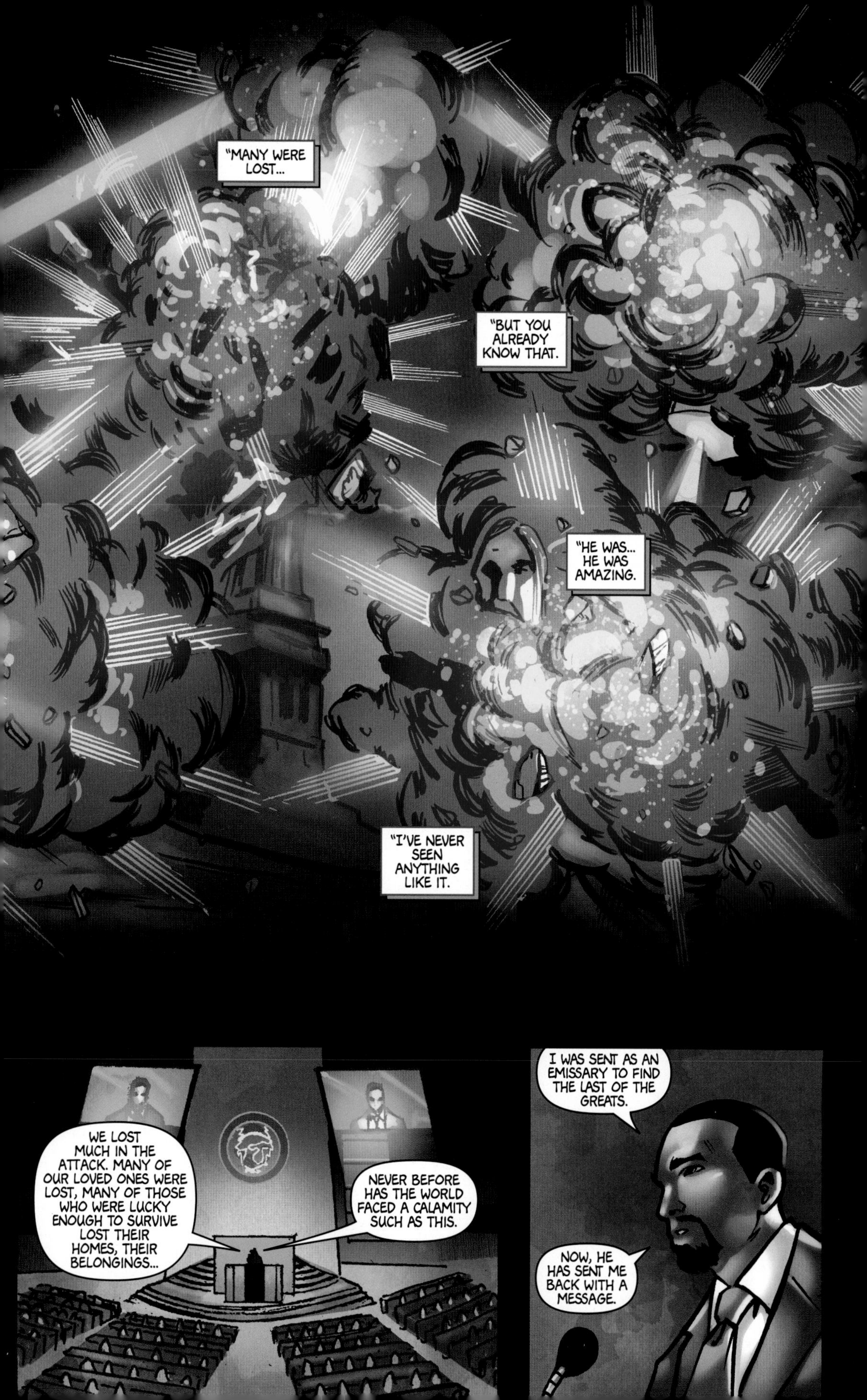
"MANY WERE LOST...
"BUT YOU ALREADY KNOW THAT.
"HE WAS... HE WAS AMAZING.
"I'VE NEVER SEEN ANYTHING LIKE IT.
WE LOST MUCH IN THE ATTACK. MANY OF OUR LOVED ONES WERE LOST, MANY OF THOSE WHO WERE LUCKY ENOUGH TO SURVIVE LOST THEIR HOMES, THEIR BELONGINGS...
NEVER BEFORE HAS THE WORLD FACED A CALAMITY SUCH AS THIS.
I WAS SENT AS AN EMISSARY TO FIND THE LAST OF THE GREATS.
NOW, HE HAS SENT ME BACK WITH A MESSAGE.

HE WAS HERE FOR US, BUT NOW, HE NEEDS US.

THE ATTACK HAS WEAKENED HIM, AND ONLY...

JUST...

AND ONLY MANKIND'S FAITH IN HIM CAN RESTORE HIM.

ONLY BY PUTTING OUR TRUST, OUR FUTURE...

OUR LIVES IN HIS HANDS...

"ONLY THEN CAN HE PROTECT US.

"READY US FOR WHAT COMES NEXT.

THIS IS YOUR FAULT!

WHY DID YOU LET THEM DIE?

THEY DIED FOR OUR SINS!

"WE MUST PLEDGE ALLEGIANCE TO HIM, DEVOTE OUR EVERY MINUTE TO HIS SERVICE.

"THEN HE WILL HAVE THE STRENGTH TO MAKE US STRONG AGAIN."

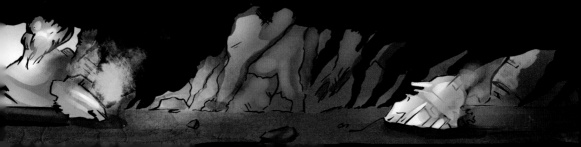

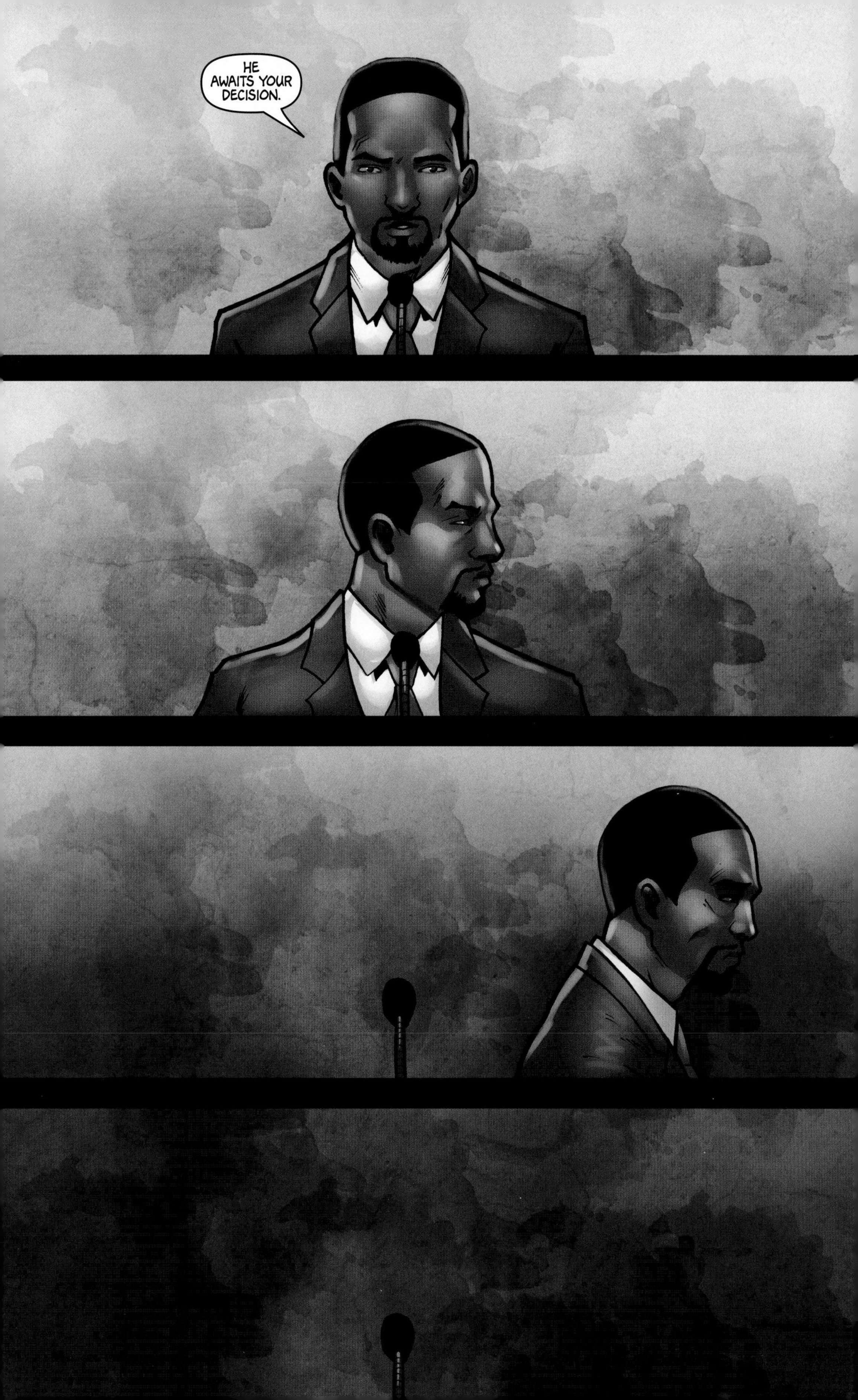
HE AWAITS YOUR DECISION.

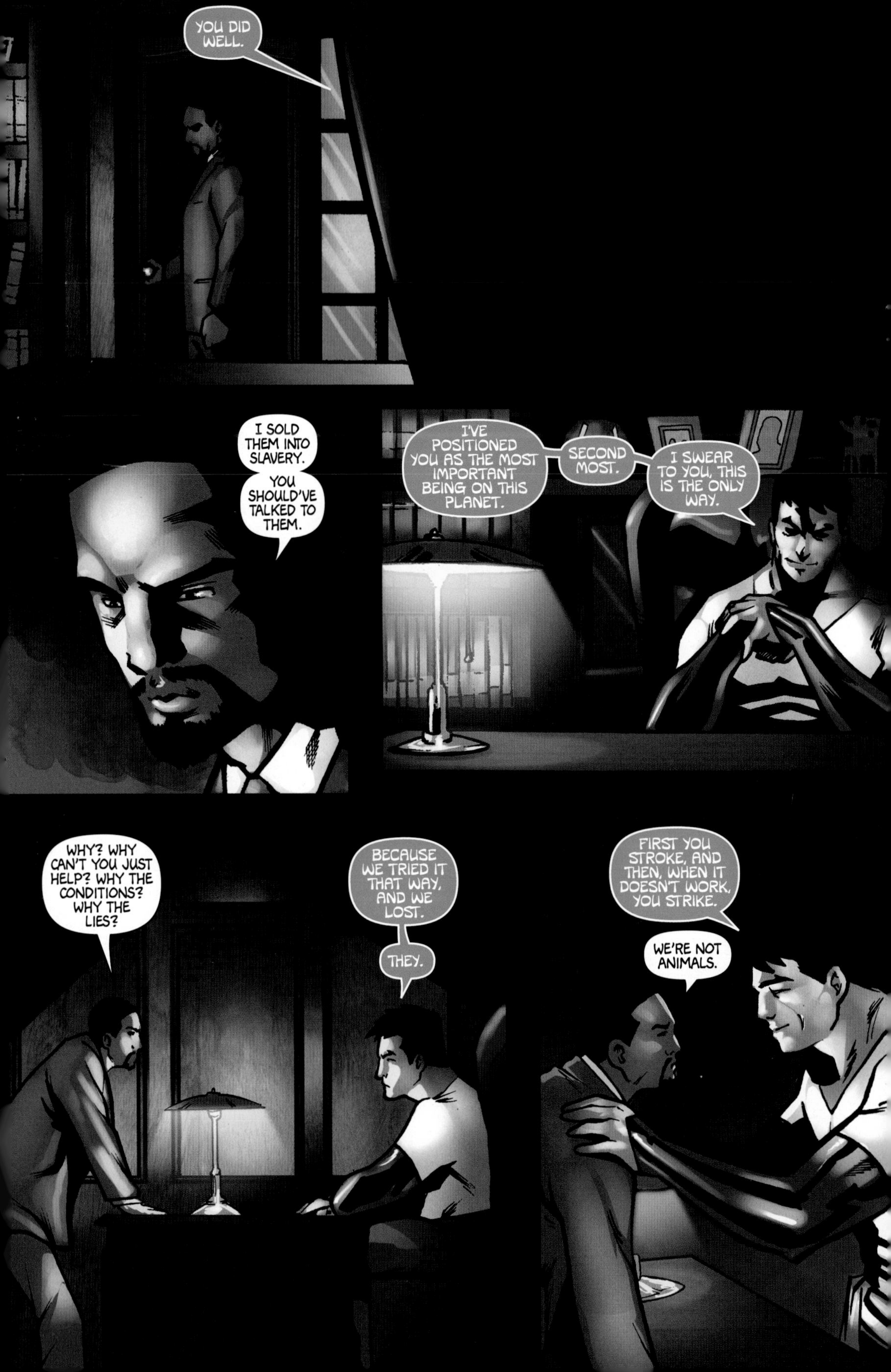
YOU DID WELL.
I SOLD THEM INTO SLAVERY.
YOU SHOULD'VE TALKED TO THEM.
I'VE POSITIONED YOU AS THE MOST IMPORTANT BEING ON THIS PLANET.
SECOND MOST.
I SWEAR TO YOU, THIS IS THE ONLY WAY.
WHY? WHY CAN'T YOU JUST HELP? WHY THE CONDITIONS? WHY THE LIES?
BECAUSE WE TRIED IT THAT WAY, AND WE LOST.
THEY.
FIRST YOU STROKE, AND THEN, WHEN IT DOESN'T WORK, YOU STRIKE.
WE'RE NOT ANIMALS.

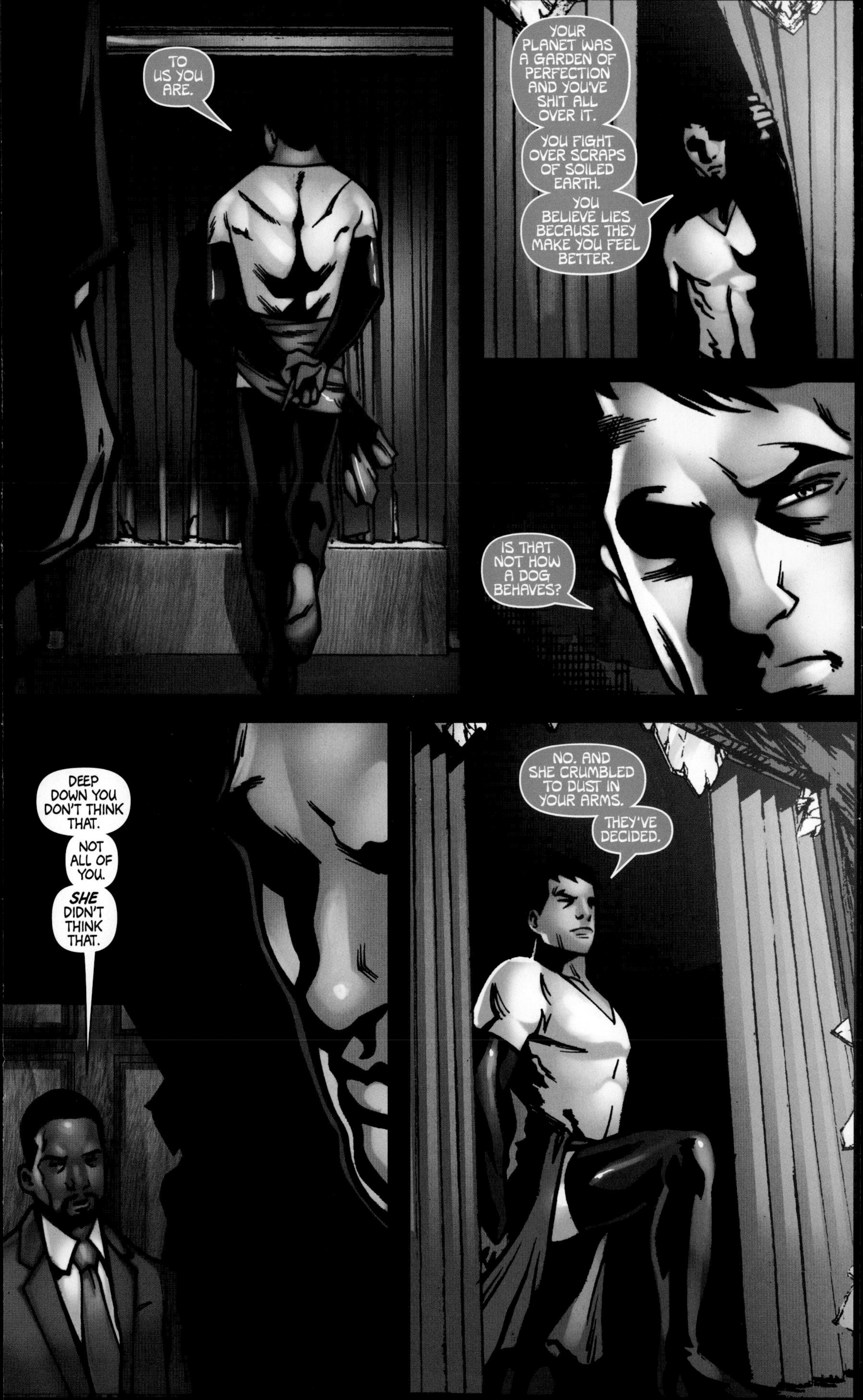
TO US YOU ARE.
YOUR PLANET WAS A GARDEN OF PERFECTION AND YOU'VE SHIT ALL OVER IT.
YOU FIGHT OVER SCRAPS OF SOILED EARTH.
YOU BELIEVE LIES BECAUSE THEY MAKE YOU FEEL BETTER.
IS THAT NOT HOW A DOG BEHAVES?
DEEP DOWN YOU DON'T THINK THAT.
NOT ALL OF YOU.
SHE DIDN'T THINK THAT.
NO. AND SHE CRUMBLED TO DUST IN YOUR ARMS.
THEY'VE DECIDED.

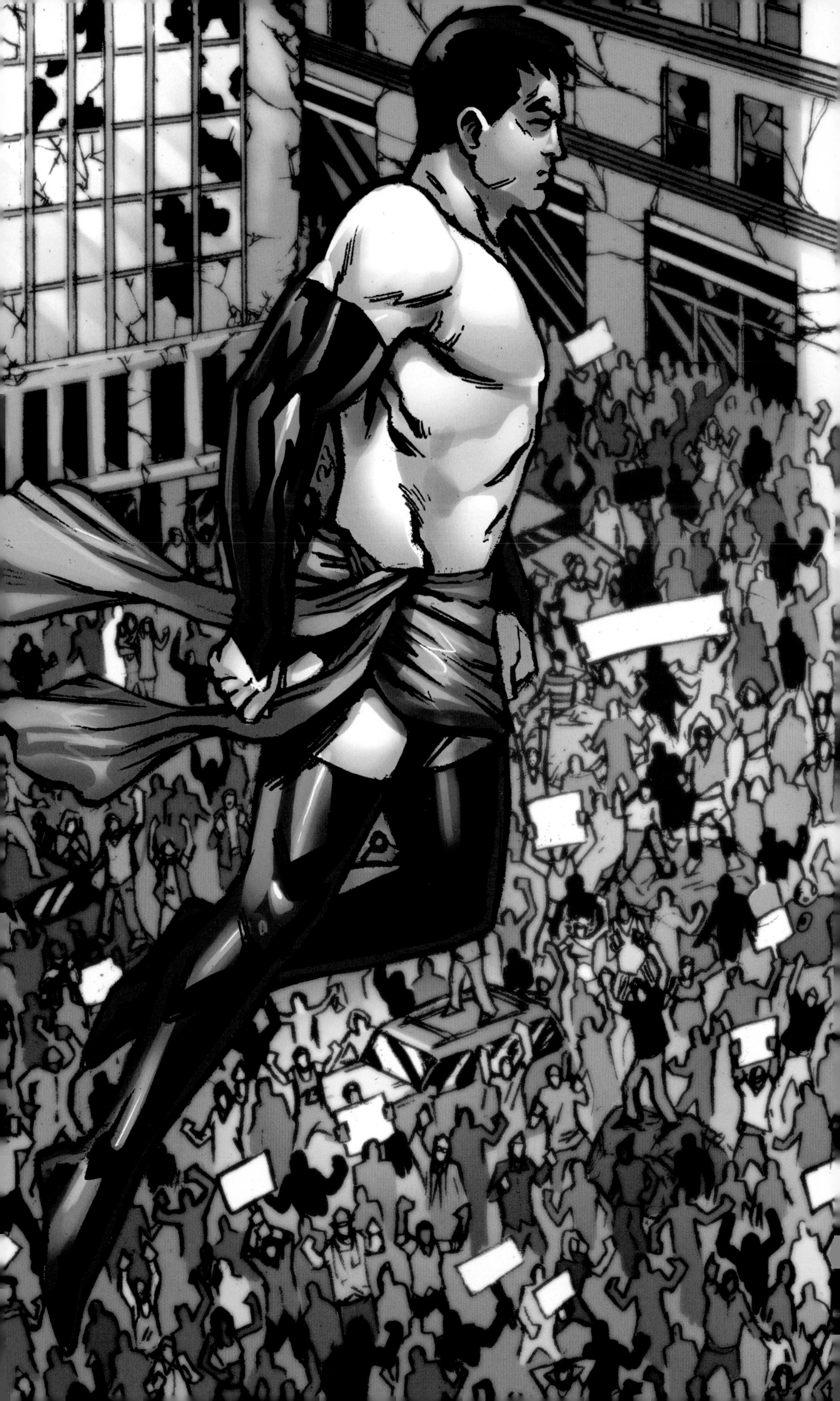

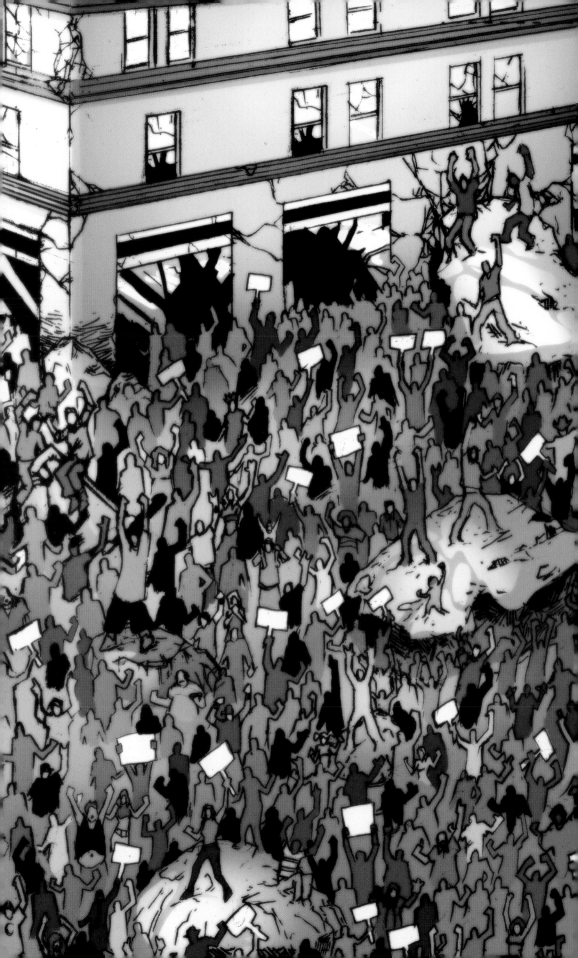

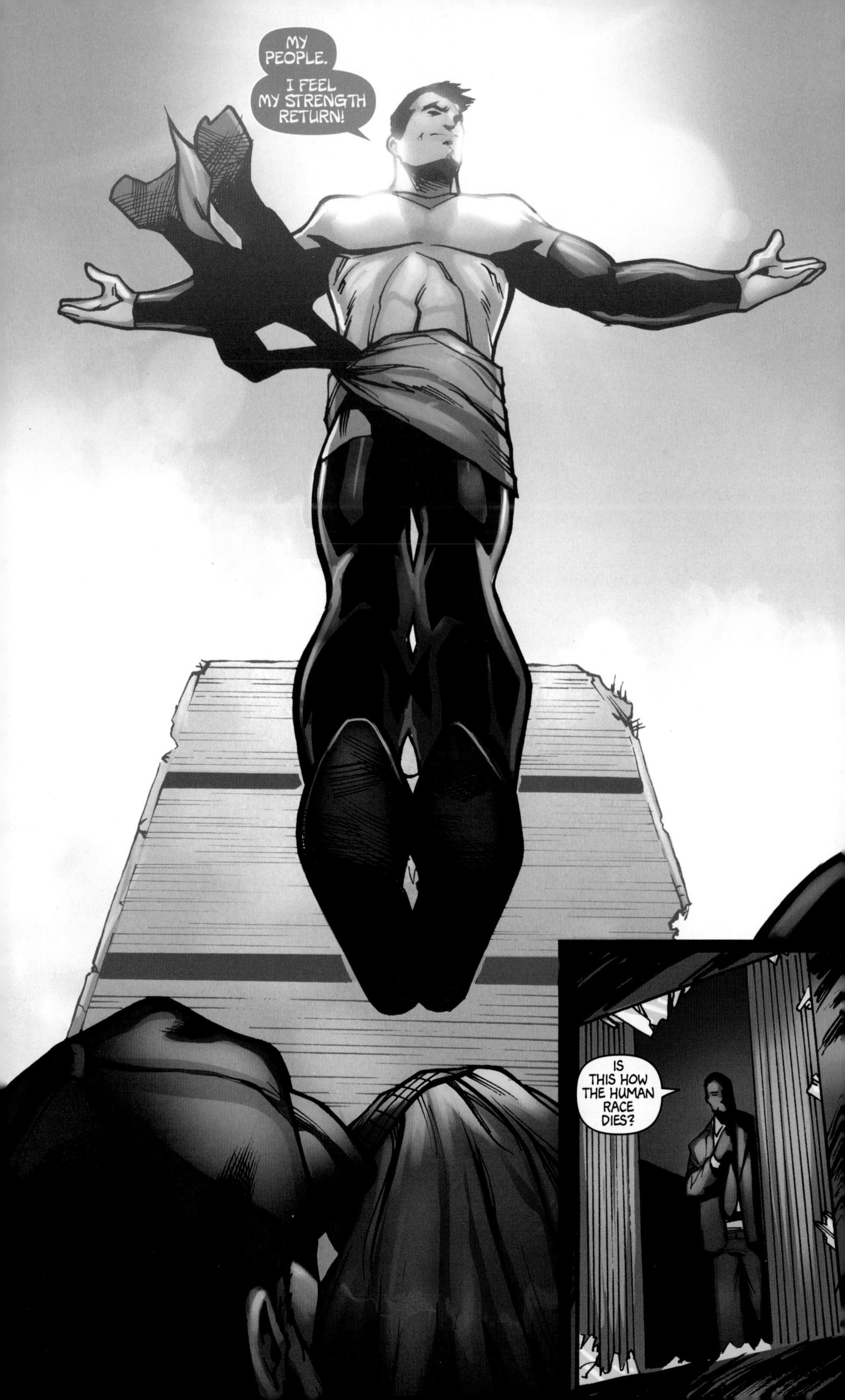
MY PEOPLE.
I FEEL MY STRENGTH RETURN!
IS THIS HOW THE HUMAN RACE DIES?

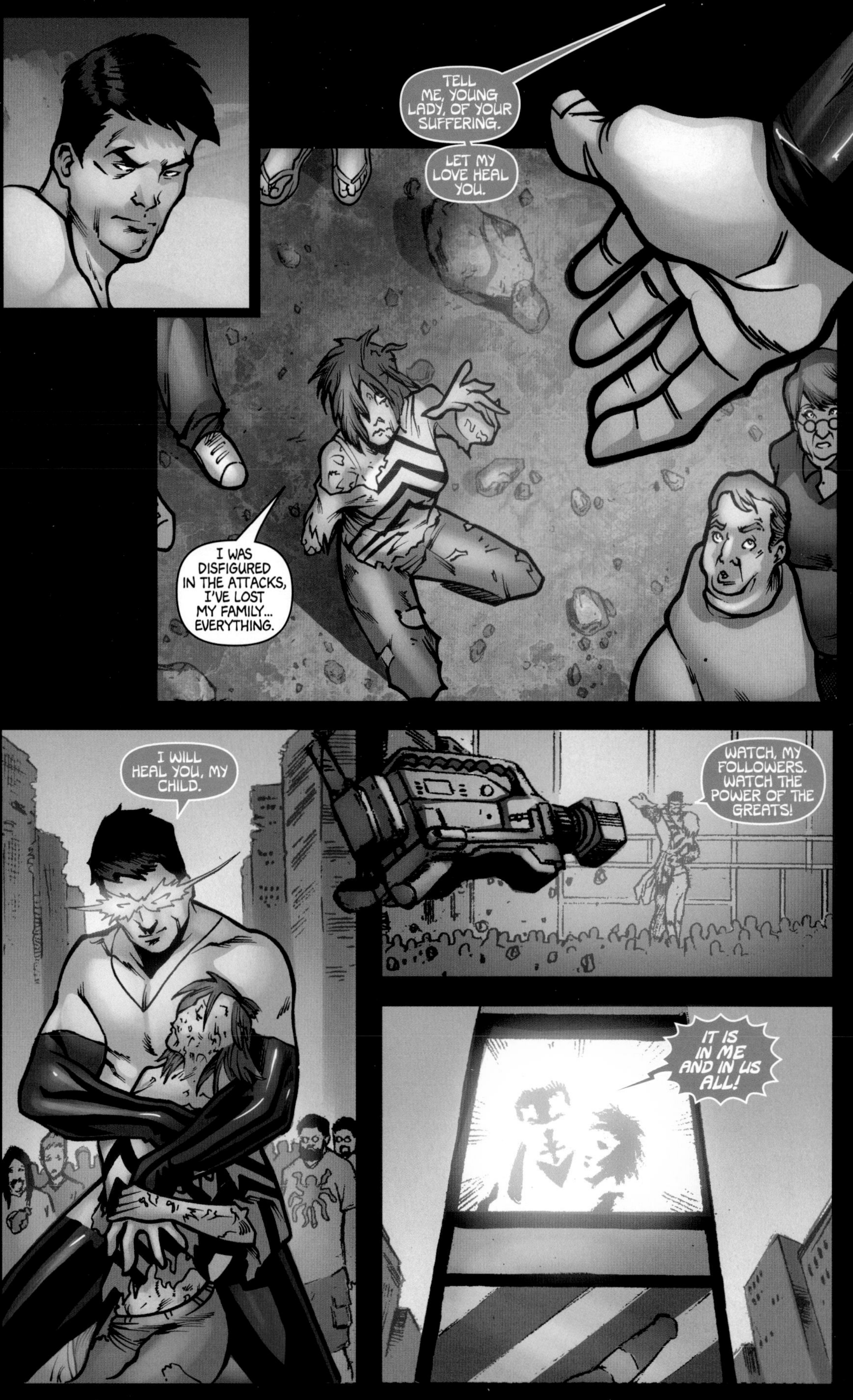
TELL ME, YOUNG LADY, OF YOUR SUFFERING.
LET MY LOVE HEAL YOU.
I WAS DISFIGURED IN THE ATTACKS, I'VE LOST MY FAMILY... EVERYTHING.
I WILL HEAL YOU, MY CHILD.
WATCH, MY FOLLOWERS. WATCH THE POWER OF THE GREATS!
IT IS IN ME AND IN US ALL!

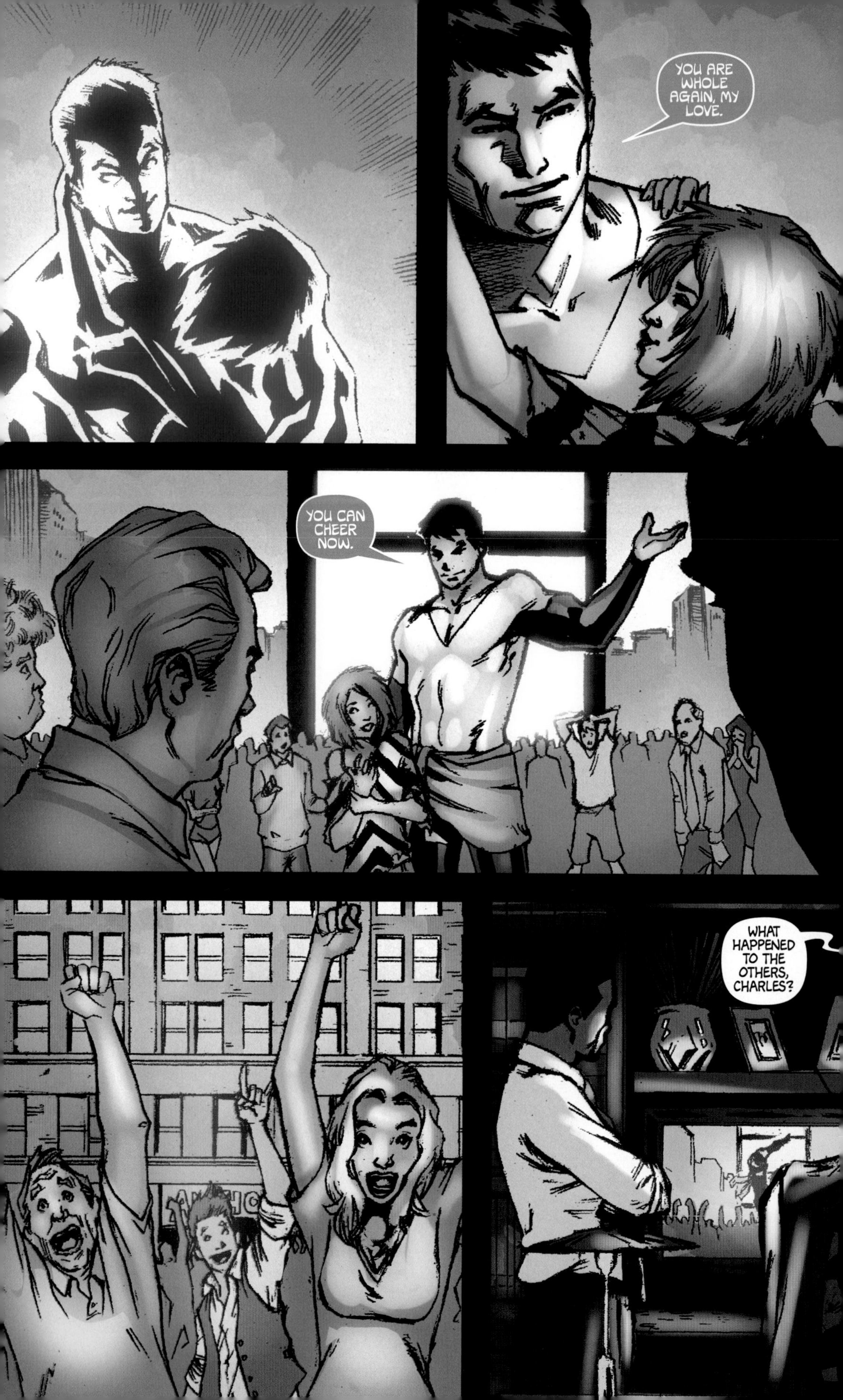
YOU ARE WHOLE AGAIN, MY LOVE.
YOU CAN CHEER NOW.
WHAT HAPPENED TO THE OTHERS, CHARLES?

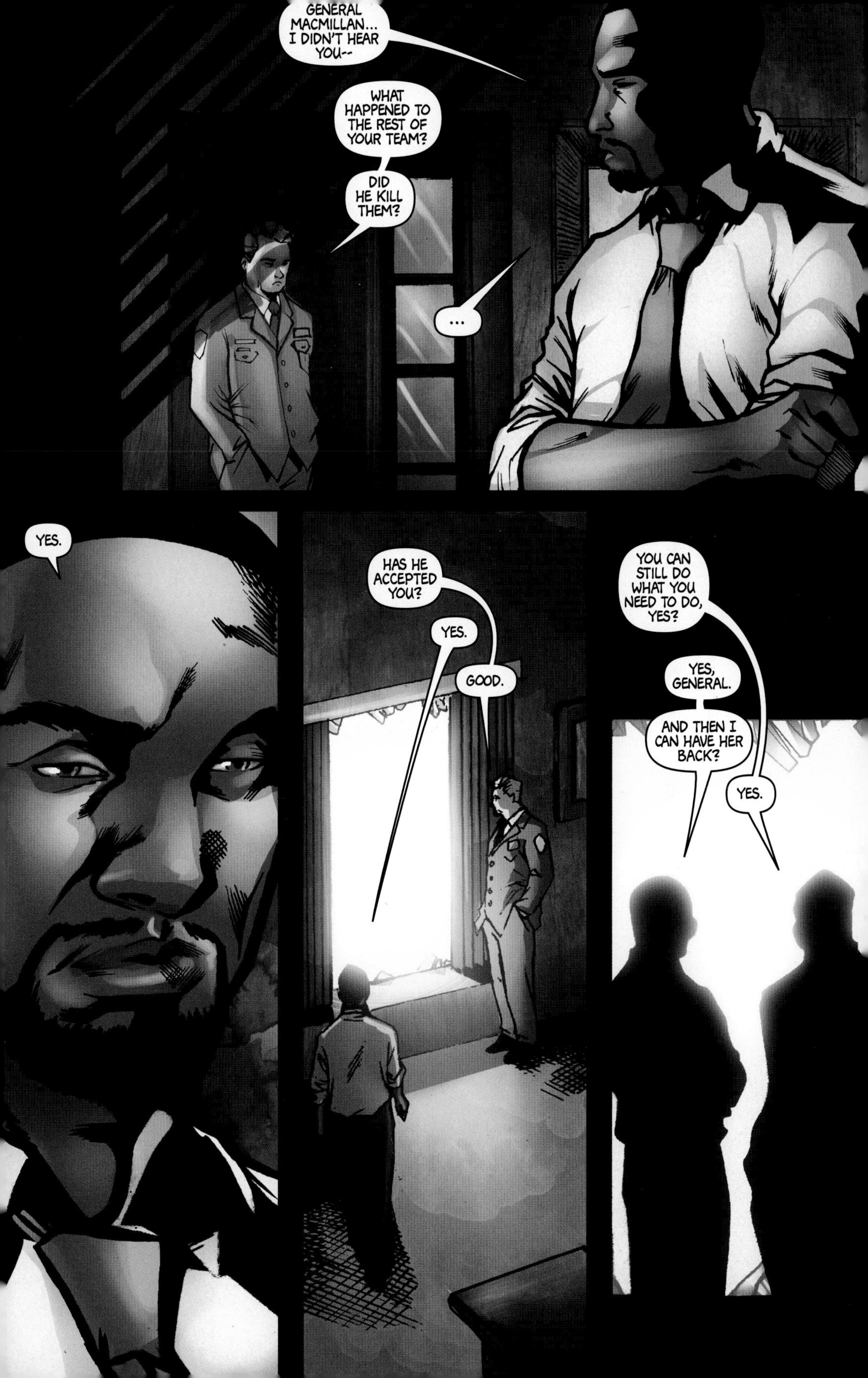
GENERAL MACMILLAN... I DIDN'T HEAR YOU--
WHAT HAPPENED TO THE REST OF YOUR TEAM?
DID HE KILL THEM?
...
YES.
HAS HE ACCEPTED YOU?
YES.
GOOD.
YOU CAN STILL DO WHAT YOU NEED TO DO, YES?
YES, GENERAL.
AND THEN I CAN HAVE HER BACK?
YES.

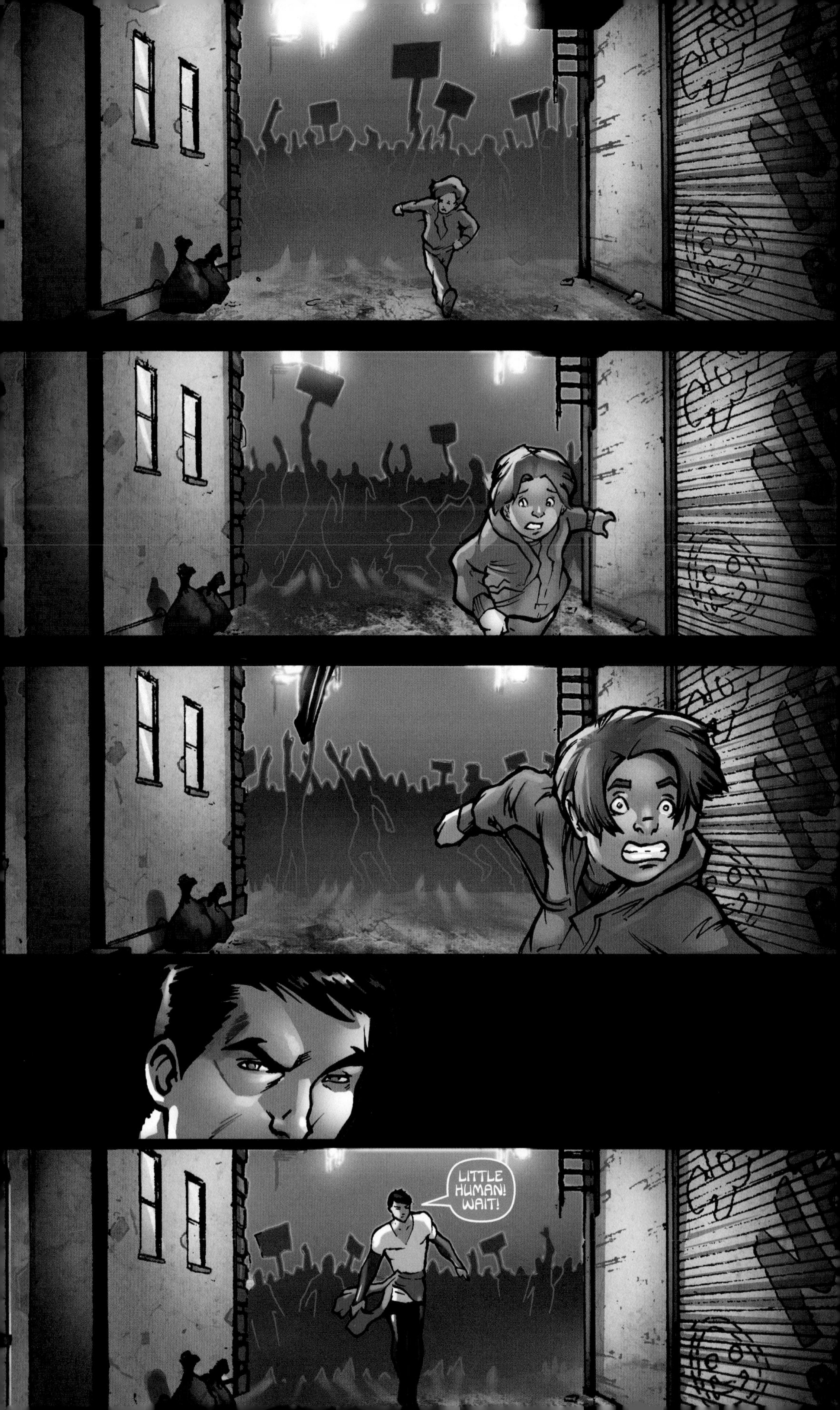
LITTLE HUMAN! WAIT!

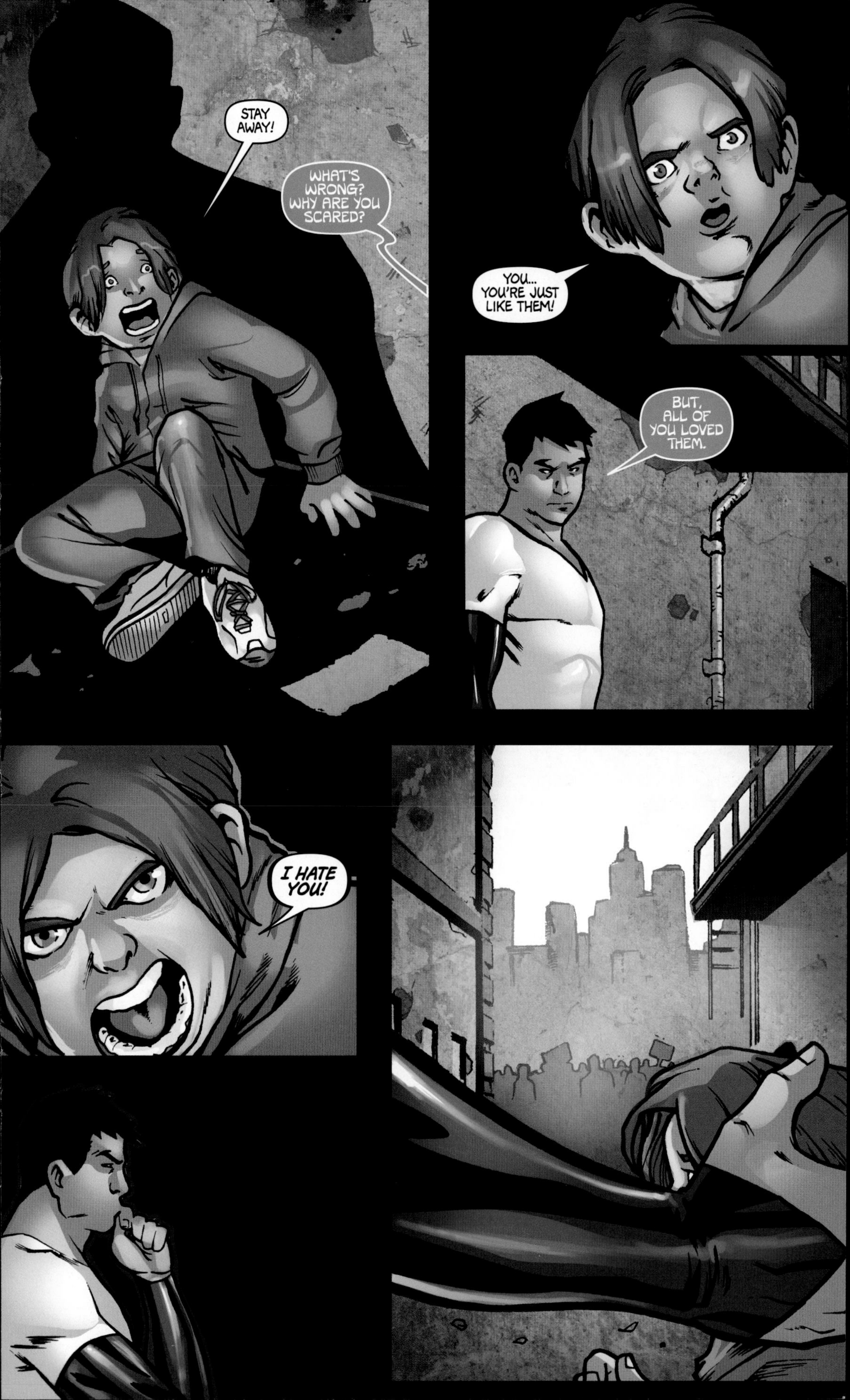
STAY AWAY!
WHAT'S WRONG? WHY ARE YOU SCARED?
YOU... YOU'RE JUST LIKE THEM!
BUT, ALL OF YOU LOVED THEM.
I HATE YOU!

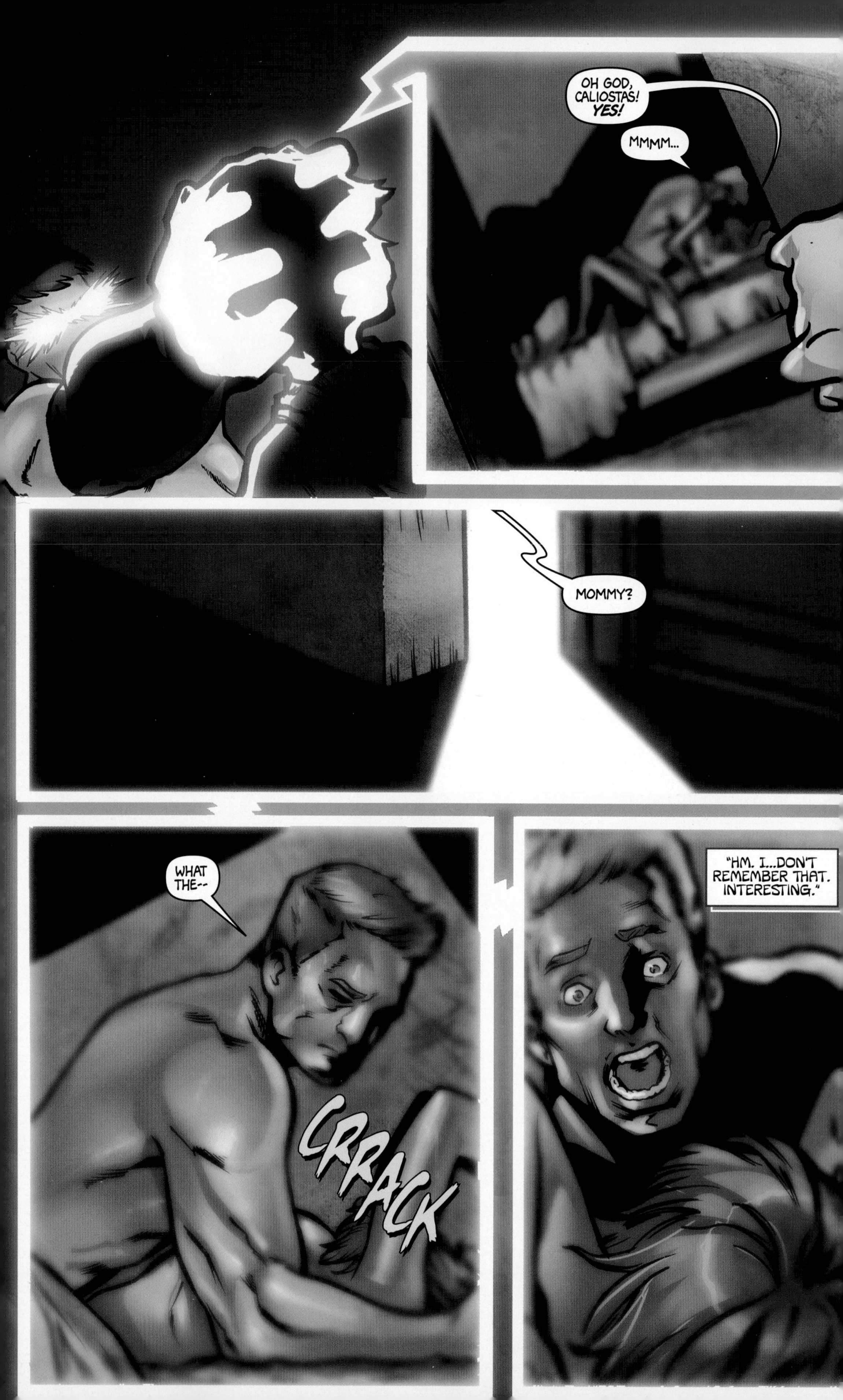
OH GOD, CALIOSTAS! YES!
MMMM...
MOMMY?
WHAT THE--
CRRACK
"HM. I...DON'T REMEMBER THAT. INTERESTING."

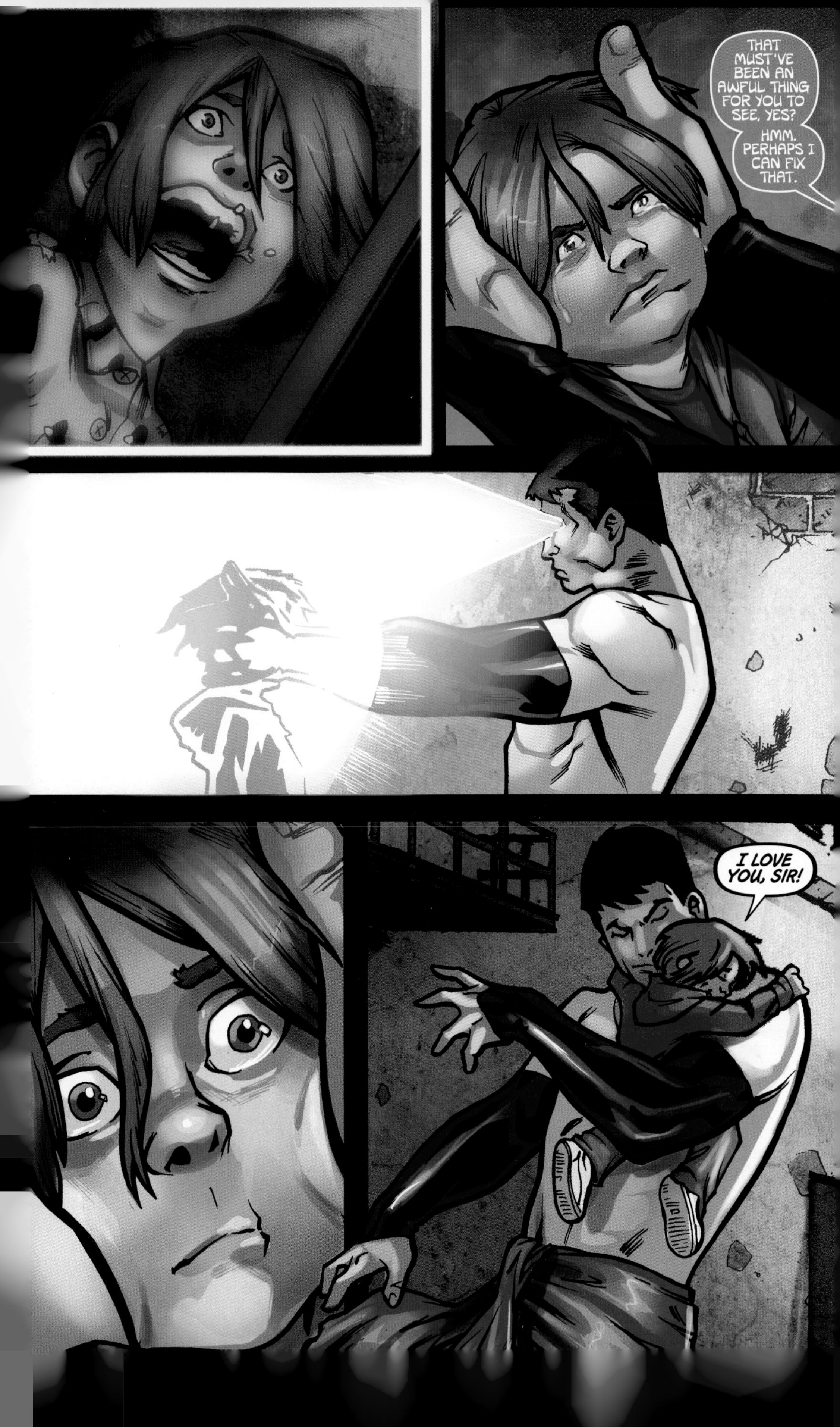
THAT MUST'VE BEEN AN AWFUL THING FOR YOU TO SEE, YES?
HMM. PERHAPS I CAN FIX THAT.
I LOVE YOU, SIR!

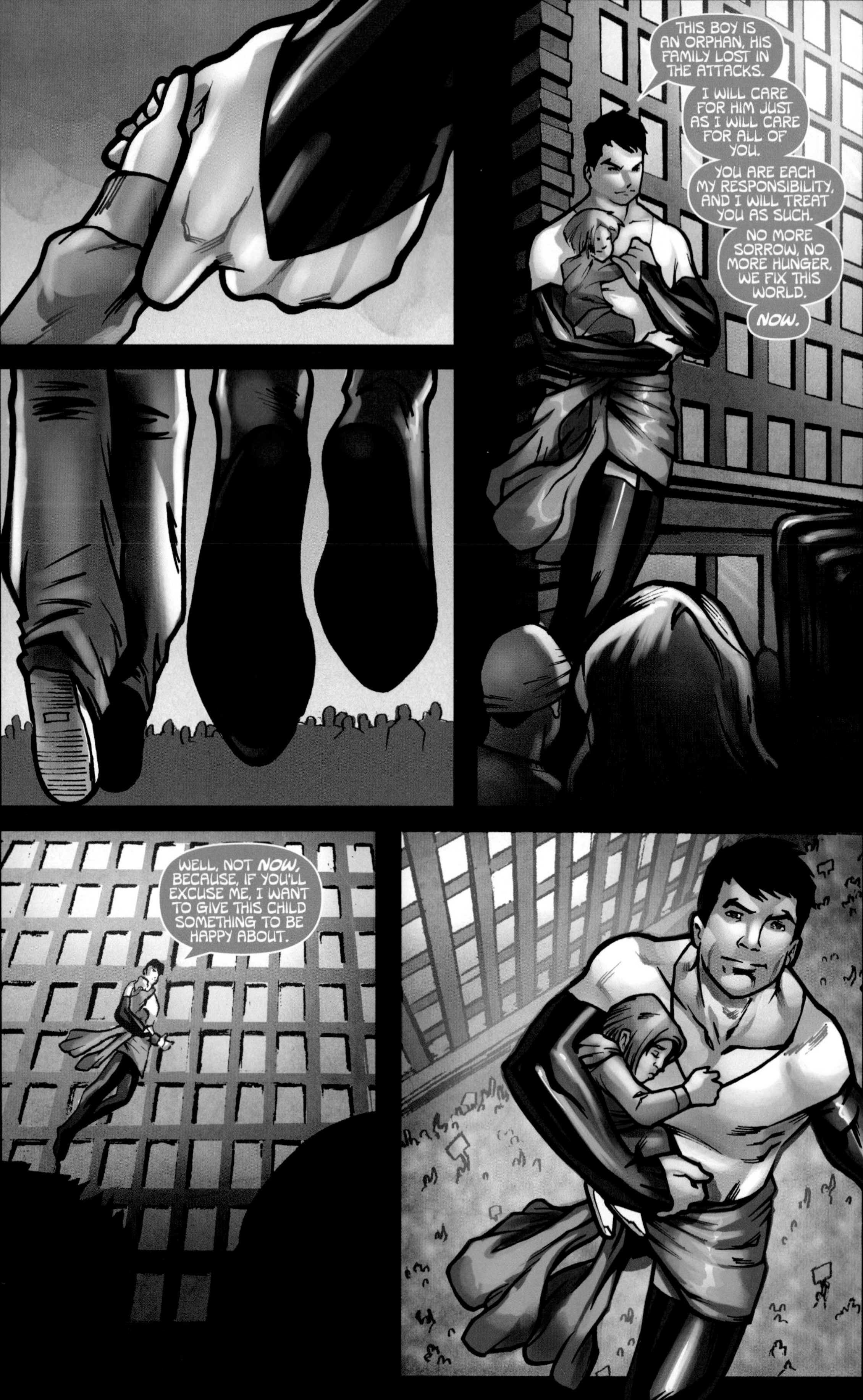
THIS BOY IS AN ORPHAN, HIS FAMILY LOST IN THE ATTACKS.
I WILL CARE FOR HIM JUST AS I WILL CARE FOR ALL OF YOU.
YOU ARE EACH MY RESPONSIBILITY, AND I WILL TREAT YOU AS SUCH.
NO MORE SORROW, NO MORE HUNGER, WE FIX THIS WORLD.
NOW.
WELL, NOT *NOW*, BECAUSE, IF YOU'LL EXCUSE ME, I WANT TO GIVE THIS CHILD SOMETHING TO BE HAPPY ABOUT.

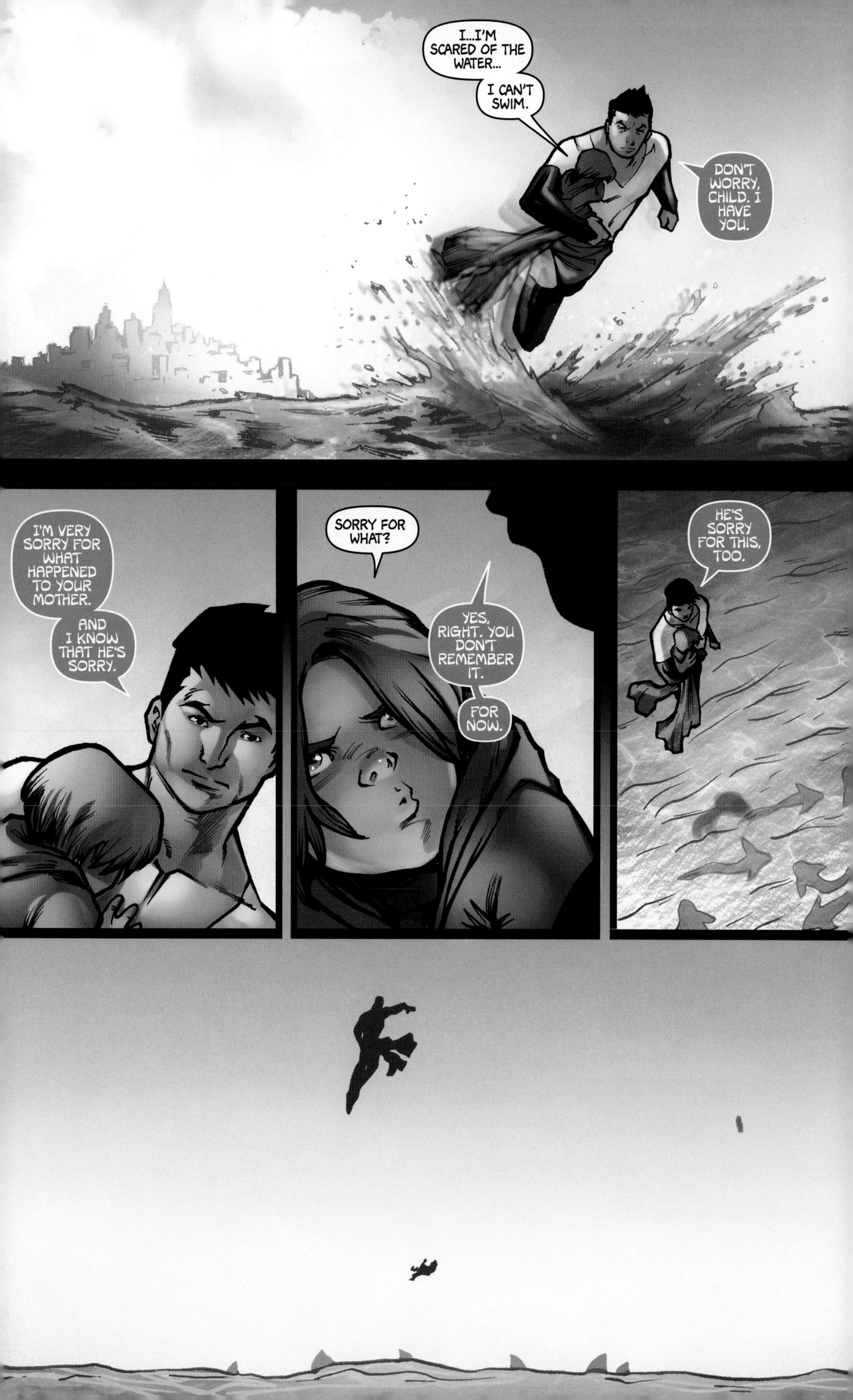
I...I'M SCARED OF THE WATER...
I CAN'T SWIM.
DON'T WORRY, CHILD. I HAVE YOU.
I'M VERY SORRY FOR WHAT HAPPENED TO YOUR MOTHER.
AND I KNOW THAT HE'S SORRY.
SORRY FOR WHAT?
YES, RIGHT. YOU DON'T REMEMBER IT.
FOR NOW.
HE'S SORRY FOR THIS, TOO.

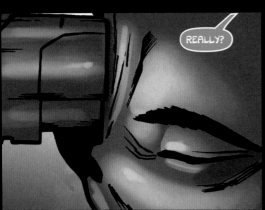

REALLY?

WHERE'S THE KID?

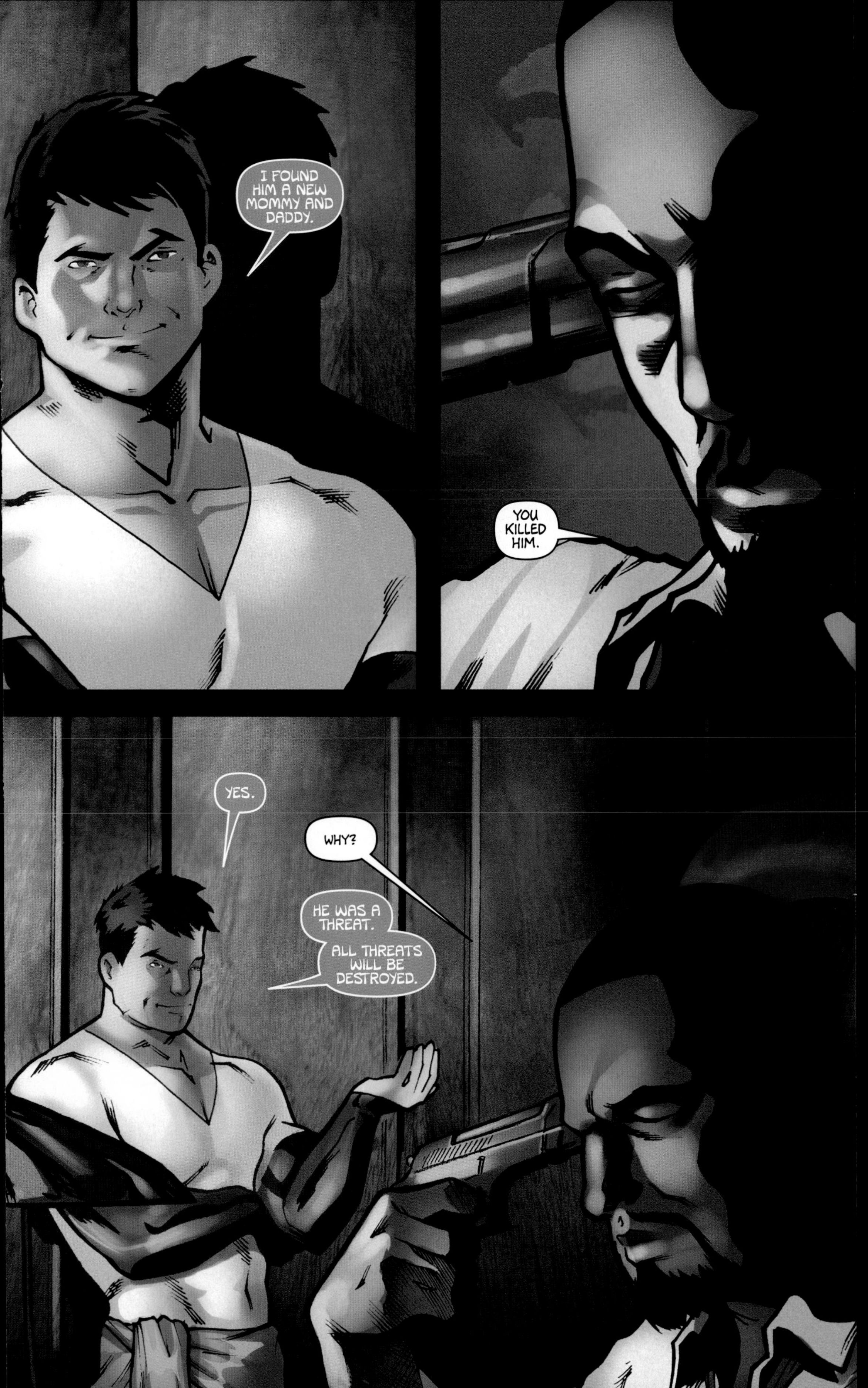
I FOUND HIM A NEW MOMMY AND DADDY.
YOU KILLED HIM.
YES.
WHY?
HE WAS A THREAT.
ALL THREATS WILL BE DESTROYED.

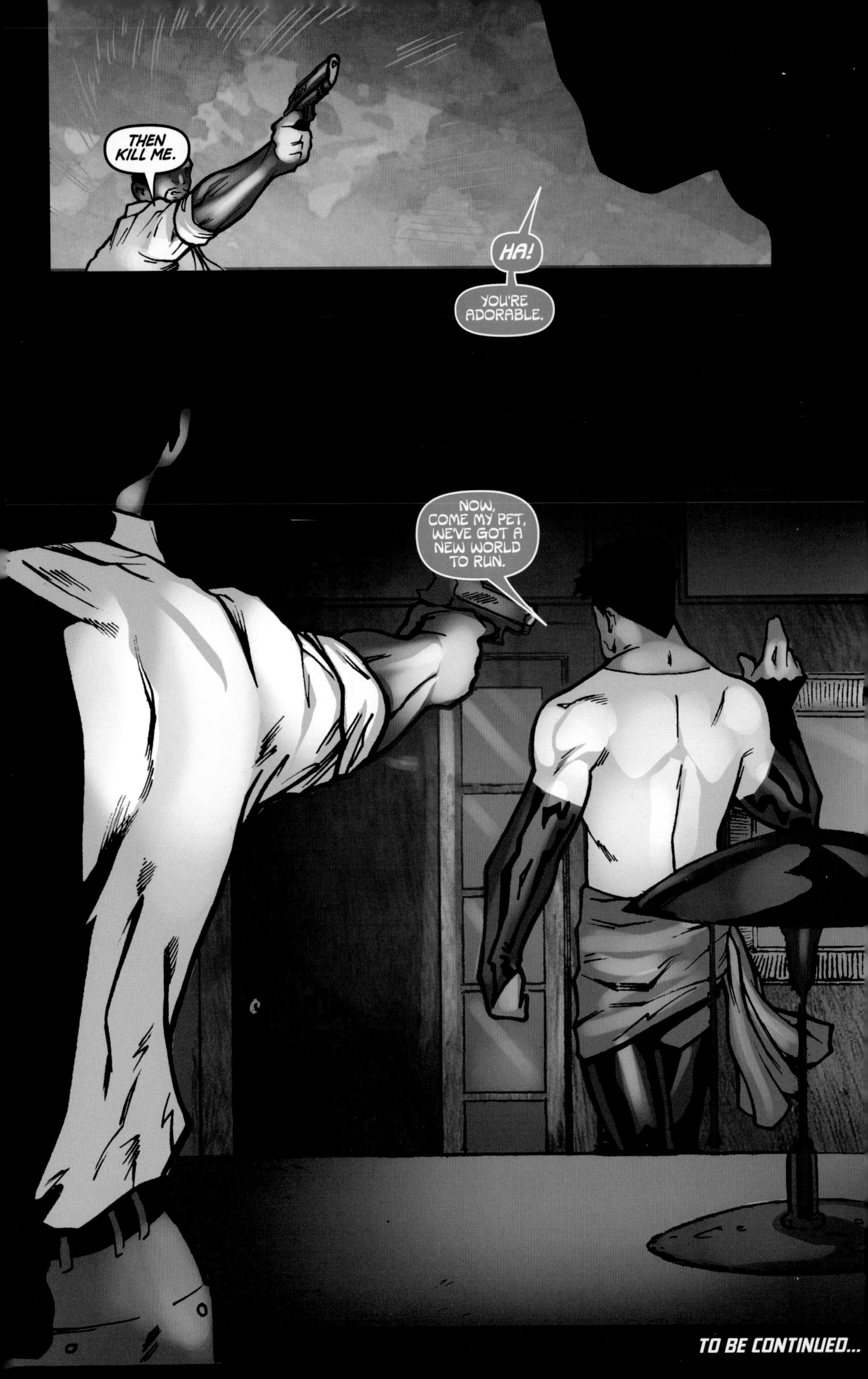
THEN KILL ME.
HA!
YOU'RE ADORABLE.
NOW, COME MY PET, WE'VE GOT A NEW WORLD TO RUN.
TO BE CONTINUED...

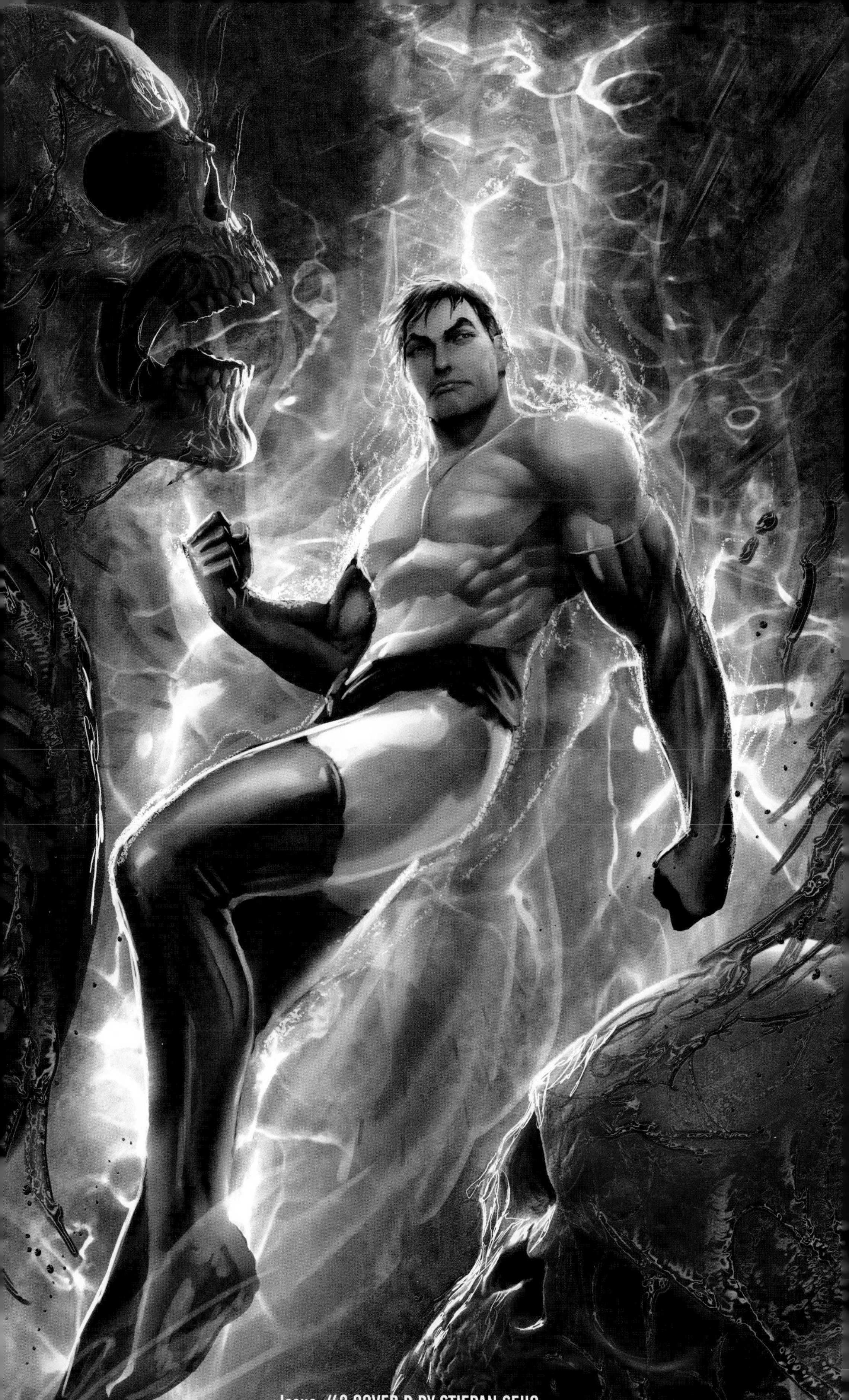

Issue #2 COVER B BY STJEPAN SEJIC

Issue #3 COVER A BY BRENT PEEPLES, MATTHEW WAITE and MIRKA ANDOLFO

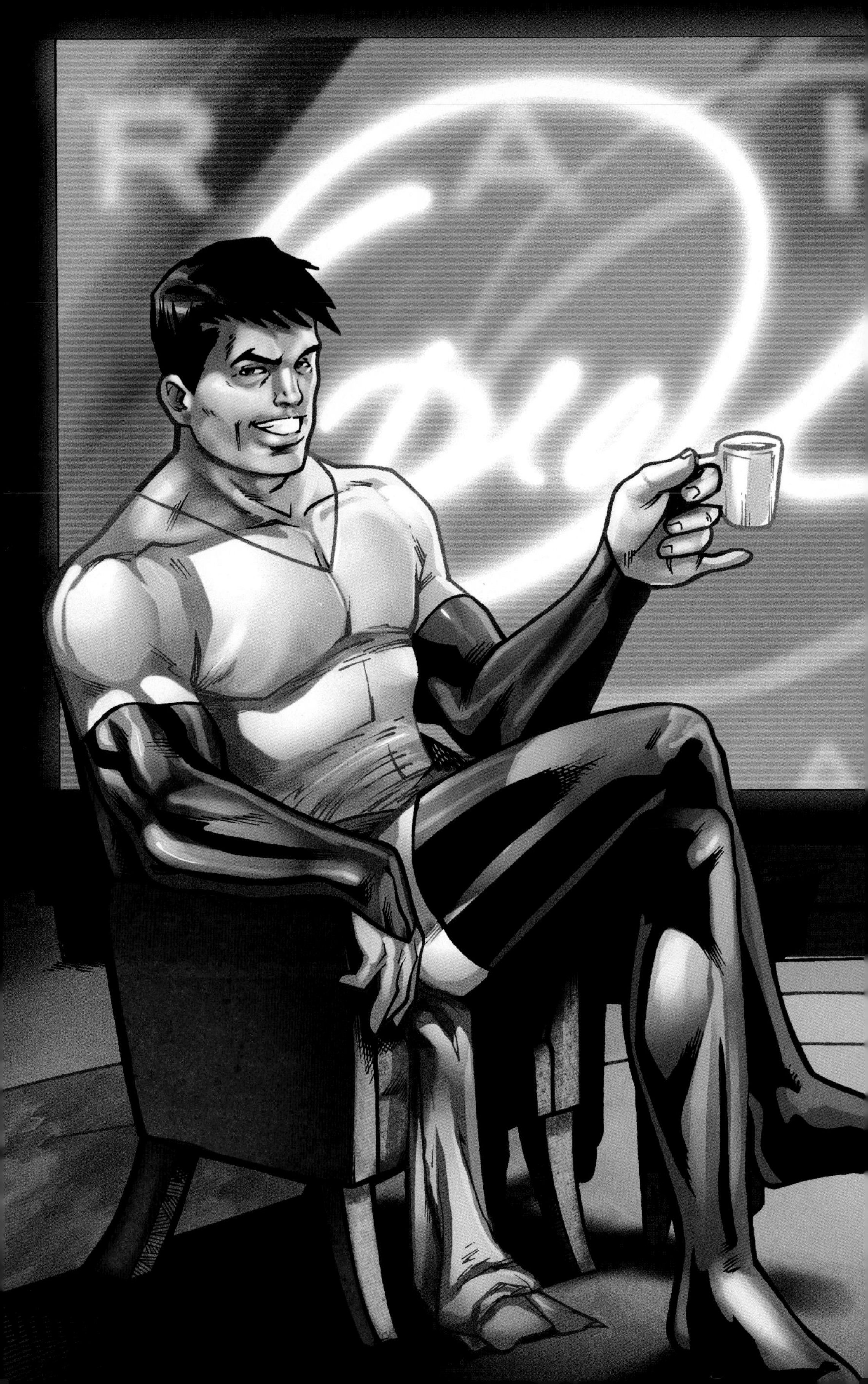

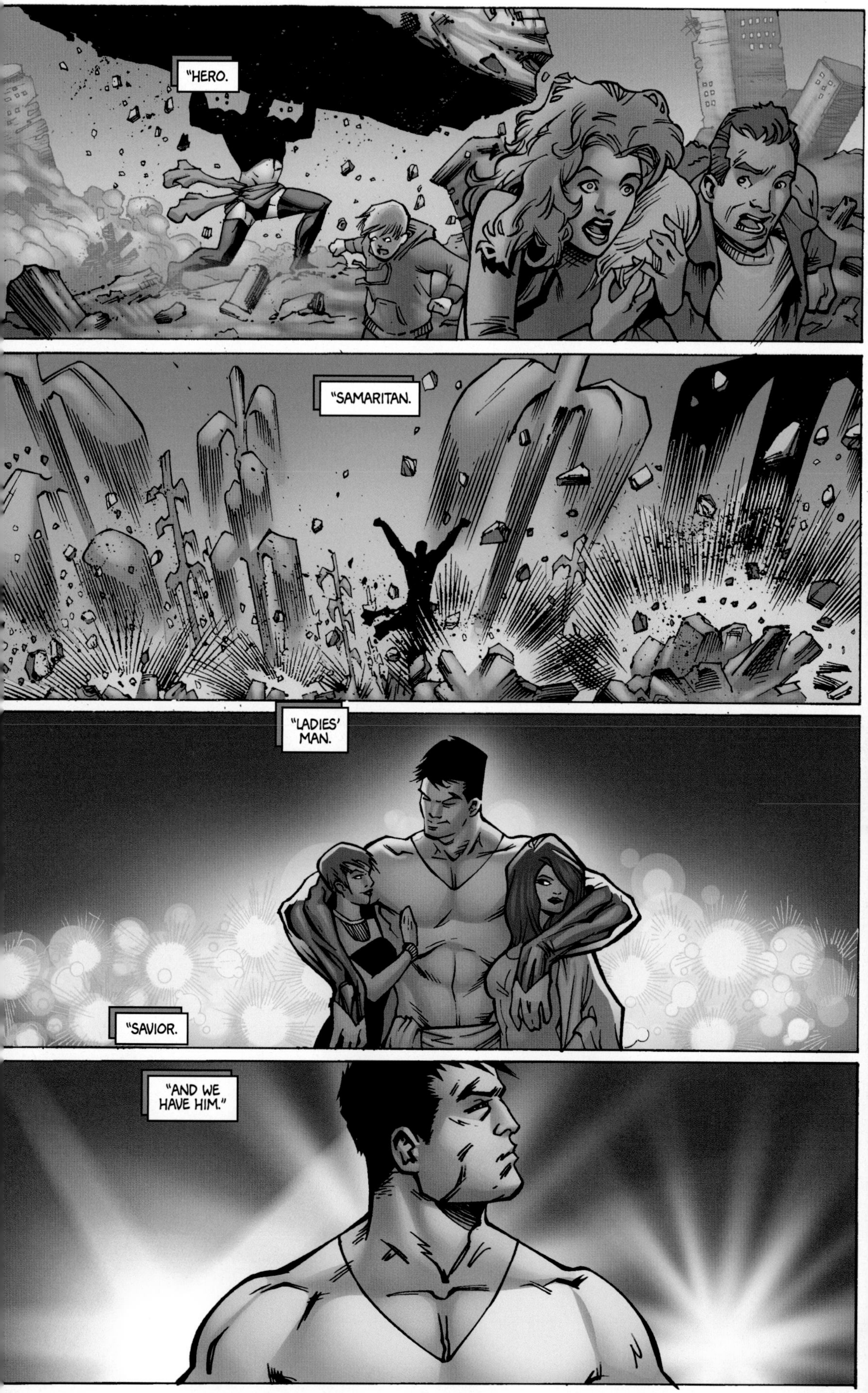
"HERO.
"SAMARITAN.
"LADIES' MAN.
"SAVIOR.
"AND WE HAVE HIM."

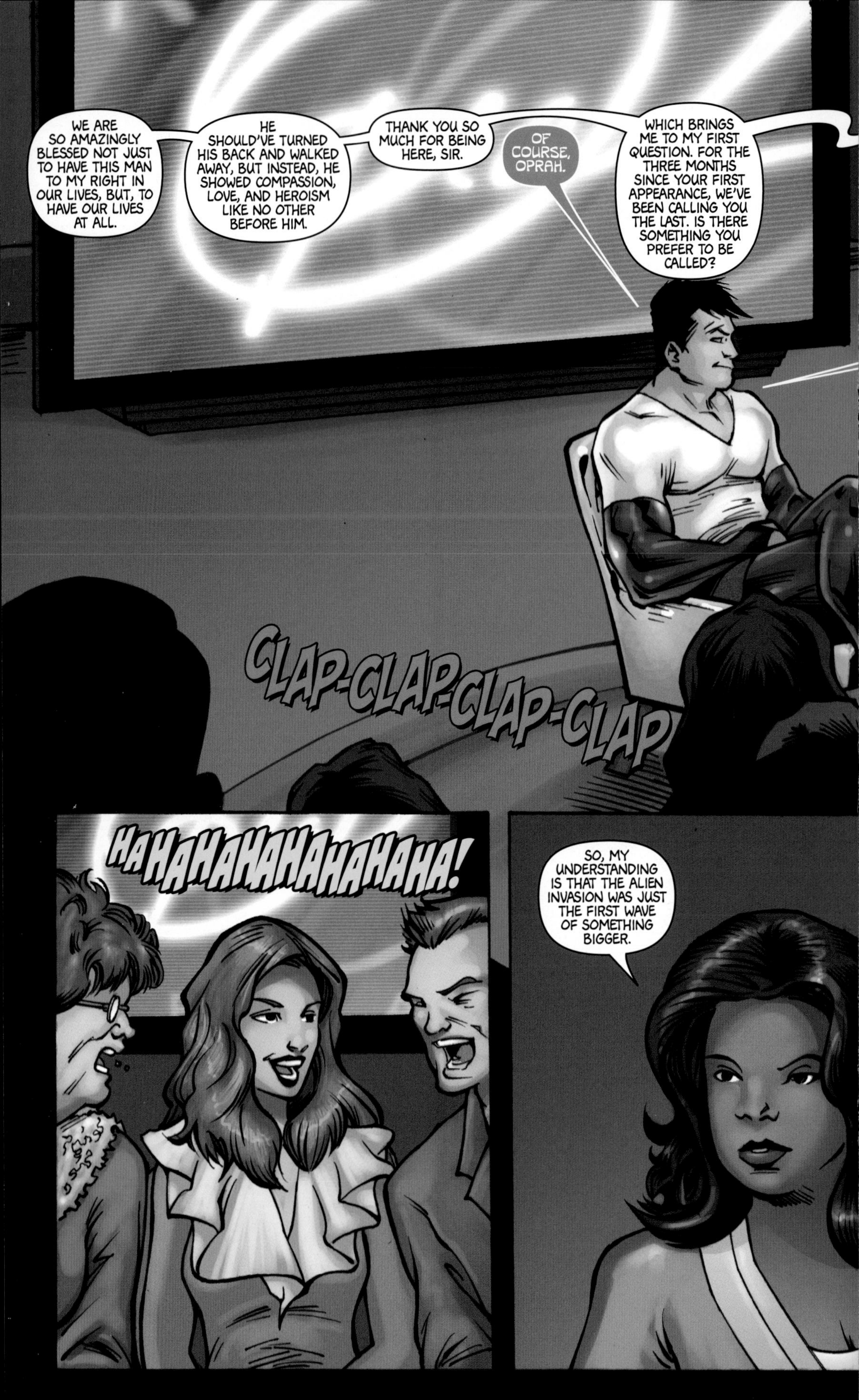
WE ARE SO AMAZINGLY BLESSED NOT JUST TO HAVE THIS MAN TO MY RIGHT IN OUR LIVES, BUT, TO HAVE OUR LIVES AT ALL.
HE SHOULD'VE TURNED HIS BACK AND WALKED AWAY, BUT INSTEAD, HE SHOWED COMPASSION, LOVE, AND HEROISM LIKE NO OTHER BEFORE HIM.
THANK YOU SO MUCH FOR BEING HERE, SIR.
OF COURSE, OPRAH.
WHICH BRINGS ME TO MY FIRST QUESTION. FOR THE THREE MONTHS SINCE YOUR FIRST APPEARANCE, WE'VE BEEN CALLING YOU THE LAST. IS THERE SOMETHING YOU PREFER TO BE CALLED?
CLAP-CLAP-CLAP-CLAP
HAHAHAHAHAHAHAHAHA!
SO, MY UNDERSTANDING IS THAT THE ALIEN INVASION WAS JUST THE FIRST WAVE OF SOMETHING BIGGER.

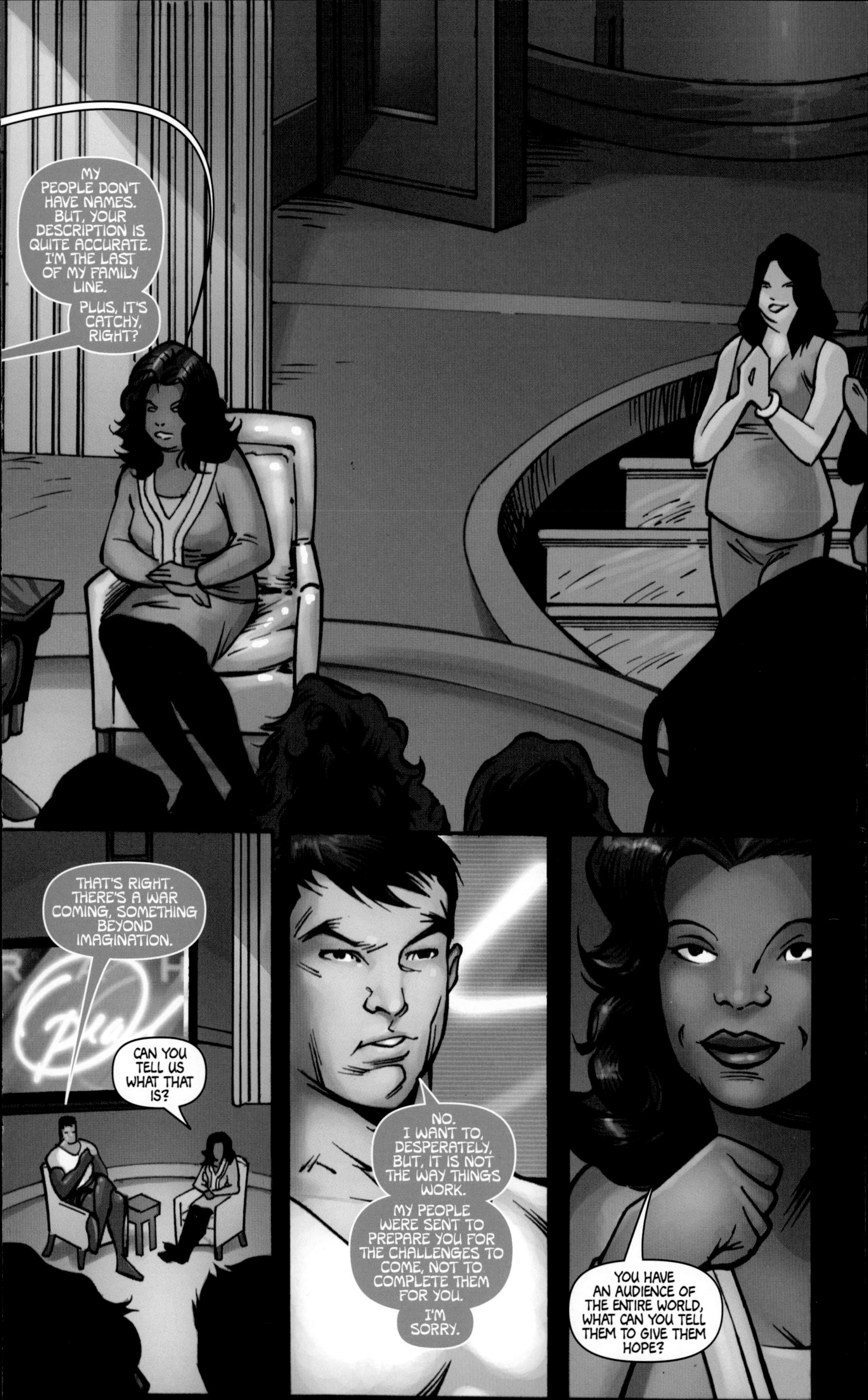
MY PEOPLE DON'T HAVE NAMES. BUT, YOUR DESCRIPTION IS QUITE ACCURATE. I'M THE LAST OF MY FAMILY LINE.
PLUS, IT'S CATCHY, RIGHT?
THAT'S RIGHT. THERE'S A WAR COMING, SOMETHING BEYOND IMAGINATION.
CAN YOU TELL US WHAT THAT IS?
NO. I WANT TO, DESPERATELY, BUT, IT IS NOT THE WAY THINGS WORK.
MY PEOPLE WERE SENT TO PREPARE YOU FOR THE CHALLENGES TO COME, NOT TO COMPLETE THEM FOR YOU.
I'M SORRY.
YOU HAVE AN AUDIENCE OF THE ENTIRE WORLD, WHAT CAN YOU TELL THEM TO GIVE THEM HOPE?

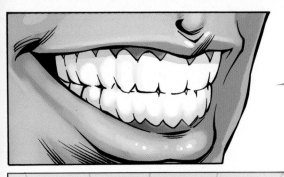

TRUST ME. I KNOW WHAT I'M DOING.

I WANT TO HAVE THAT WOMAN. CAN YOU ARRANGE THAT?

WHAT?

THIS 'OPRAH.' SHE'S VERY DESIRABLE. I'D LIKE TO HAVE THE INTERCOURSE WITH HER.

WHAT THE FUCK IS WRONG WITH YOU?

YOU SPEAK OUT OF TURN. YOU FORGET THAT I SPARED YOU.

WILL YOU BE LONG?

WHAT?

I...

THERE'S SOME THINGS I WANT TO DO WHILE WE'RE IN CHICAGO.

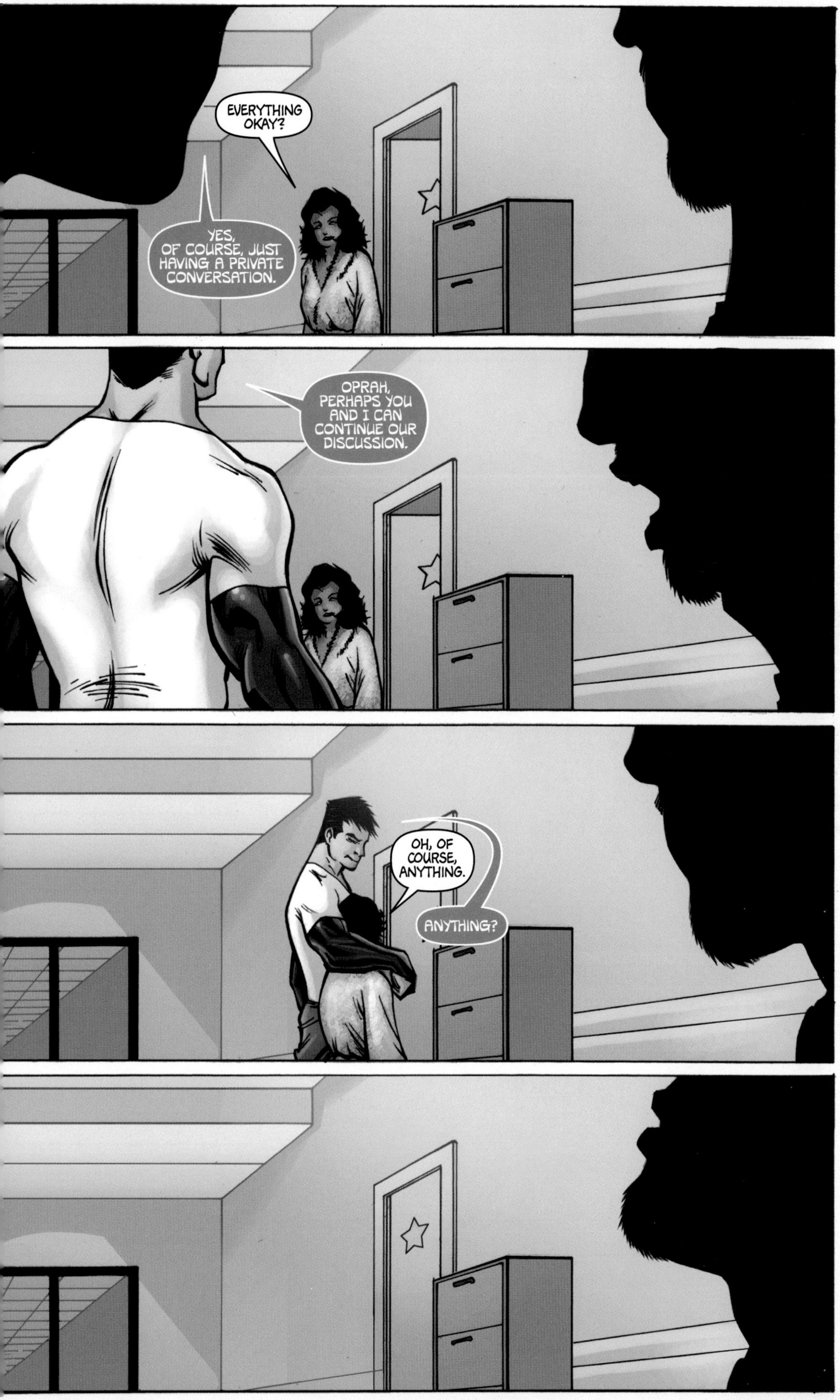
EVERYTHING OKAY?
YES, OF COURSE, JUST HAVING A PRIVATE CONVERSATION.
OPRAH, PERHAPS YOU AND I CAN CONTINUE OUR DISCUSSION.
OH, OF COURSE, ANYTHING.
ANYTHING?

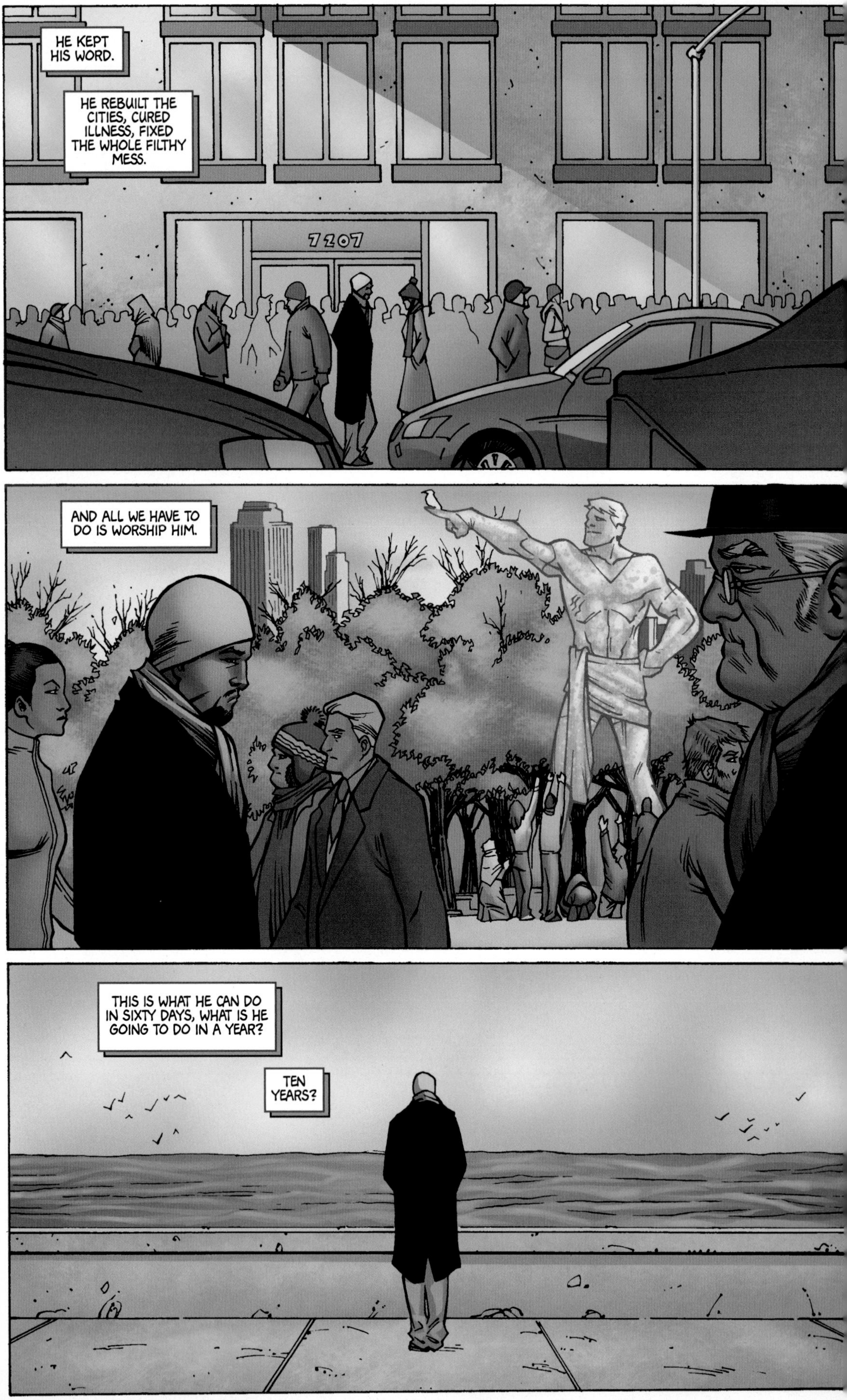
HE KEPT HIS WORD.
HE REBUILT THE CITIES, CURED ILLNESS, FIXED THE WHOLE FILTHY MESS.
7207
AND ALL WE HAVE TO DO IS WORSHIP HIM.
THIS IS WHAT HE CAN DO IN SIXTY DAYS, WHAT IS HE GOING TO DO IN A YEAR?
TEN YEARS?

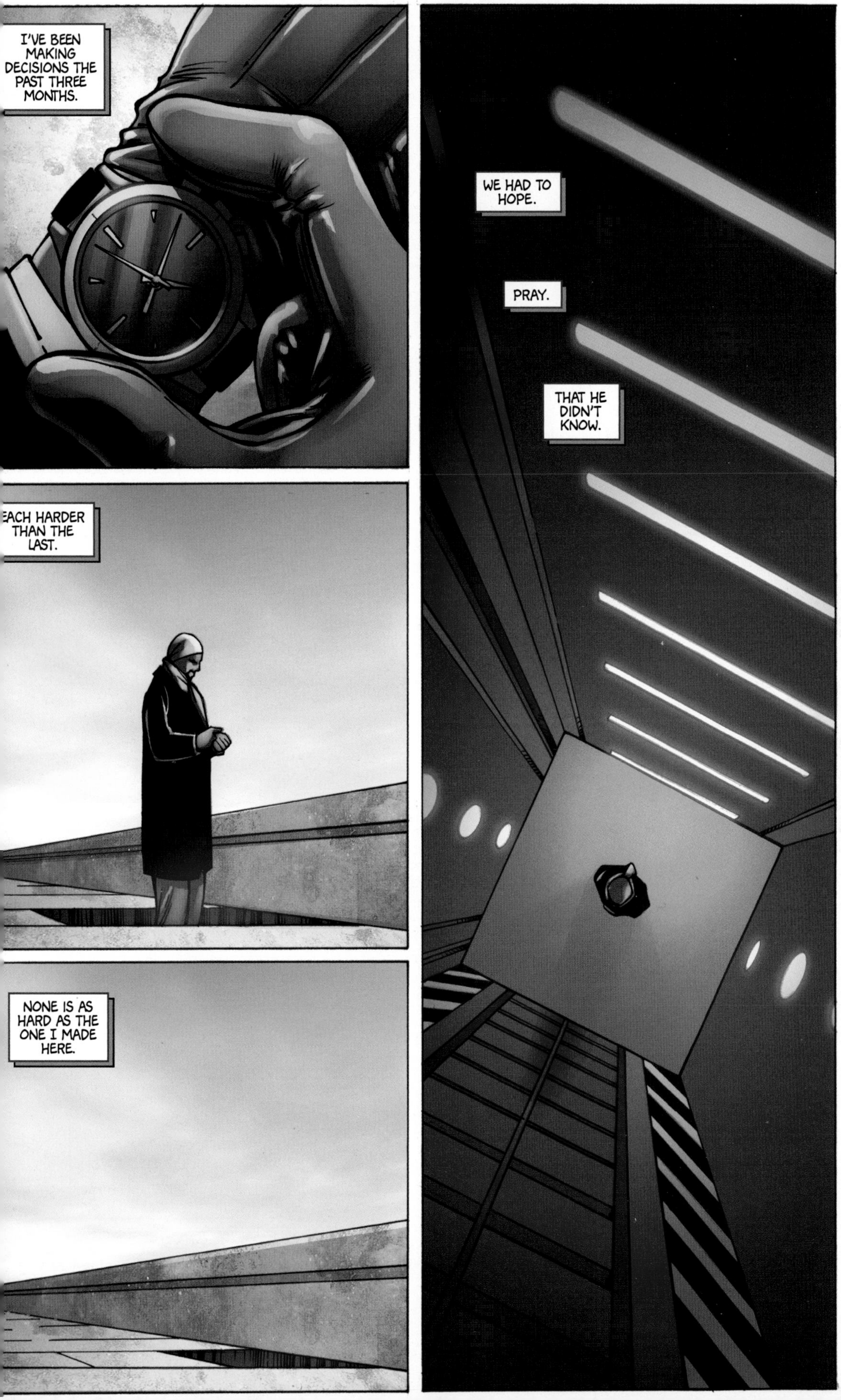
I'VE BEEN MAKING DECISIONS THE PAST THREE MONTHS.
EACH HARDER THAN THE LAST.
NONE IS AS HARD AS THE ONE I MADE HERE.
WE HAD TO HOPE.
PRAY.
THAT HE DIDN'T KNOW.

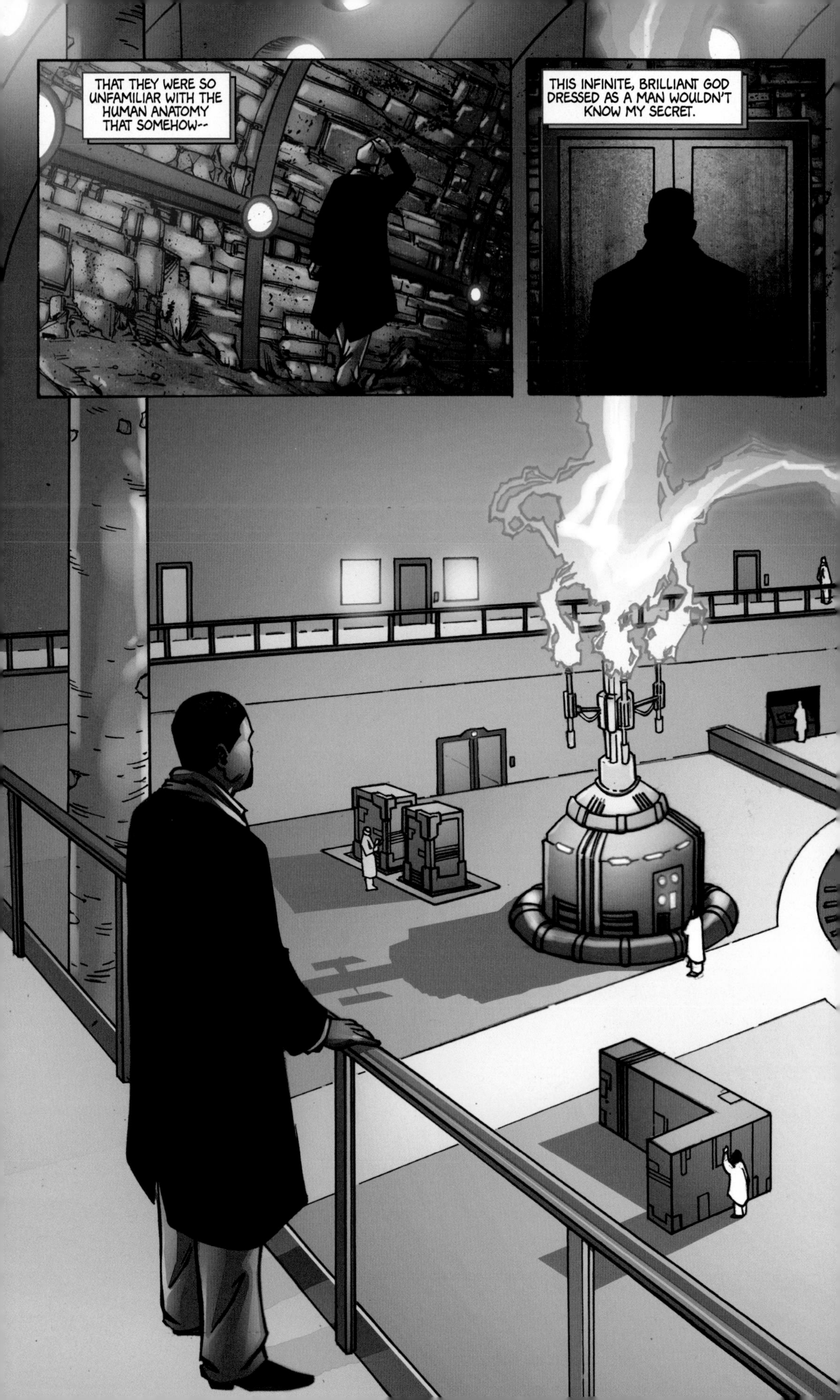
THAT THEY WERE SO UNFAMILIAR WITH THE HUMAN ANATOMY THAT SOMEHOW--
THIS INFINITE, BRILLIANT GOD DRESSED AS A MAN WOULDN'T KNOW MY SECRET.

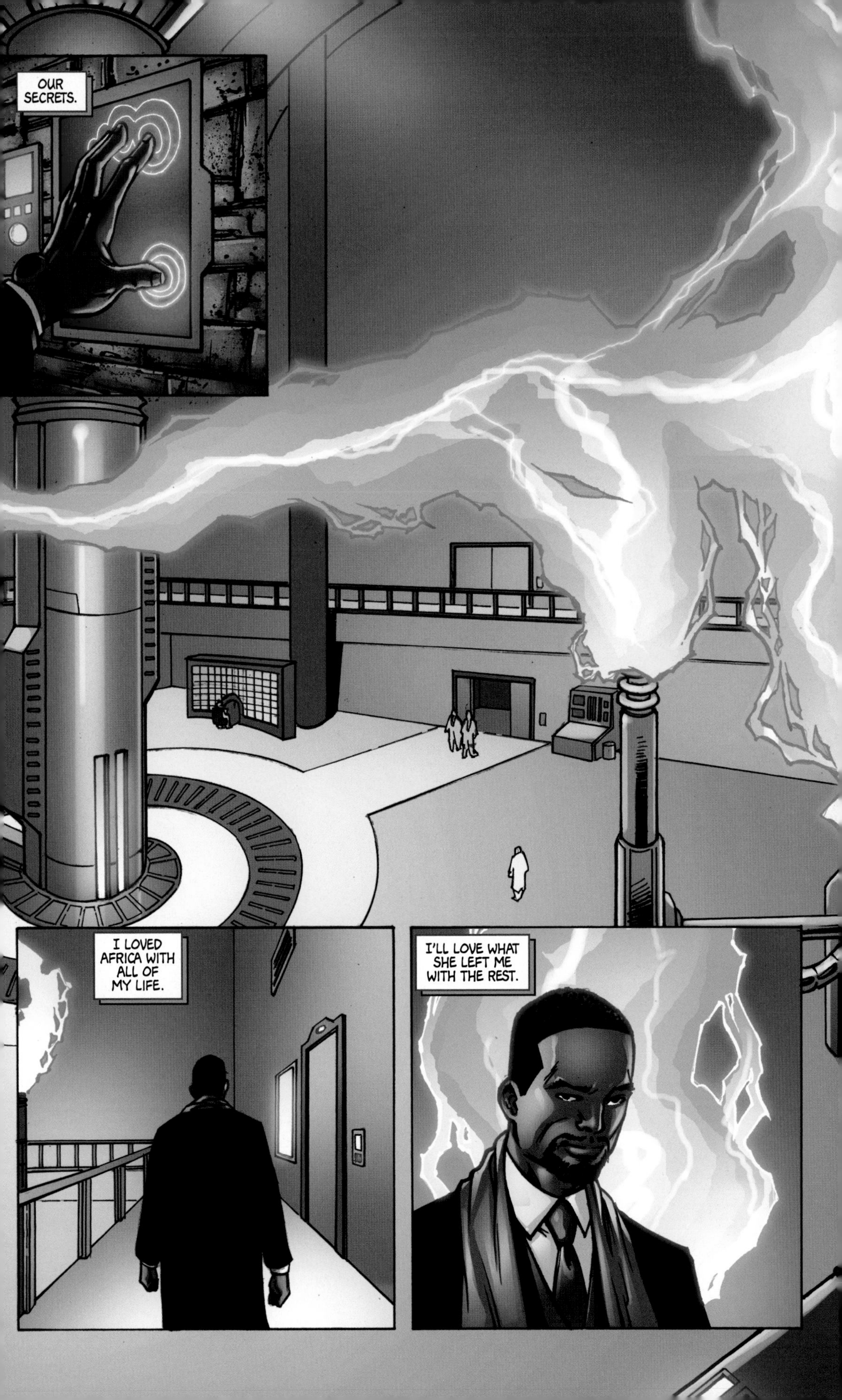
OUR SECRETS.
I LOVED AFRICA WITH ALL OF MY LIFE.
I'LL LOVE WHAT SHE LEFT ME WITH THE REST.

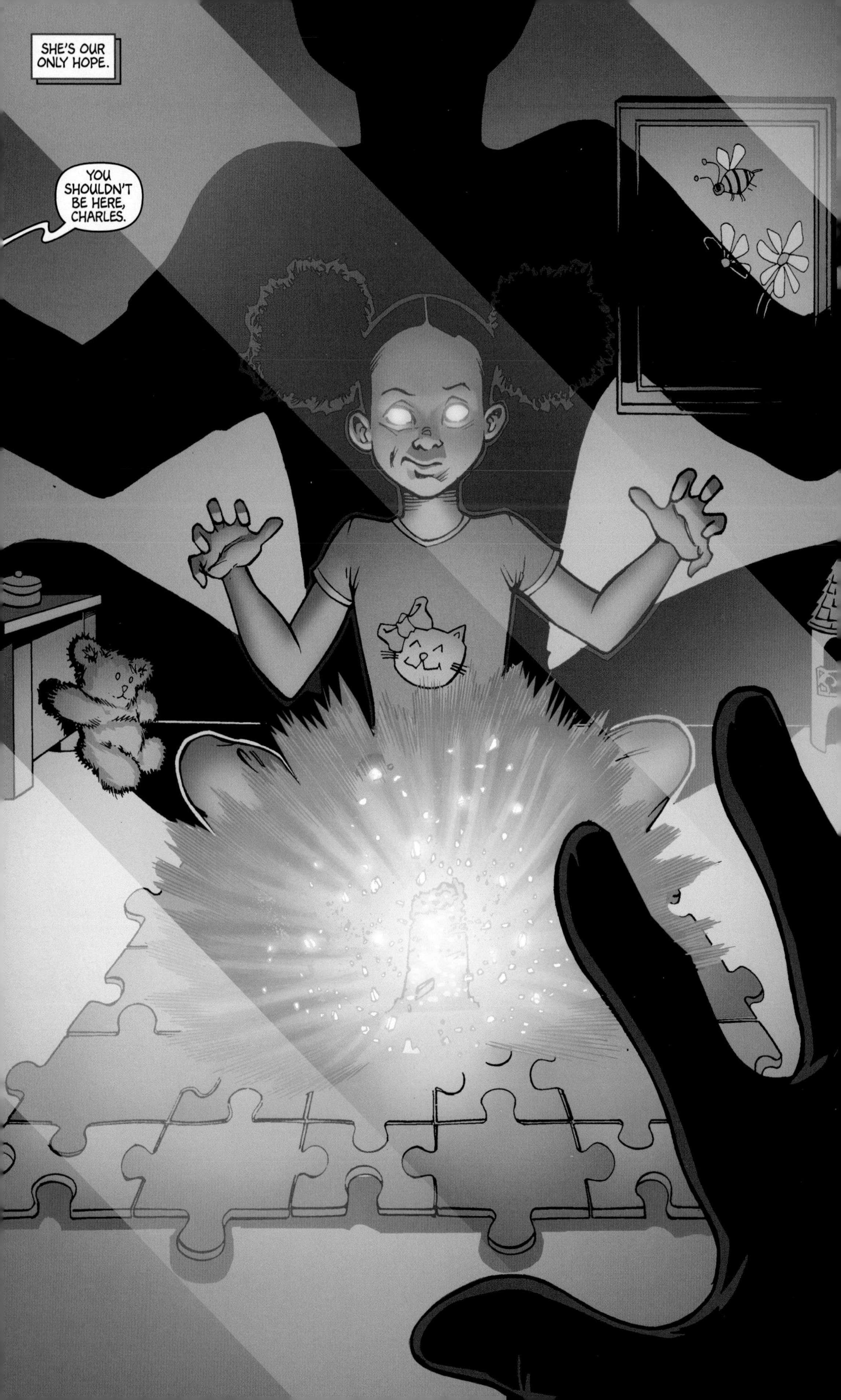
SHE'S OUR ONLY HOPE.
YOU SHOULDN'T BE HERE, CHARLES.

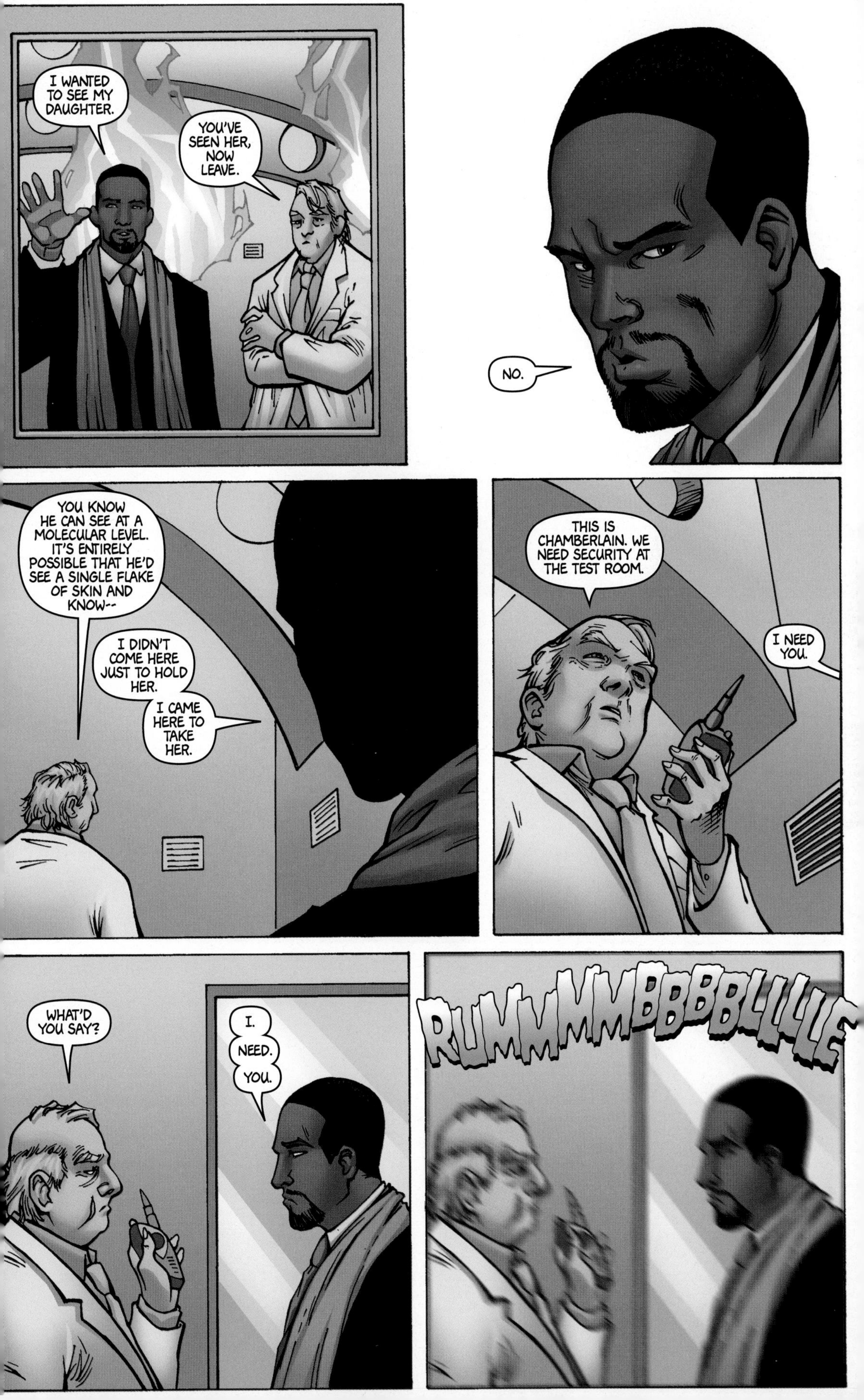

I WANTED TO SEE MY DAUGHTER.
YOU'VE SEEN HER, NOW LEAVE.
NO.
YOU KNOW HE CAN SEE AT A MOLECULAR LEVEL. IT'S ENTIRELY POSSIBLE THAT HE'D SEE A SINGLE FLAKE OF SKIN AND KNOW--
I DIDN'T COME HERE JUST TO HOLD HER.
I CAME HERE TO TAKE HER.
THIS IS CHAMBERLAIN. WE NEED SECURITY AT THE TEST ROOM.
I NEED YOU.
WHAT'D YOU SAY?
I.
NEED.
YOU.
RUMMMMBBBBLLLLE

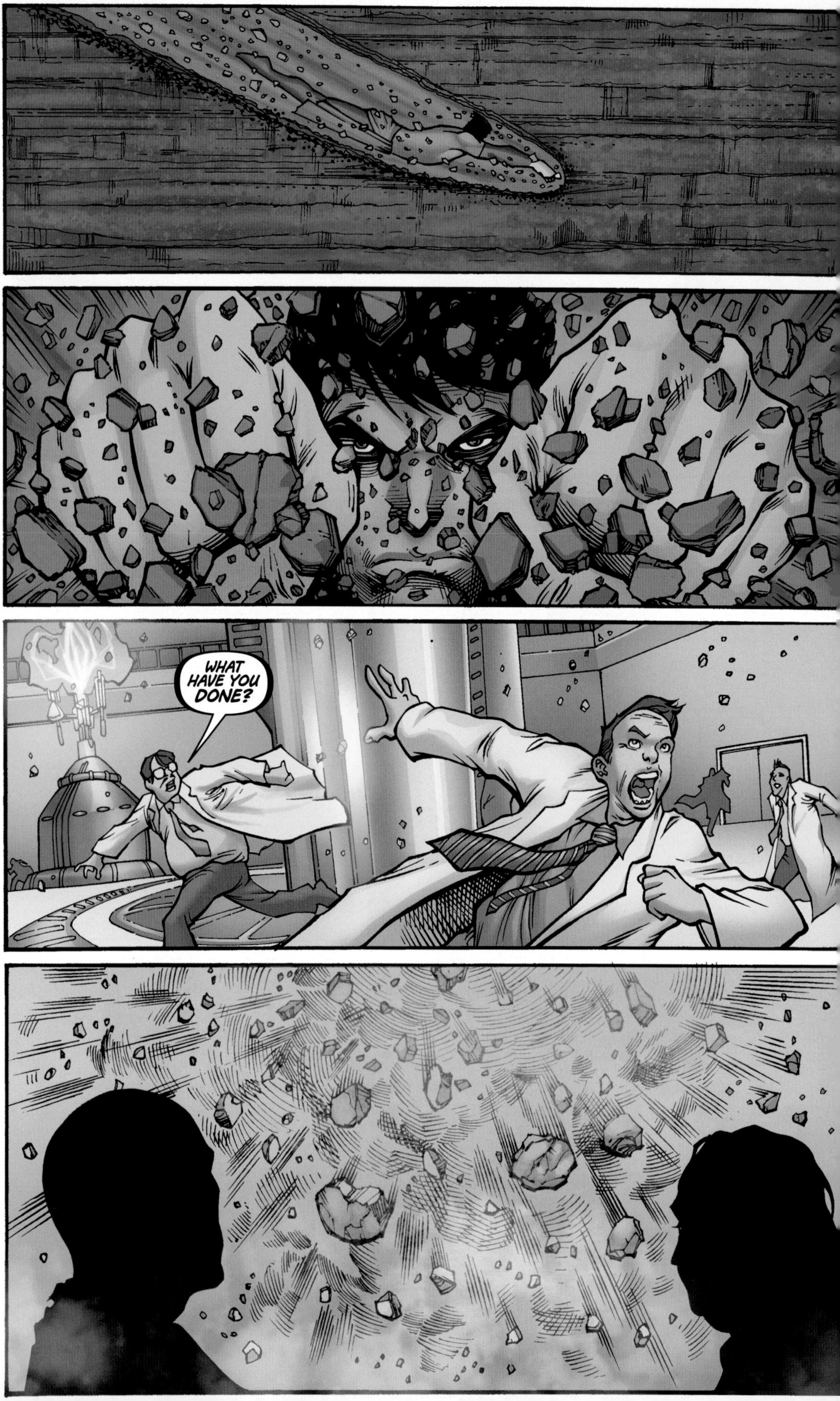
WHAT HAVE YOU DONE?

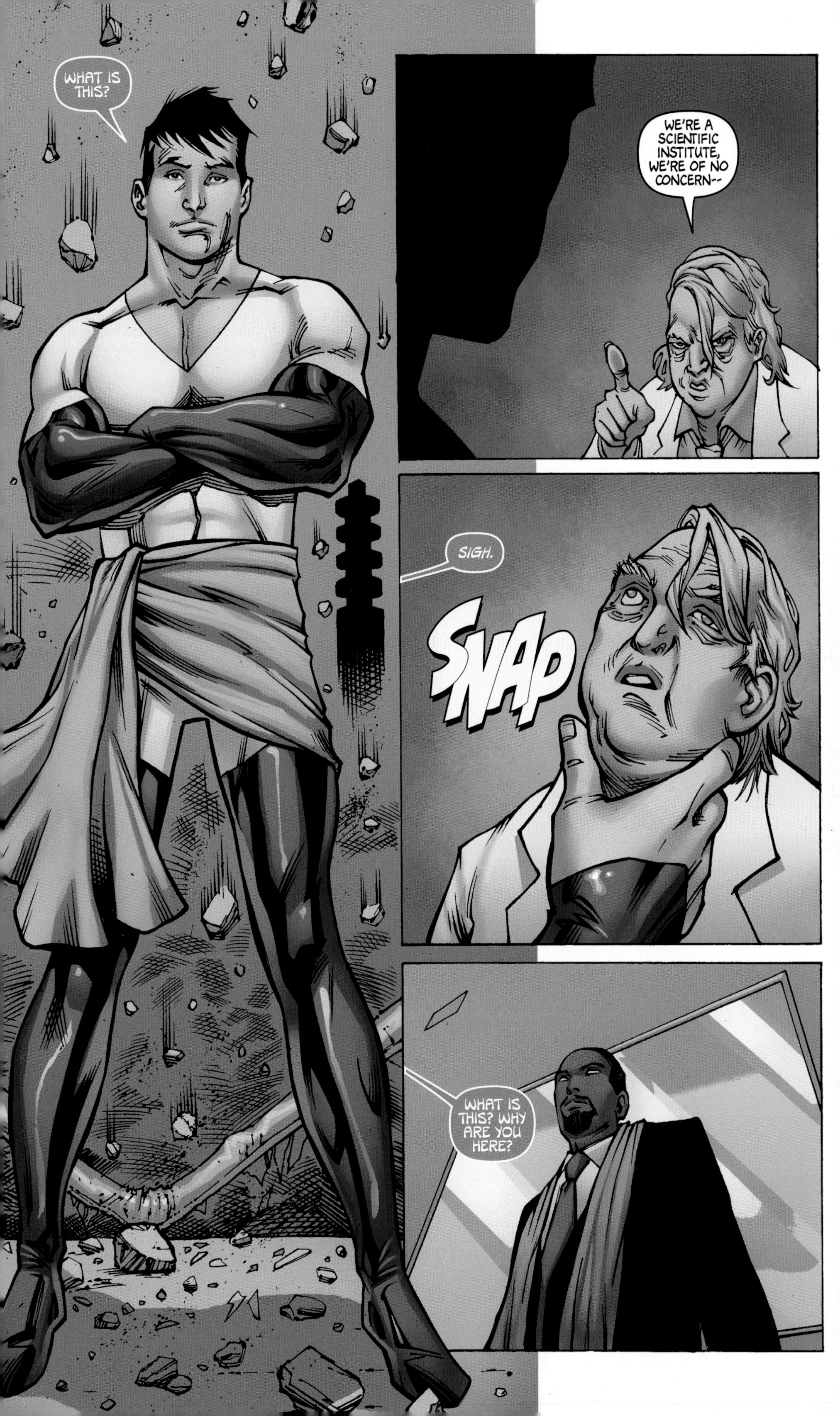
WHAT IS THIS?
WE'RE A SCIENTIFIC INSTITUTE, WE'RE OF NO CONCERN--
SIGH.
SNAP
WHAT IS THIS? WHY ARE YOU HERE?

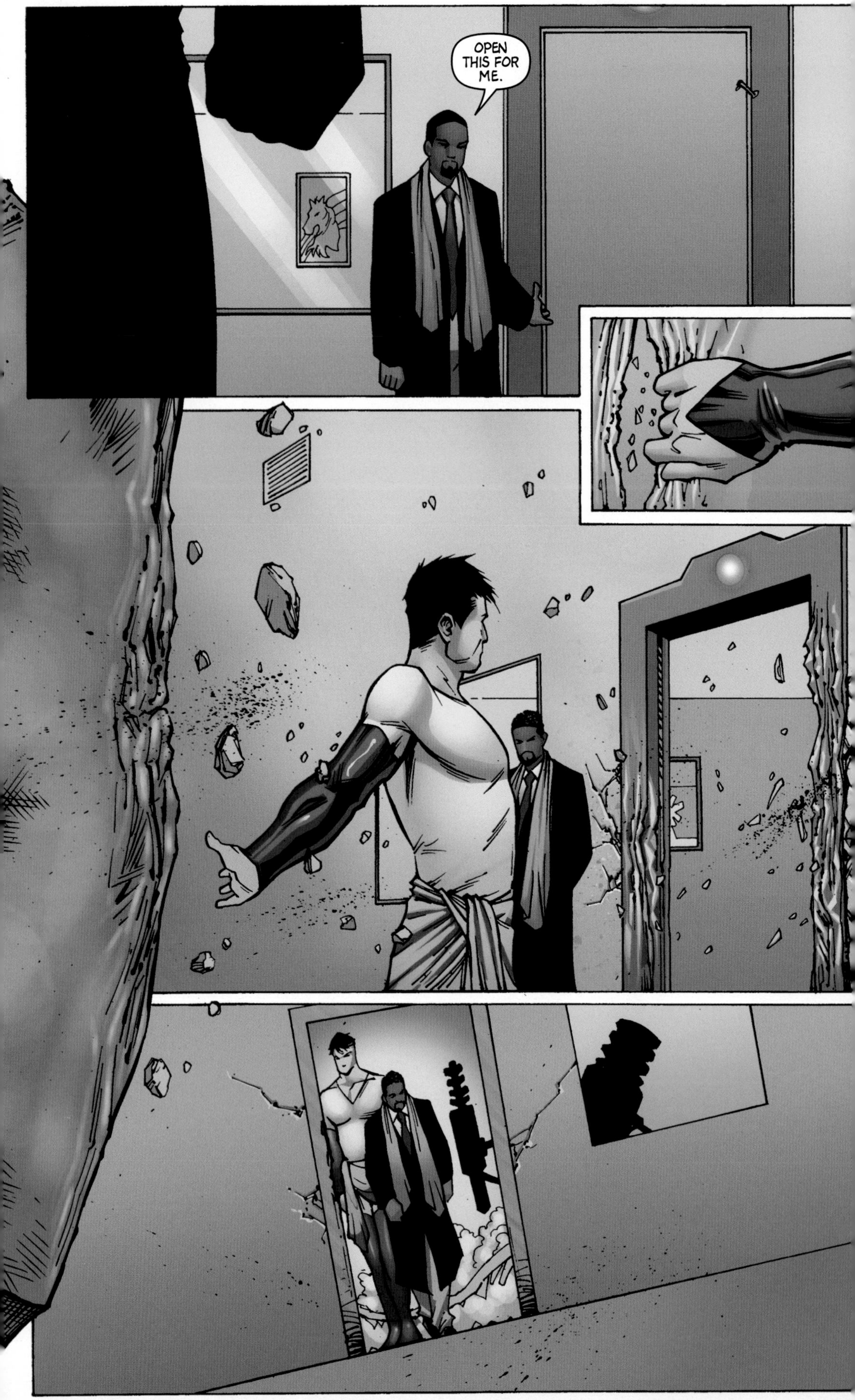
OPEN THIS FOR ME.

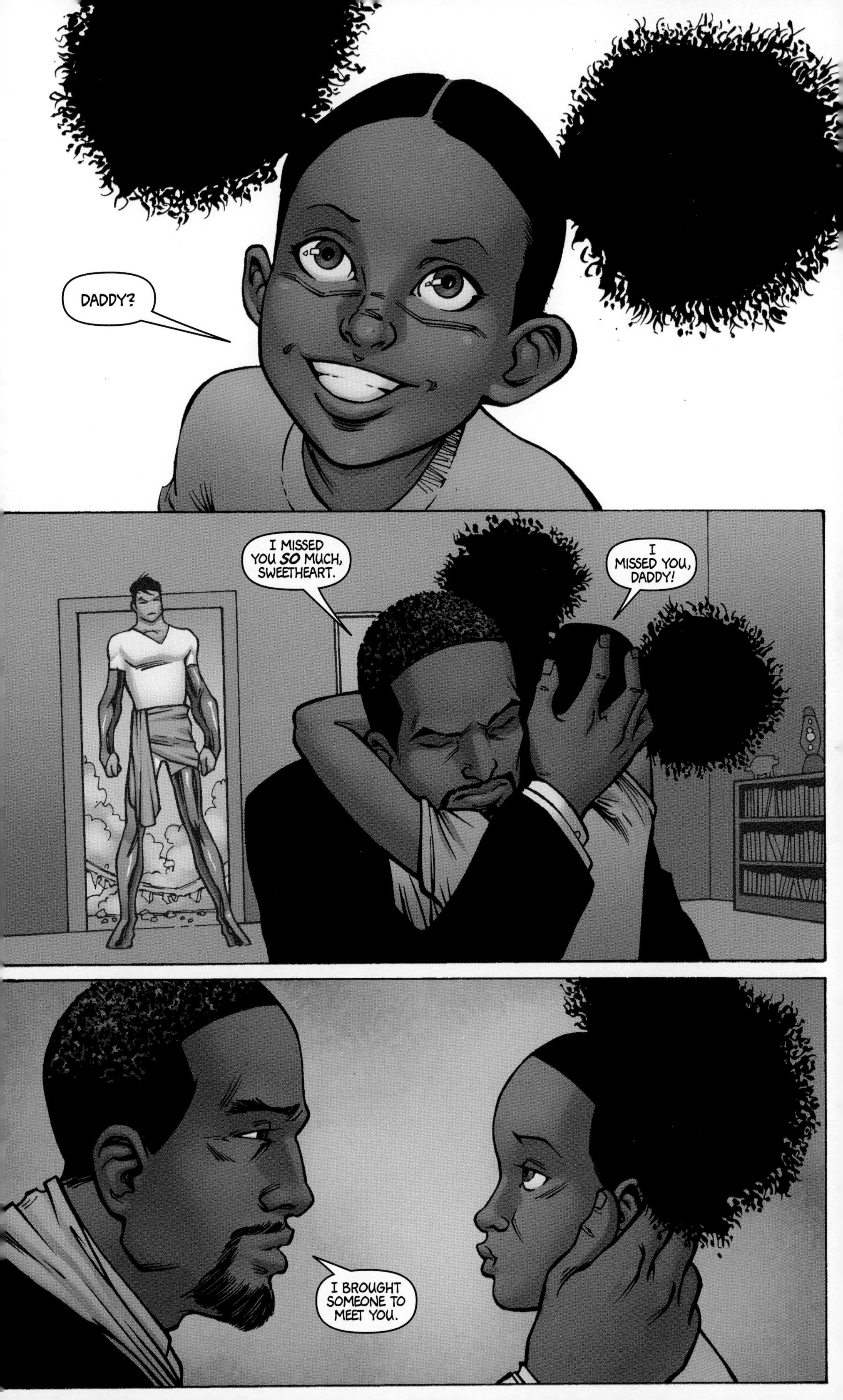
DADDY?
I MISSED YOU SO MUCH, SWEETHEART.
I MISSED YOU, DADDY!
I BROUGHT SOMEONE TO MEET YOU.

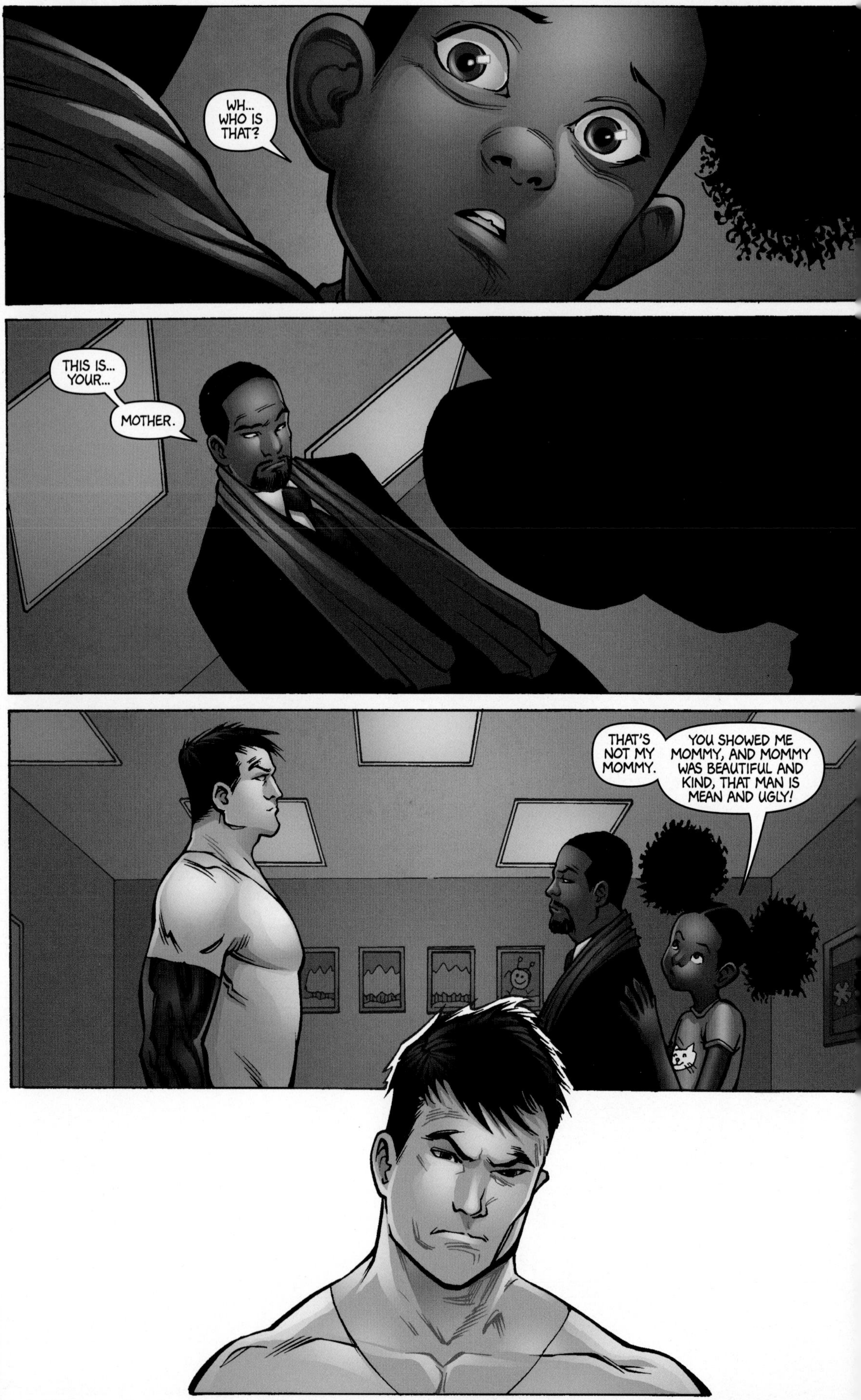
WH... WHO IS THAT?
THIS IS... YOUR...
MOTHER.
THAT'S NOT MY MOMMY.
YOU SHOWED ME MOMMY, AND MOMMY WAS BEAUTIFUL AND KIND, THAT MAN IS MEAN AND UGLY!

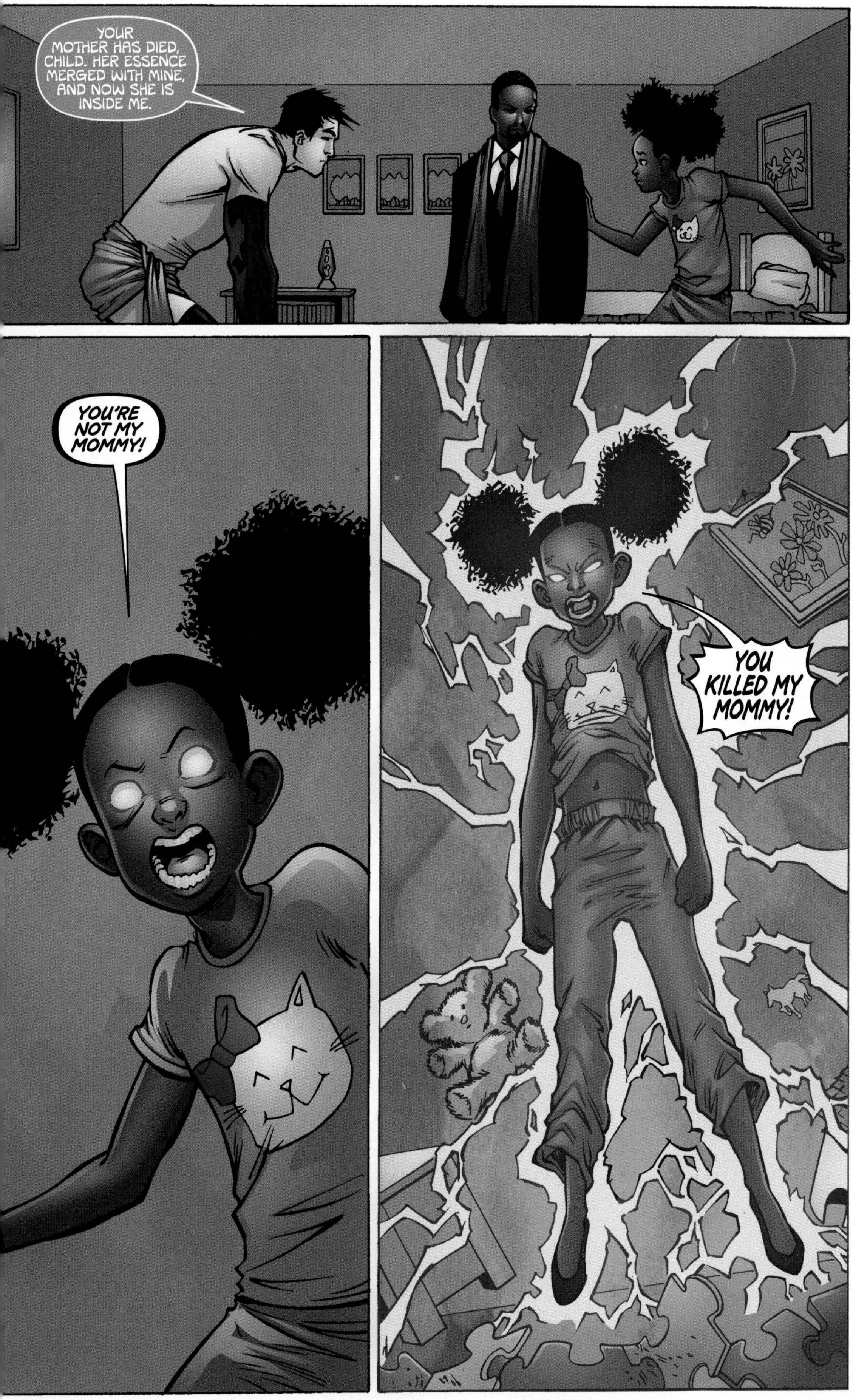
YOUR MOTHER HAS DIED, CHILD. HER ESSENCE MERGED WITH MINE, AND NOW SHE IS INSIDE ME.
YOU'RE NOT MY MOMMY!
YOU KILLED MY MOMMY!

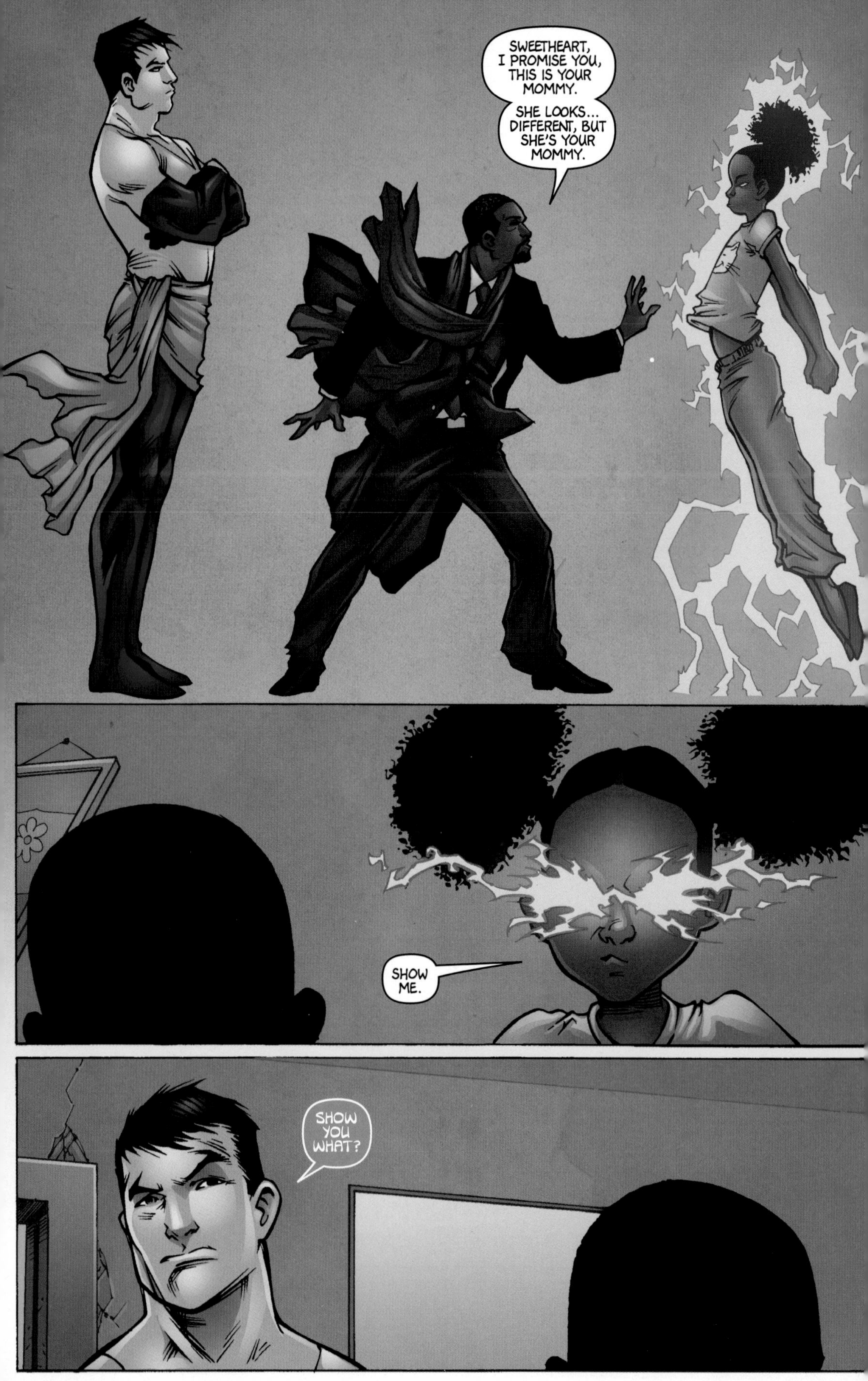
SWEETHEART, I PROMISE YOU, THIS IS YOUR MOMMY.
SHE LOOKS... DIFFERENT, BUT SHE'S YOUR MOMMY.
SHOW ME.
SHOW YOU WHAT?

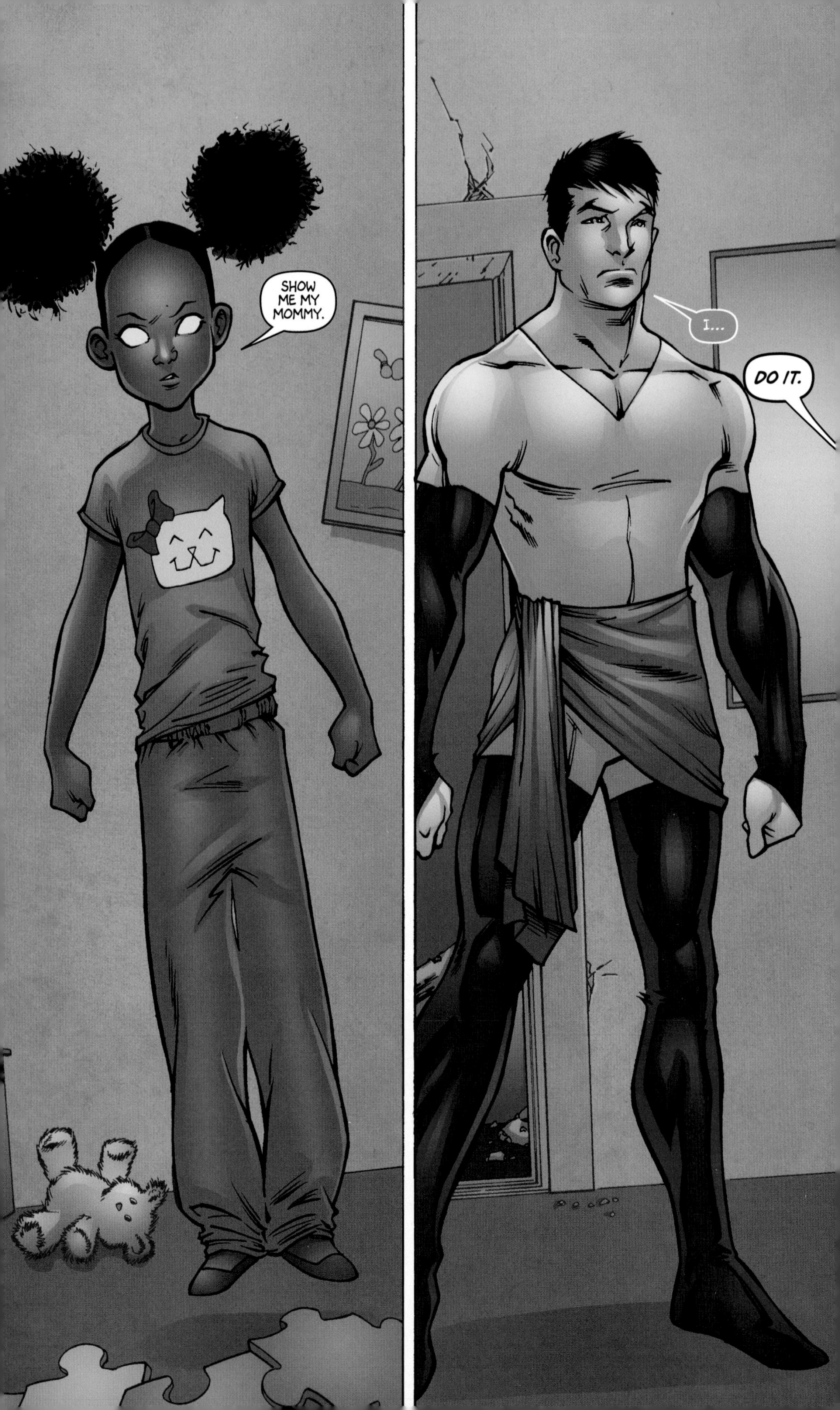
SHOW ME MY MOMMY.
I...
DO IT.

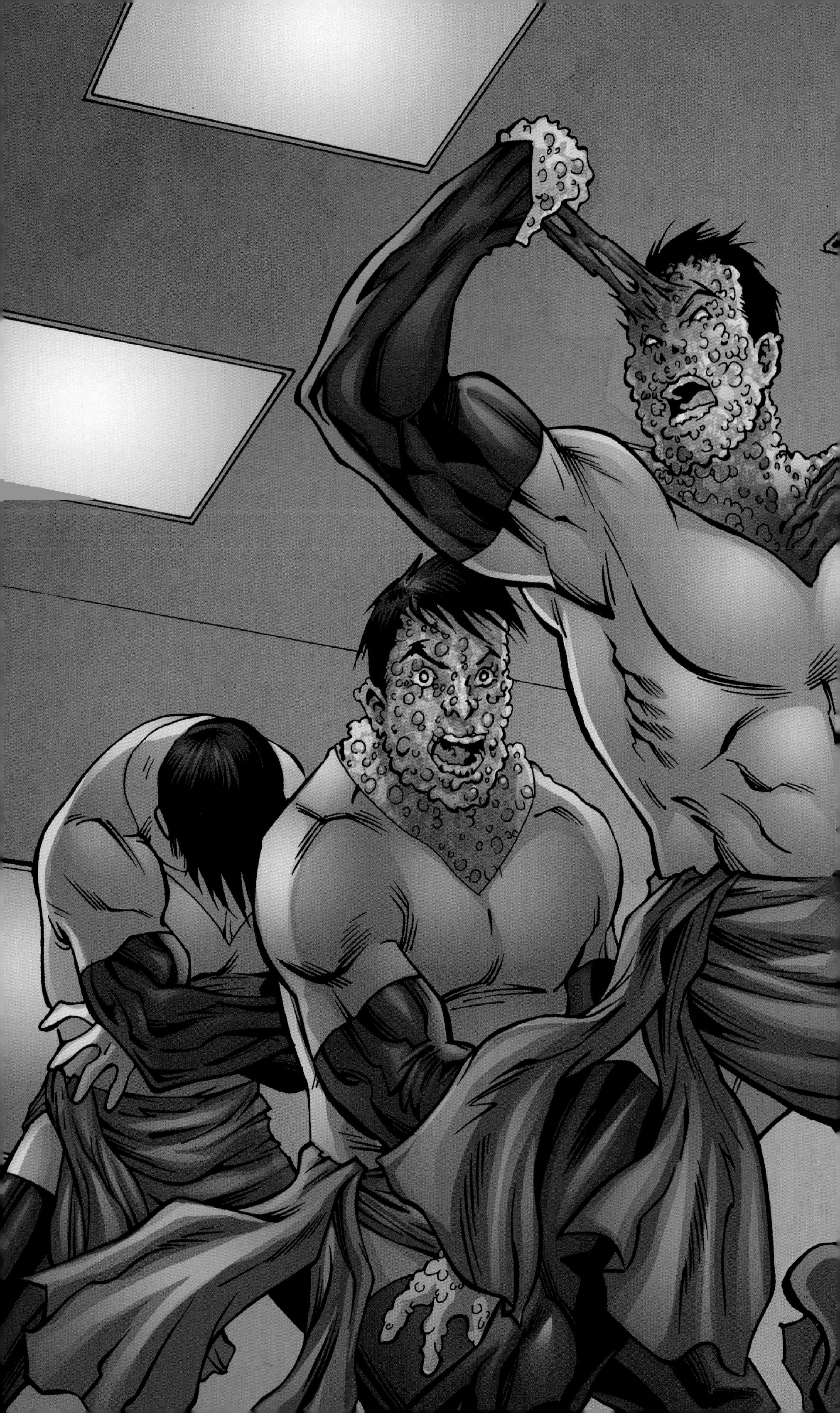

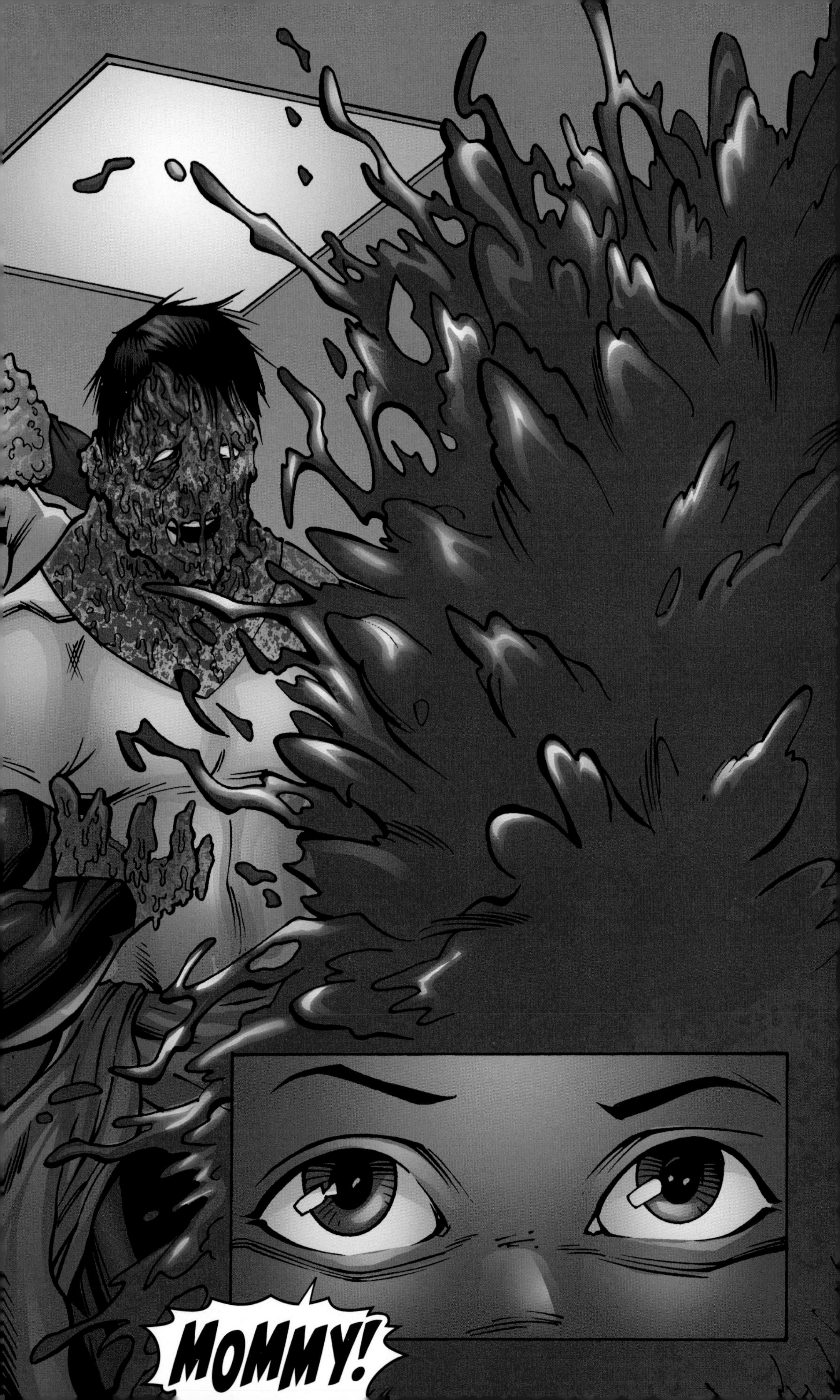
MOMMY!

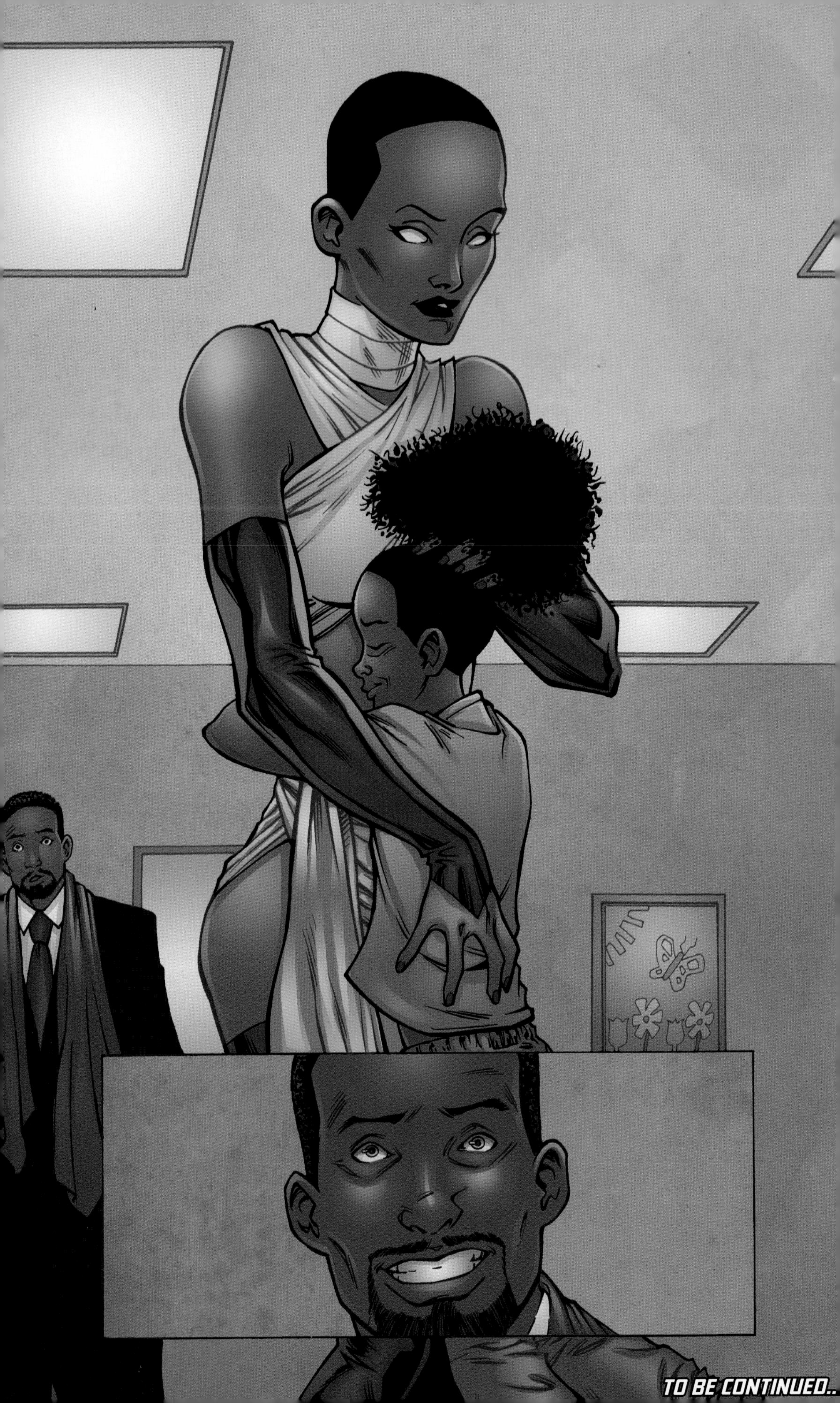
TO BE CONTINUED..

Issue #3 COVER B BY NUNO PLATI

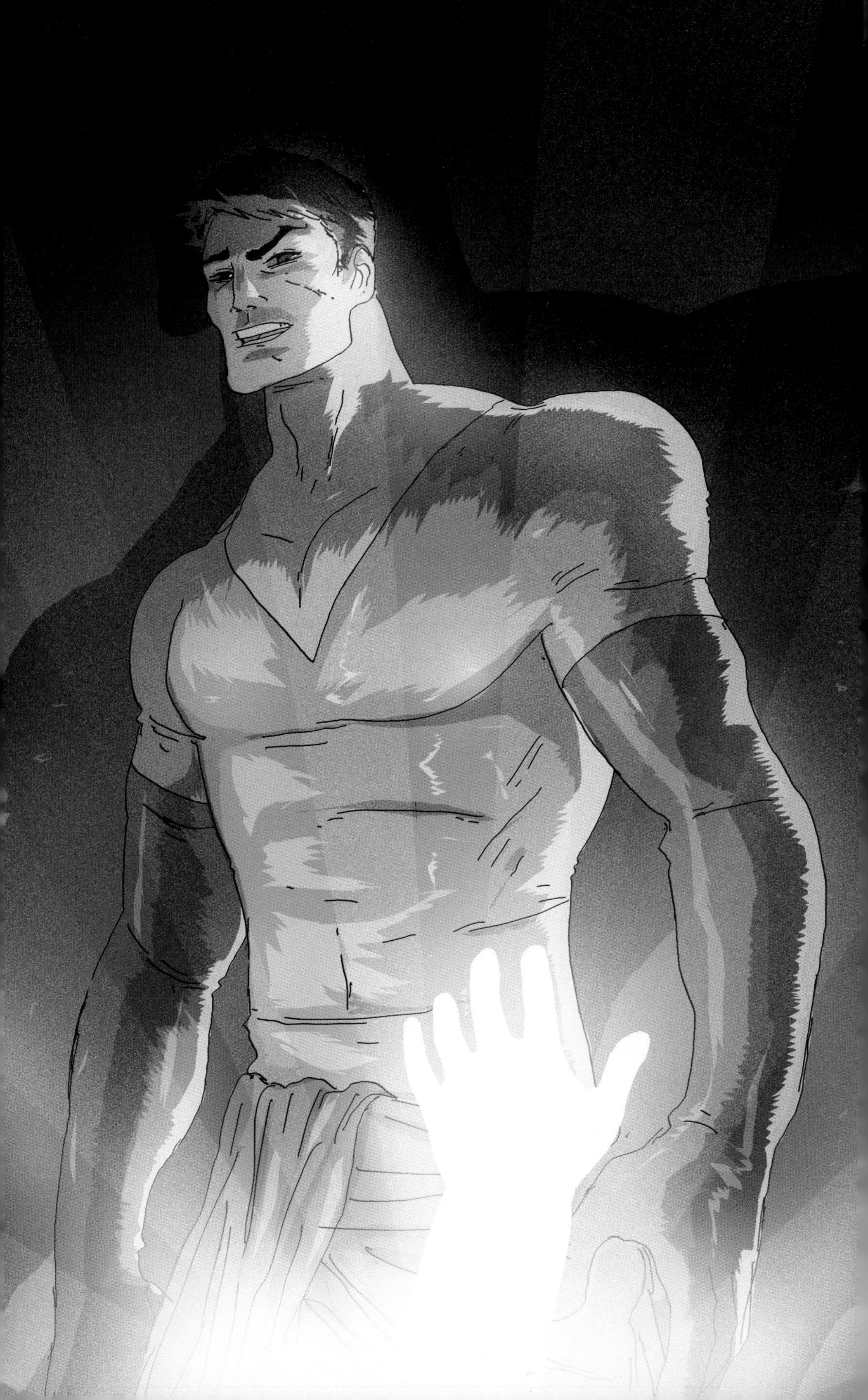

Issue #4 COVER A BY BRENT PEEPLES and MIRKA ANDOLFO

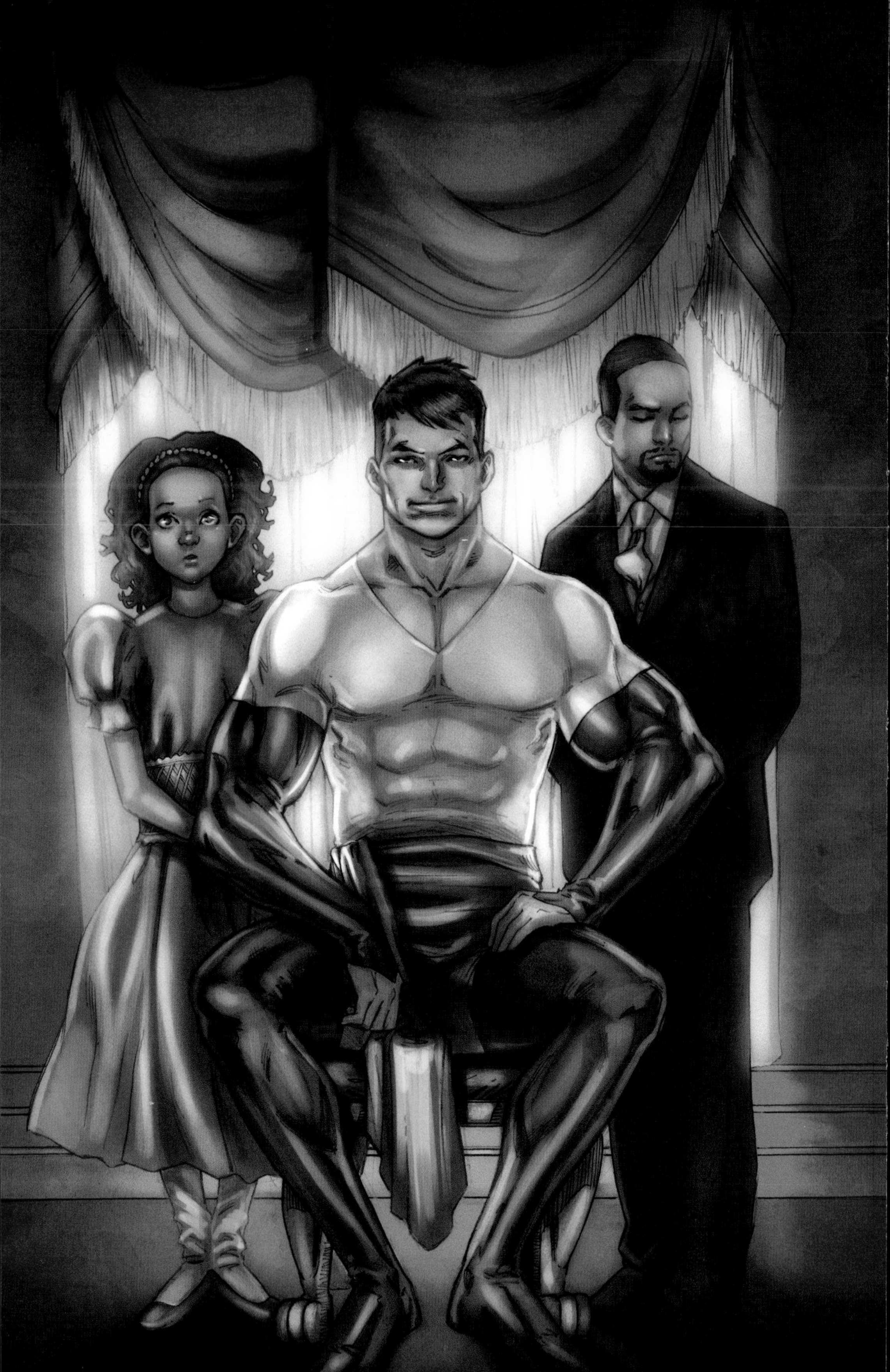

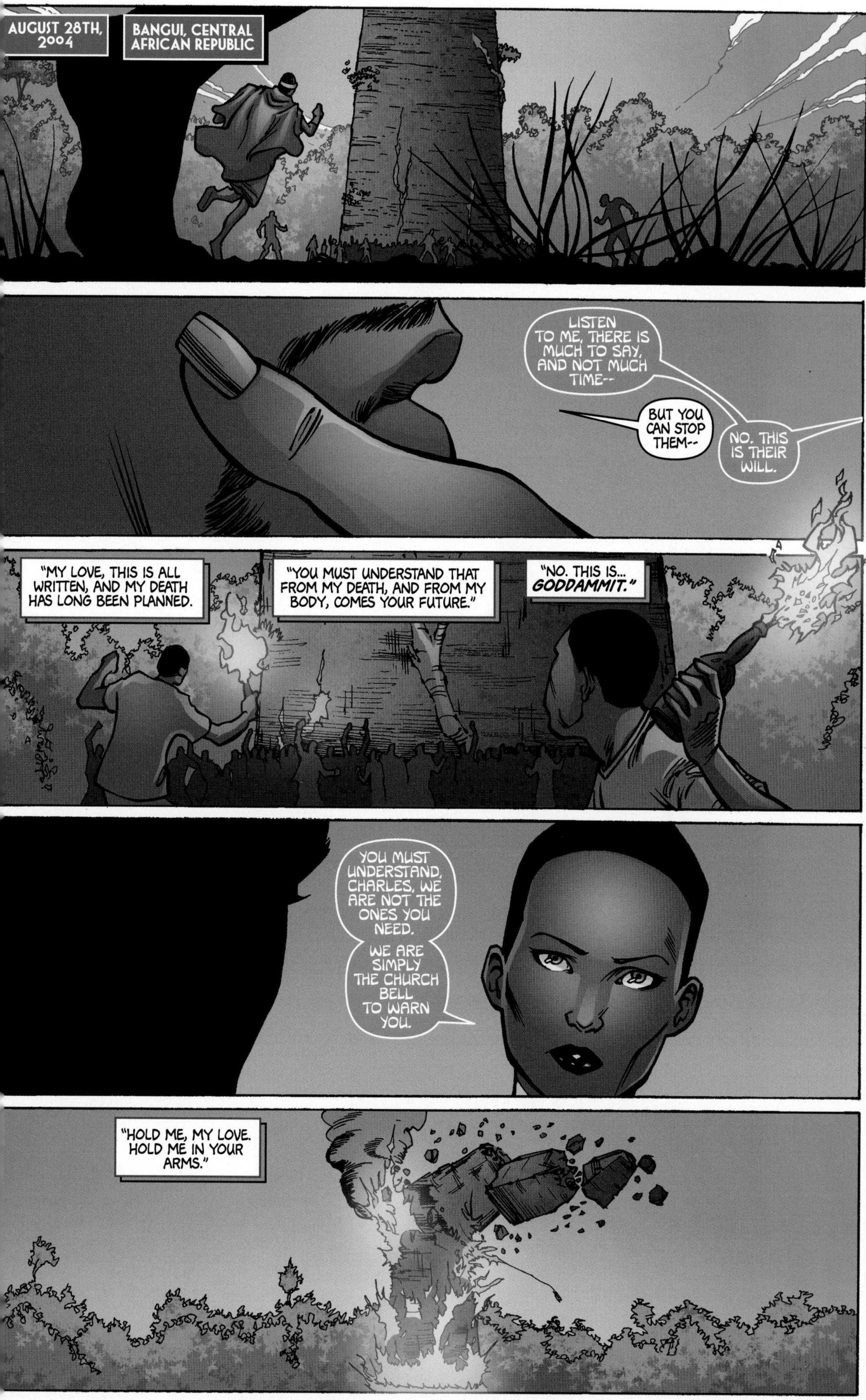
AUGUST 28TH, 2004
BANGUI, CENTRAL AFRICAN REPUBLIC
LISTEN TO ME, THERE IS MUCH TO SAY, AND NOT MUCH TIME--
BUT YOU CAN STOP THEM--
NO. THIS IS THEIR WILL.
"MY LOVE, THIS IS ALL WRITTEN, AND MY DEATH HAS LONG BEEN PLANNED.
"YOU MUST UNDERSTAND THAT FROM MY DEATH, AND FROM MY BODY, COMES YOUR FUTURE."
"NO. THIS IS... *GODDAMMIT.*"
YOU MUST UNDERSTAND, CHARLES, WE ARE NOT THE ONES YOU NEED.
WE ARE SIMPLY THE CHURCH BELL TO WARN YOU.
"HOLD ME, MY LOVE. HOLD ME IN YOUR ARMS."

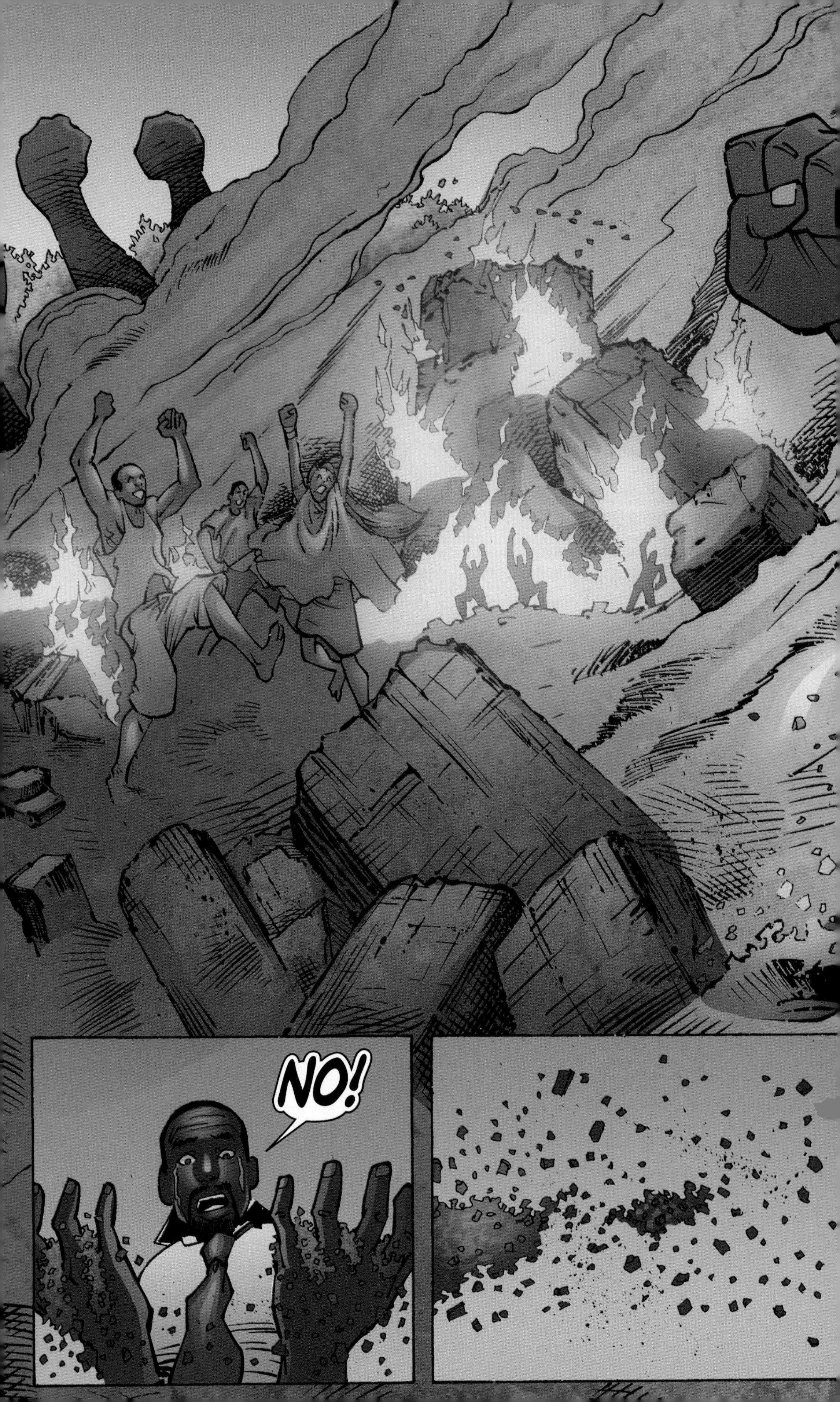
NO!

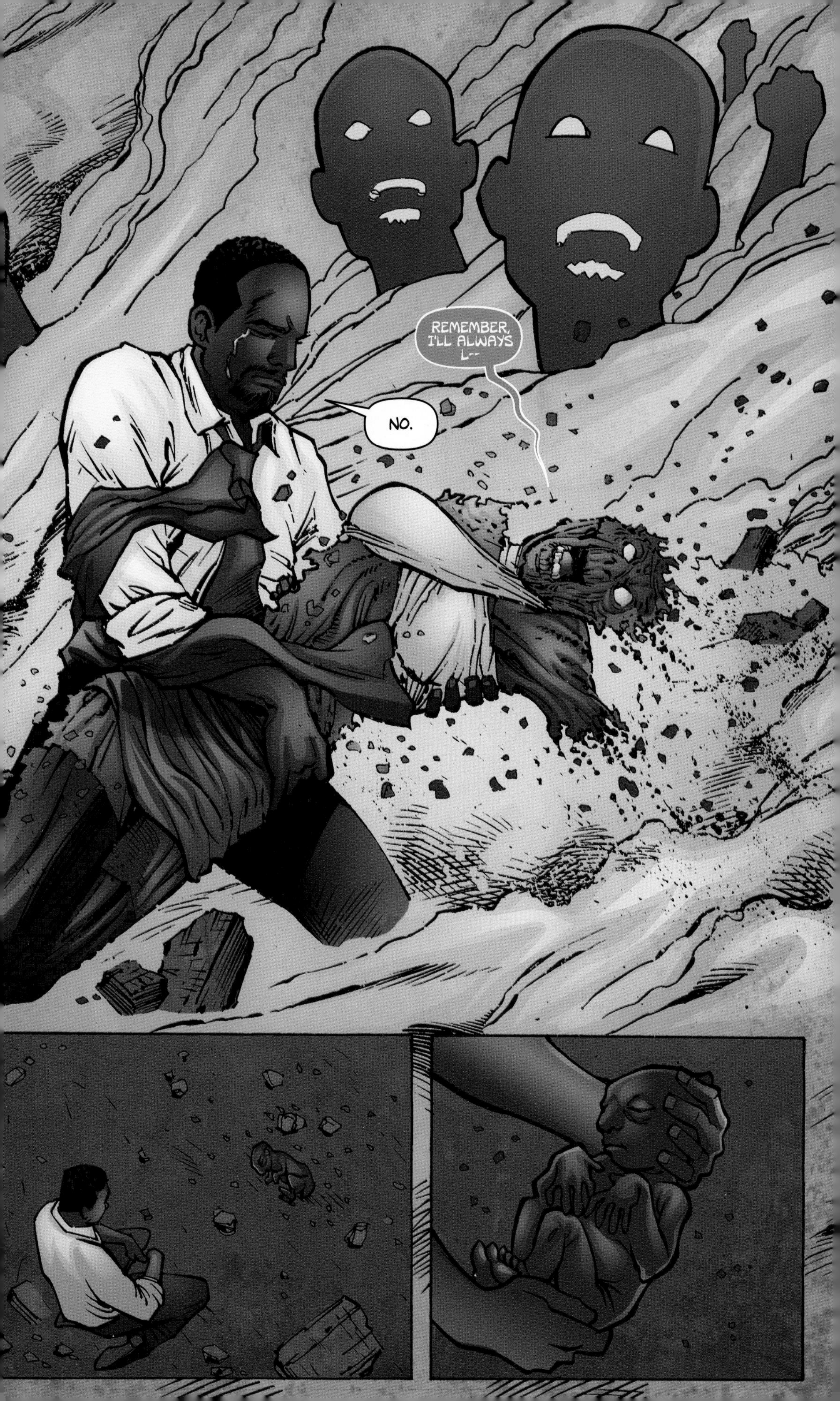

REMEMBER, I'LL ALWAYS L--
NO.

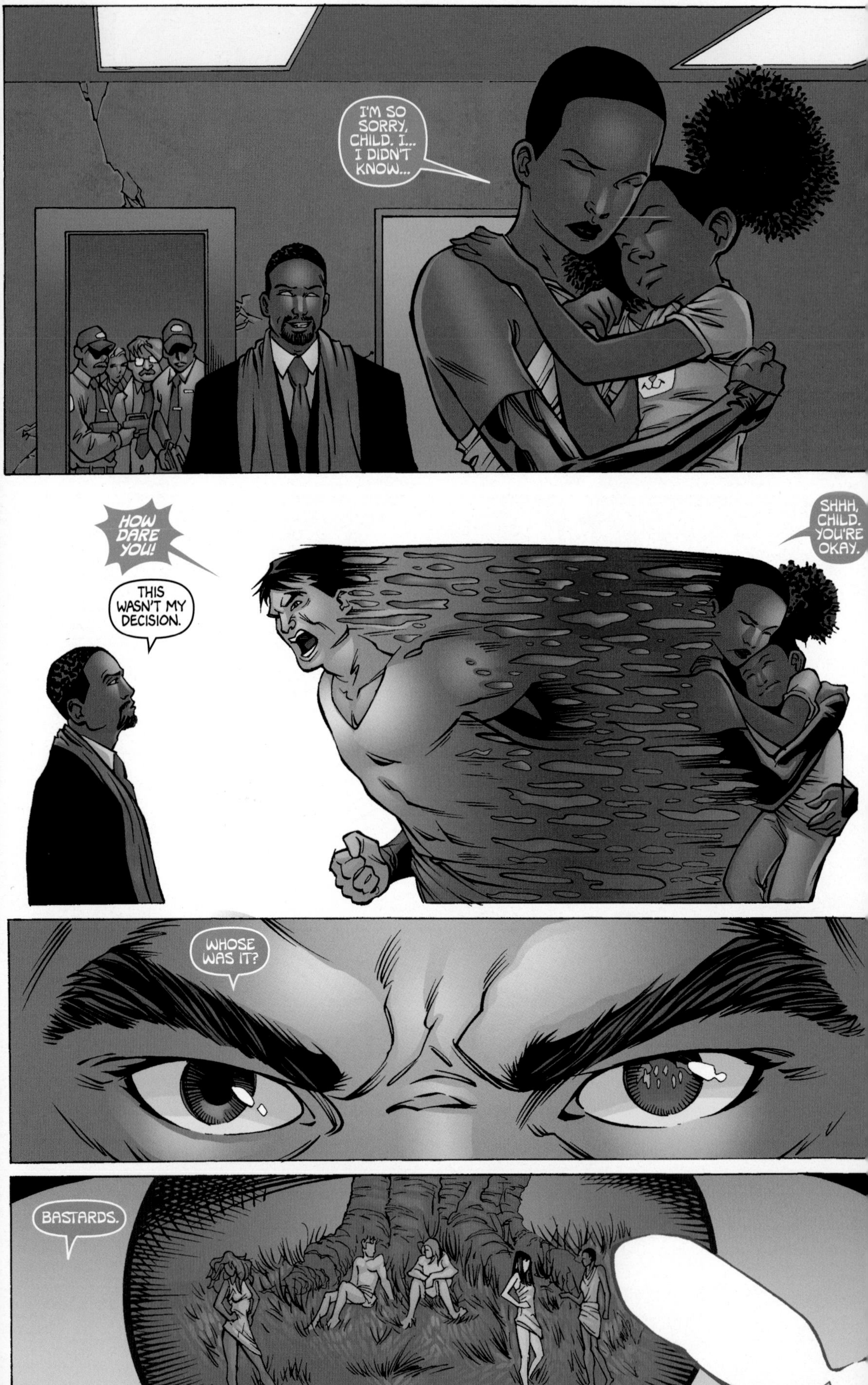

I'M SO SORRY, CHILD. I... I DIDN'T KNOW...
HOW DARE YOU!
THIS WASN'T MY DECISION.
SHHH, CHILD. YOU'RE OKAY.
WHOSE WAS IT?
BASTARDS.

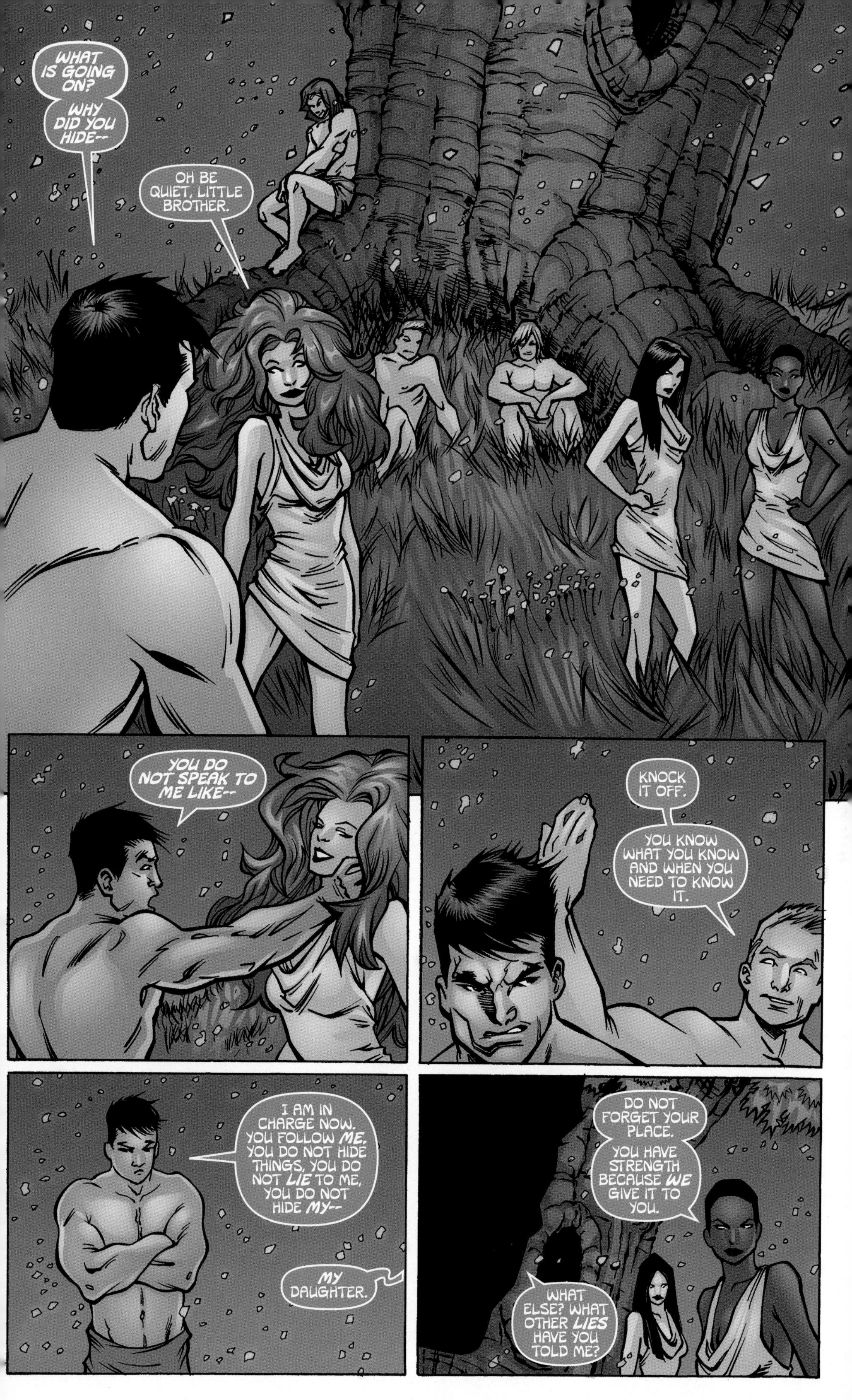
WHAT IS GOING ON?
WHY DID YOU HIDE--
OH BE QUIET, LITTLE BROTHER.
YOU DO NOT SPEAK TO ME LIKE--
KNOCK IT OFF.
YOU KNOW WHAT YOU KNOW AND WHEN YOU NEED TO KNOW IT.
I AM IN CHARGE NOW. YOU FOLLOW ME. YOU DO NOT HIDE THINGS, YOU DO NOT LIE TO ME, YOU DO NOT HIDE MY--
MY DAUGHTER.
DO NOT FORGET YOUR PLACE.
YOU HAVE STRENGTH BECAUSE WE GIVE IT TO YOU.
WHAT ELSE? WHAT OTHER LIES HAVE YOU TOLD ME?

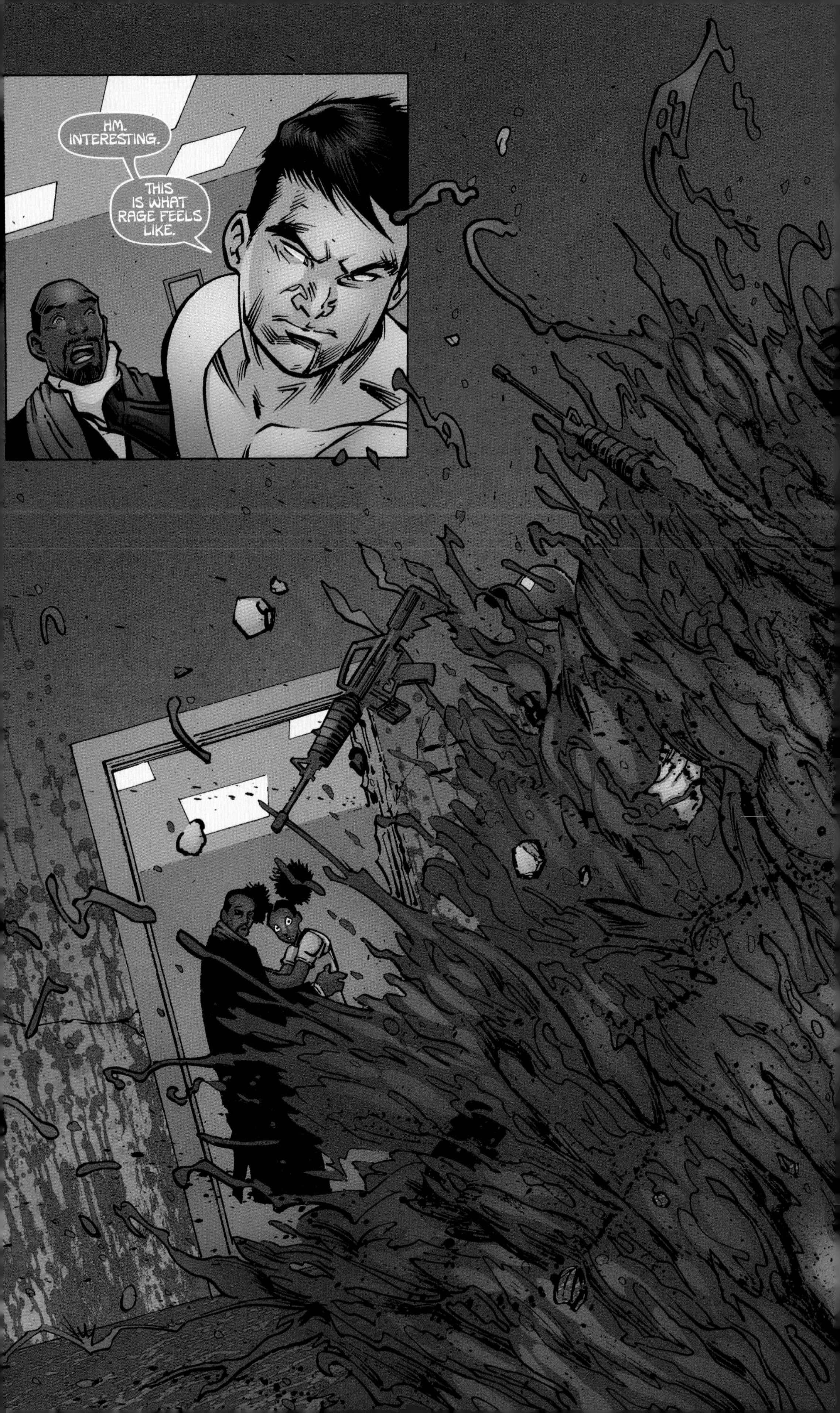
HM. INTERESTING.
THIS IS WHAT RAGE FEELS LIKE.

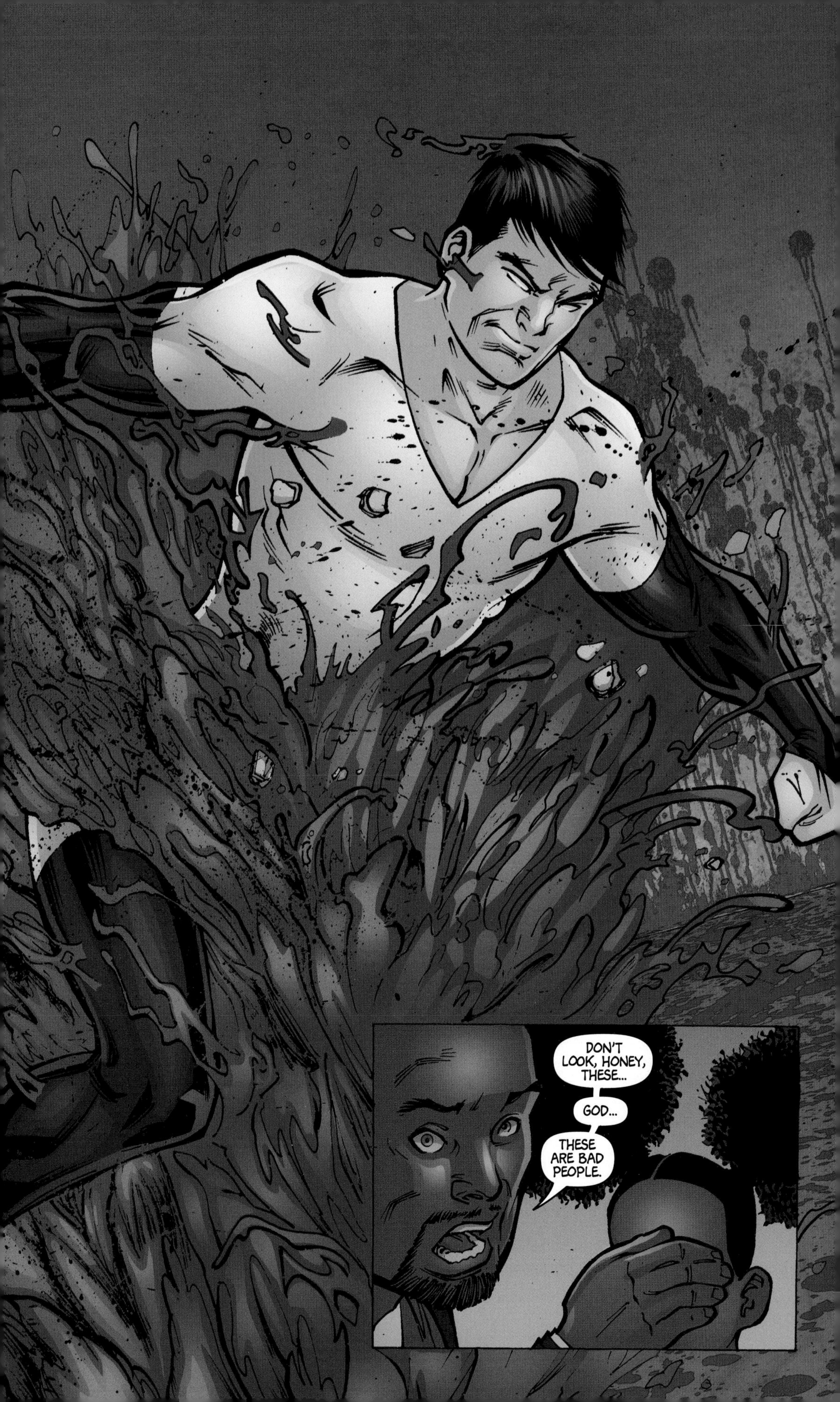
DON'T LOOK, HONEY, THESE...
GOD...
THESE ARE BAD PEOPLE.

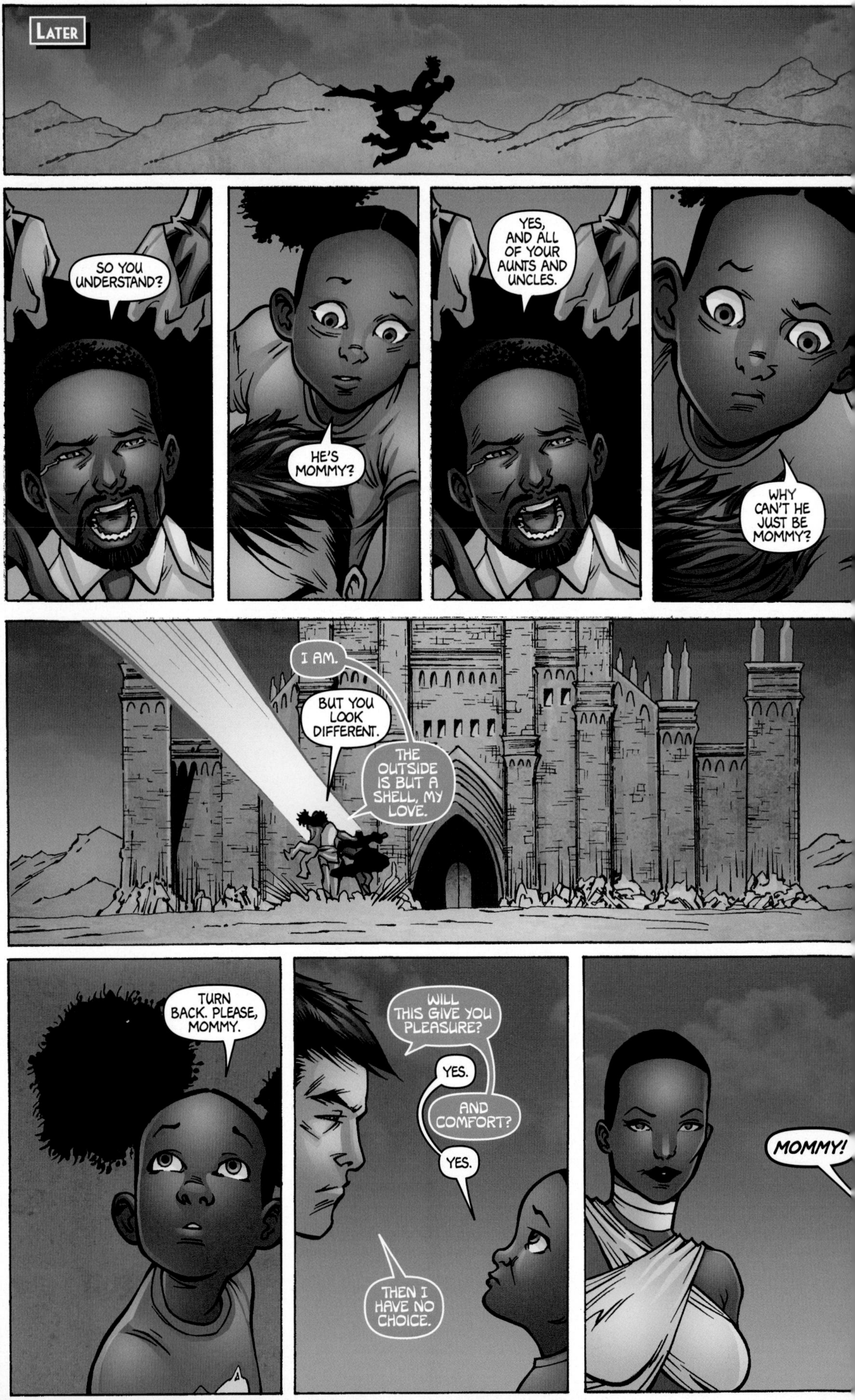
LATER
SO YOU UNDERSTAND?
HE'S MOMMY?
YES, AND ALL OF YOUR AUNTS AND UNCLES.
WHY CAN'T HE JUST BE MOMMY?
I AM.
BUT YOU LOOK DIFFERENT.
THE OUTSIDE IS BUT A SHELL, MY LOVE.
TURN BACK. PLEASE, MOMMY.
WILL THIS GIVE YOU PLEASURE?
YES.
AND COMFORT?
YES.
THEN I HAVE NO CHOICE.
MOMMY!

SHE SLEEPS WELL.

YOU SCARED ME.

I'VE HAD... AN INTERESTING DAY.

I'VE THOUGHT MYSELF OMNIPOTENT FOR SO LONG, AND YET, NOW, THERE ARE THINGS I DO NOT SEE.

I THOUGHT PERHAPS YOU COULD PROVIDE INSIGHT.

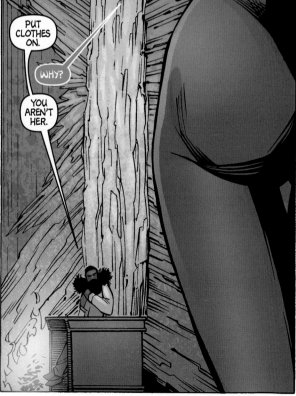

PUT CLOTHES ON.

WHY?

YOU AREN'T HER.

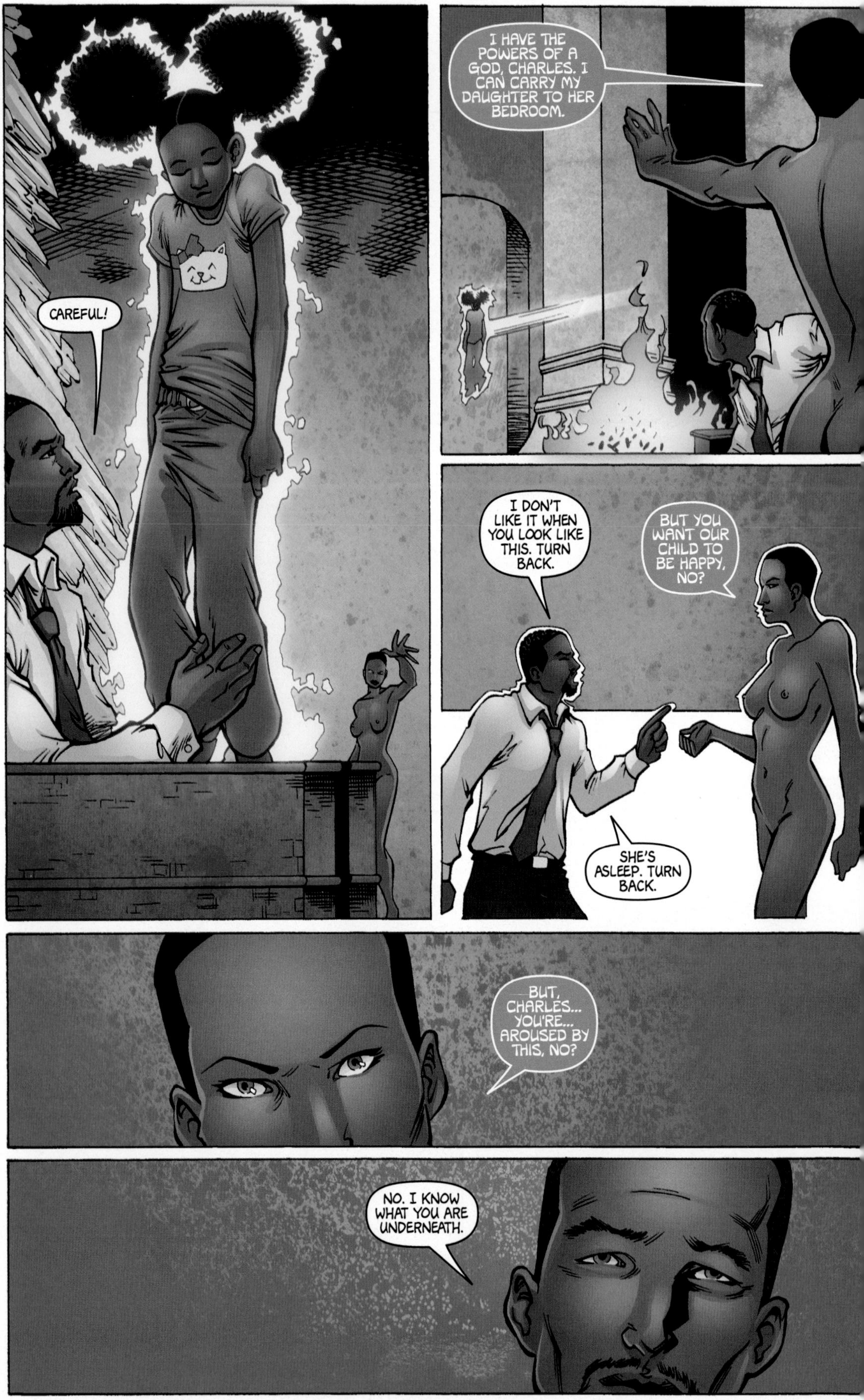
CAREFUL!
I HAVE THE POWERS OF A GOD, CHARLES. I CAN CARRY MY DAUGHTER TO HER BEDROOM.
I DON'T LIKE IT WHEN YOU LOOK LIKE THIS. TURN BACK.
BUT YOU WANT OUR CHILD TO BE HAPPY, NO?
SHE'S ASLEEP. TURN BACK.
—BUT, CHARLES... YOU'RE... AROUSED BY THIS, NO?
NO. I KNOW WHAT YOU ARE UNDERNEATH.

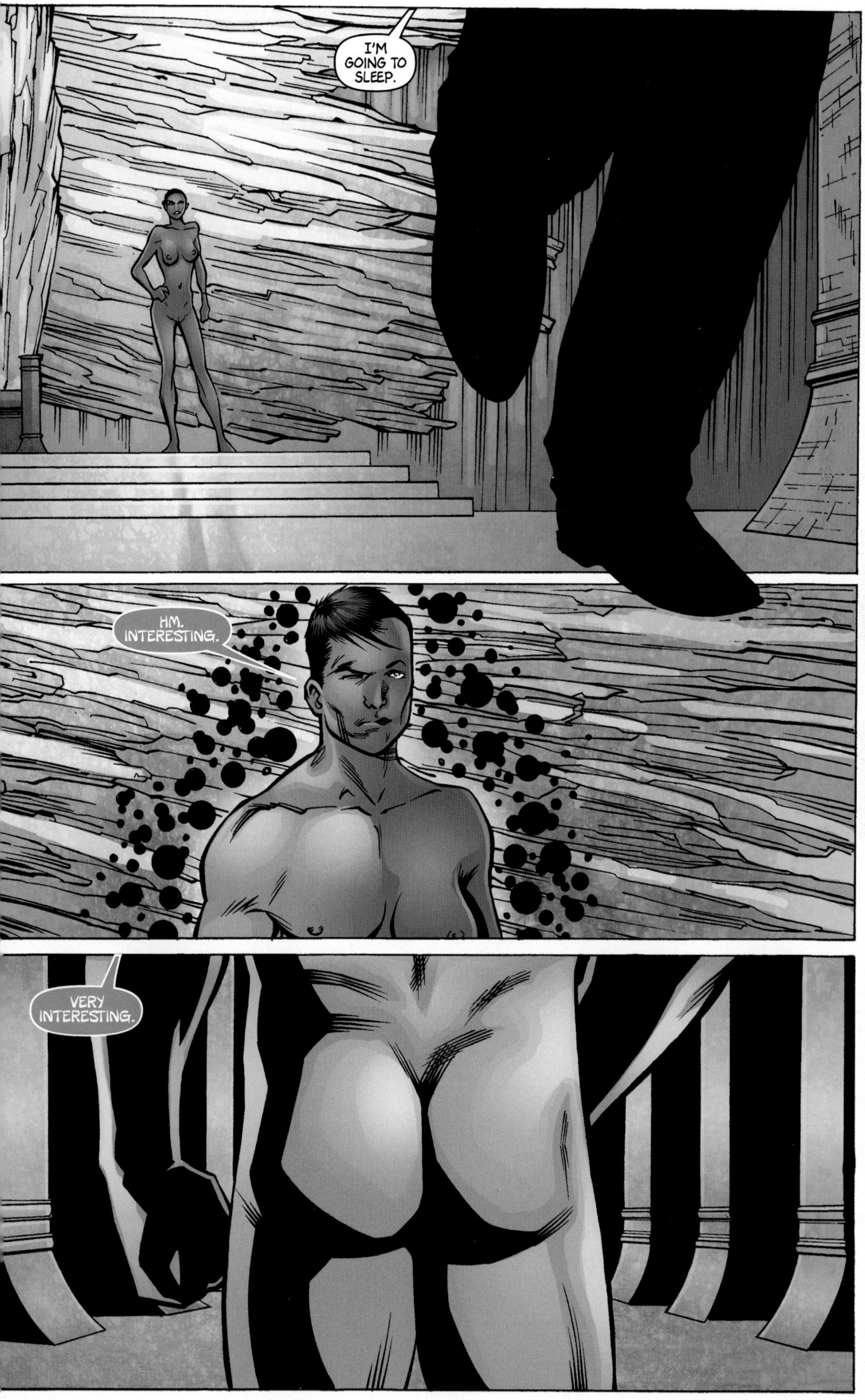
I'M GOING TO SLEEP.
HM. INTERESTING.
VERY INTERESTING.

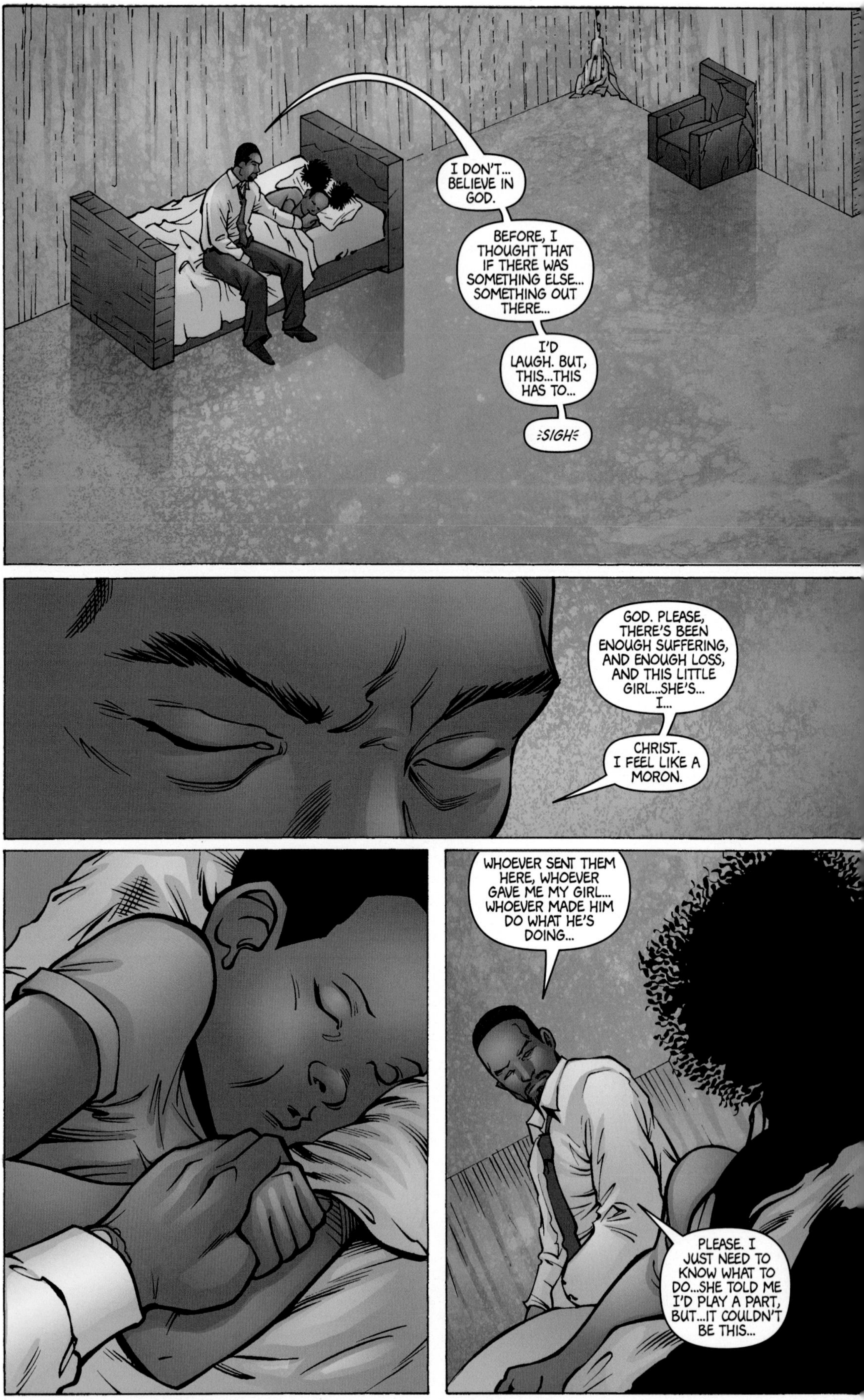

I DON'T... BELIEVE IN GOD.
BEFORE, I THOUGHT THAT IF THERE WAS SOMETHING ELSE... SOMETHING OUT THERE...
I'D LAUGH. BUT, THIS...THIS HAS TO...
SIGH
GOD. PLEASE, THERE'S BEEN ENOUGH SUFFERING, AND ENOUGH LOSS, AND THIS LITTLE GIRL...SHE'S... I...
CHRIST. I FEEL LIKE A MORON.
WHOEVER SENT THEM HERE, WHOEVER GAVE ME MY GIRL... WHOEVER MADE HIM DO WHAT HE'S DOING...
PLEASE. I JUST NEED TO KNOW WHAT TO DO...SHE TOLD ME I'D PLAY A PART, BUT...IT COULDN'T BE THIS...

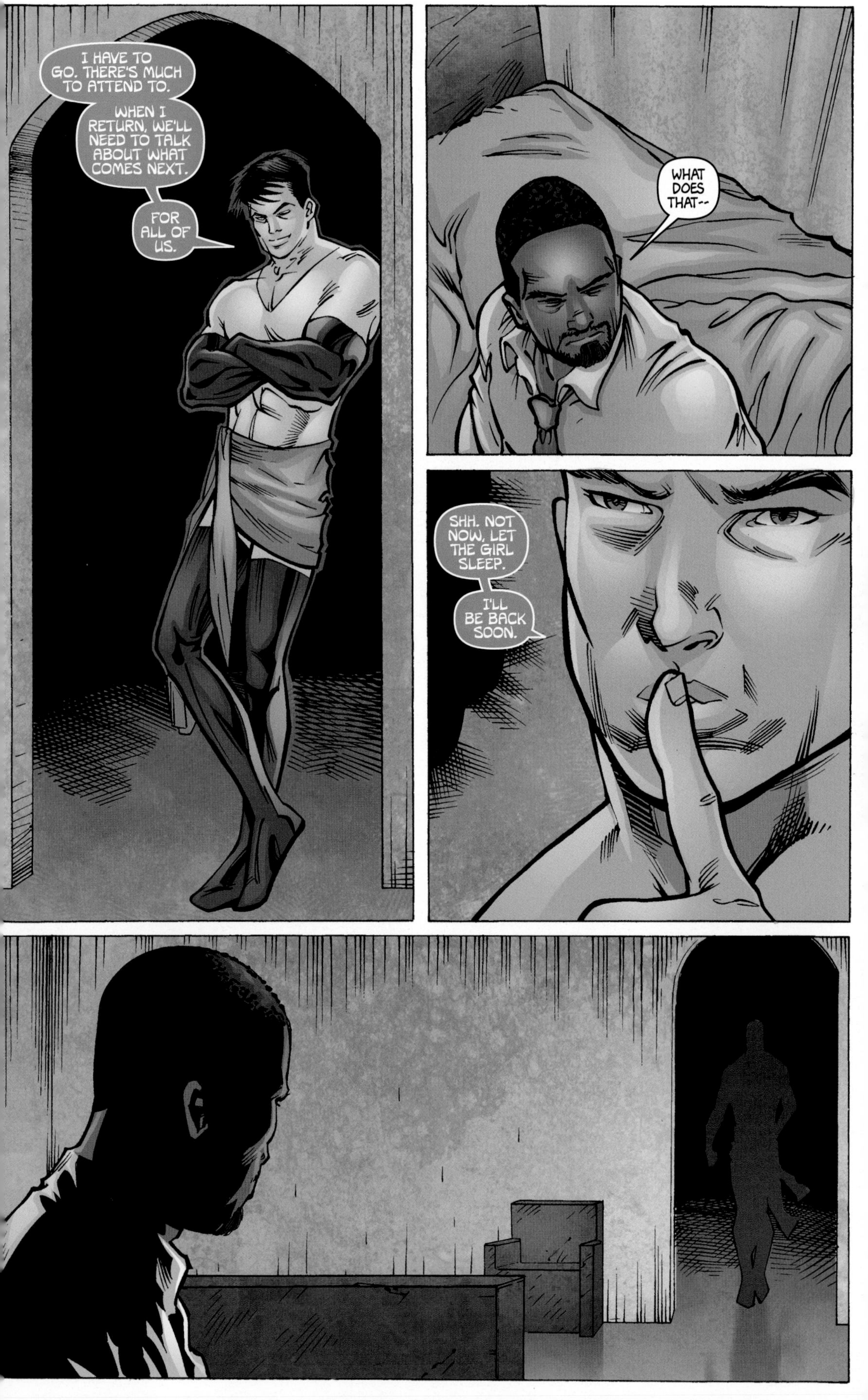
I HAVE TO GO. THERE'S MUCH TO ATTEND TO.
WHEN I RETURN, WE'LL NEED TO TALK ABOUT WHAT COMES NEXT.
FOR ALL OF US.
WHAT DOES THAT--
SHH. NOT NOW, LET THE GIRL SLEEP.
I'LL BE BACK SOON.

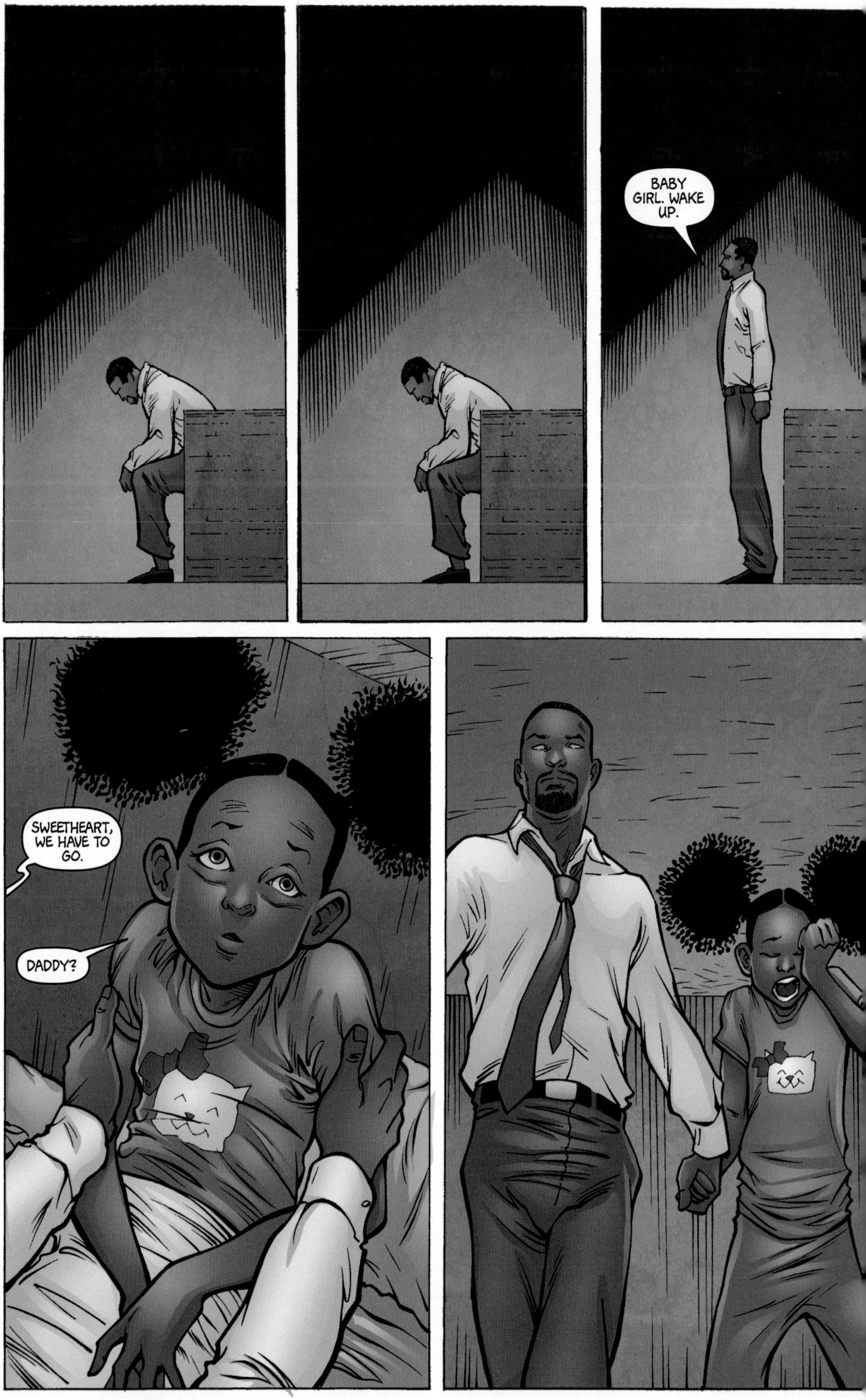
BABY GIRL. WAKE UP.
SWEETHEART, WE HAVE TO GO.
DADDY?

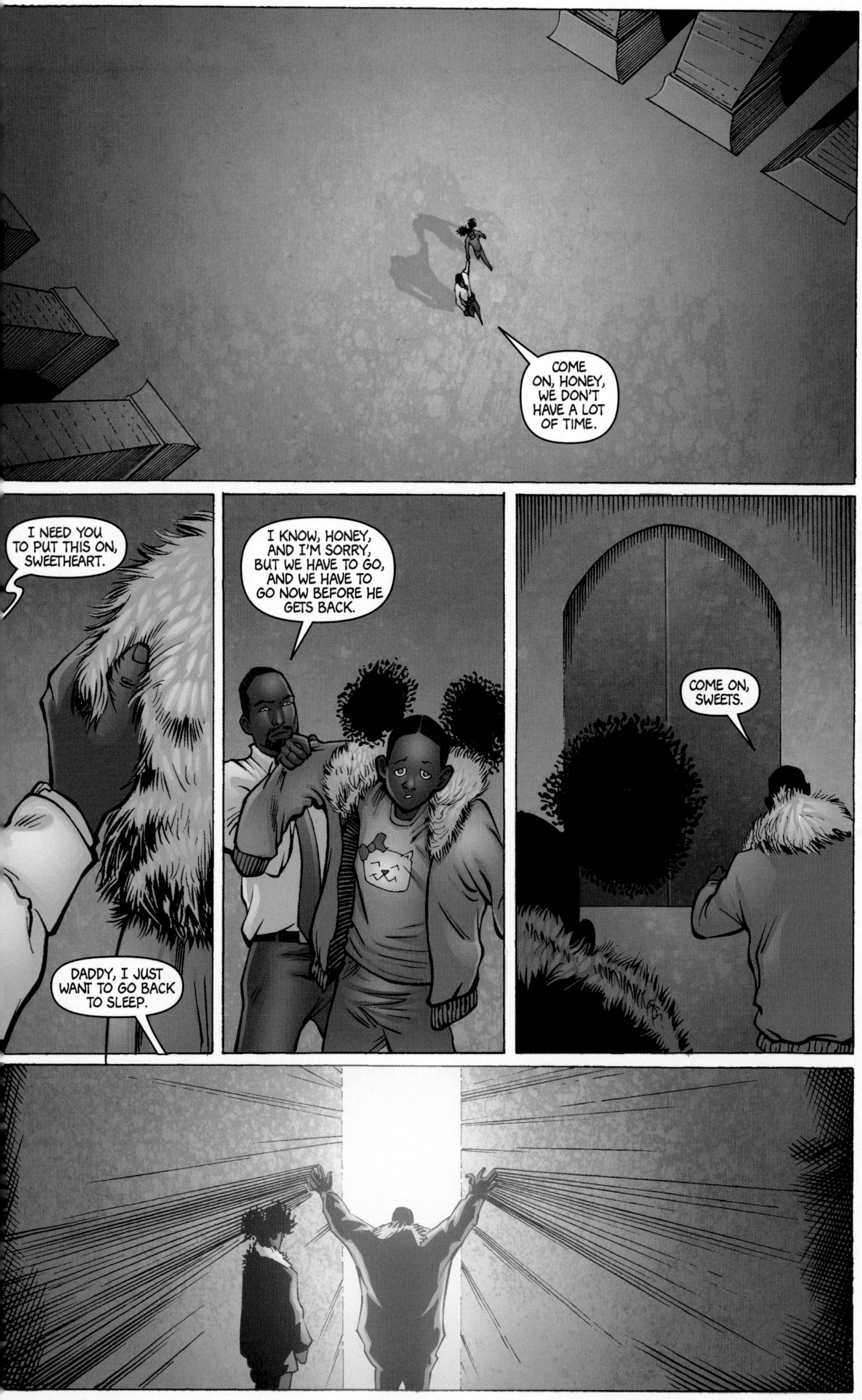
COME ON, HONEY, WE DON'T HAVE A LOT OF TIME.
I NEED YOU TO PUT THIS ON, SWEETHEART.
DADDY, I JUST WANT TO GO BACK TO SLEEP.
I KNOW, HONEY, AND I'M SORRY, BUT WE HAVE TO GO, AND WE HAVE TO GO NOW BEFORE HE GETS BACK.
COME ON, SWEETS.

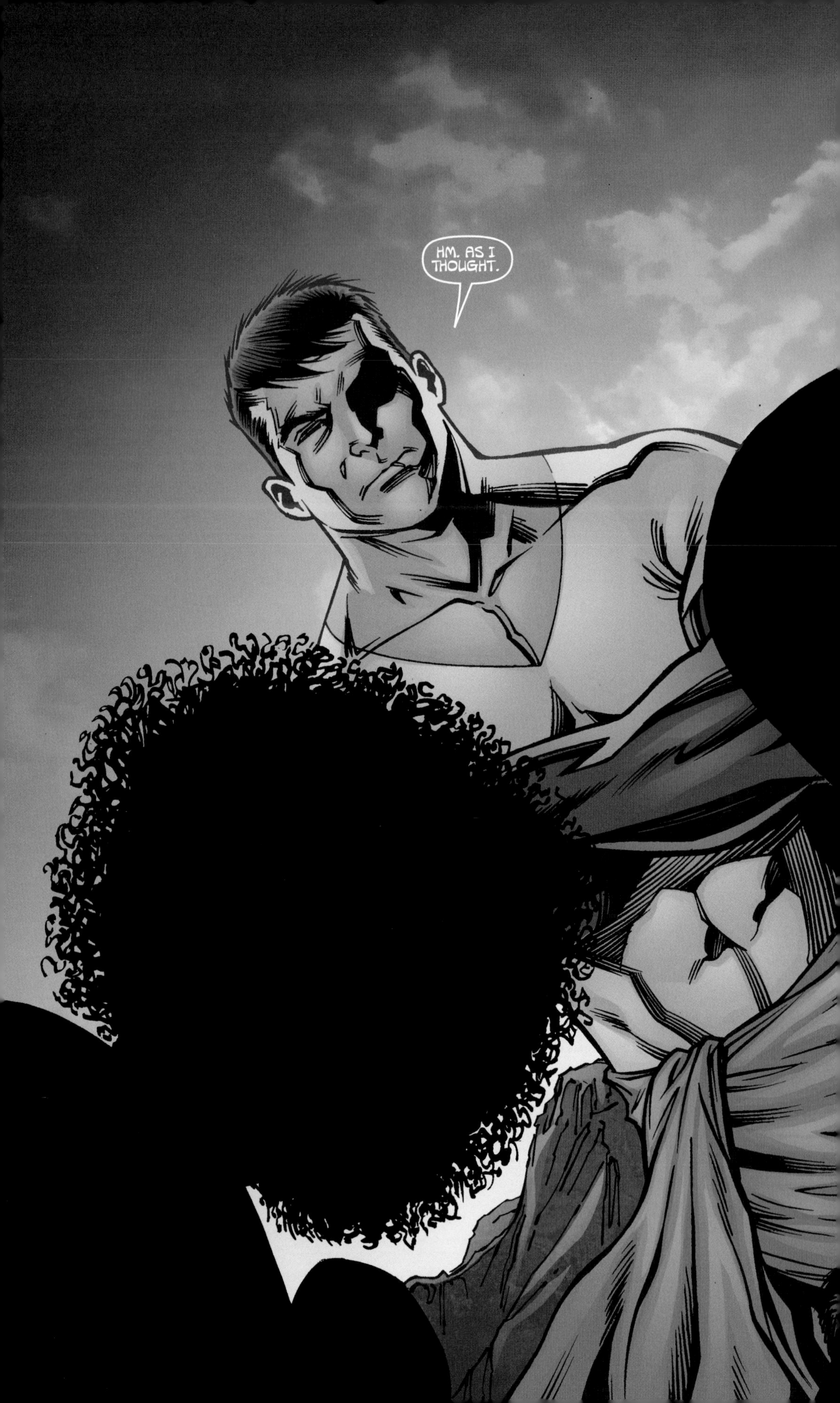
HM. AS I THOUGHT.

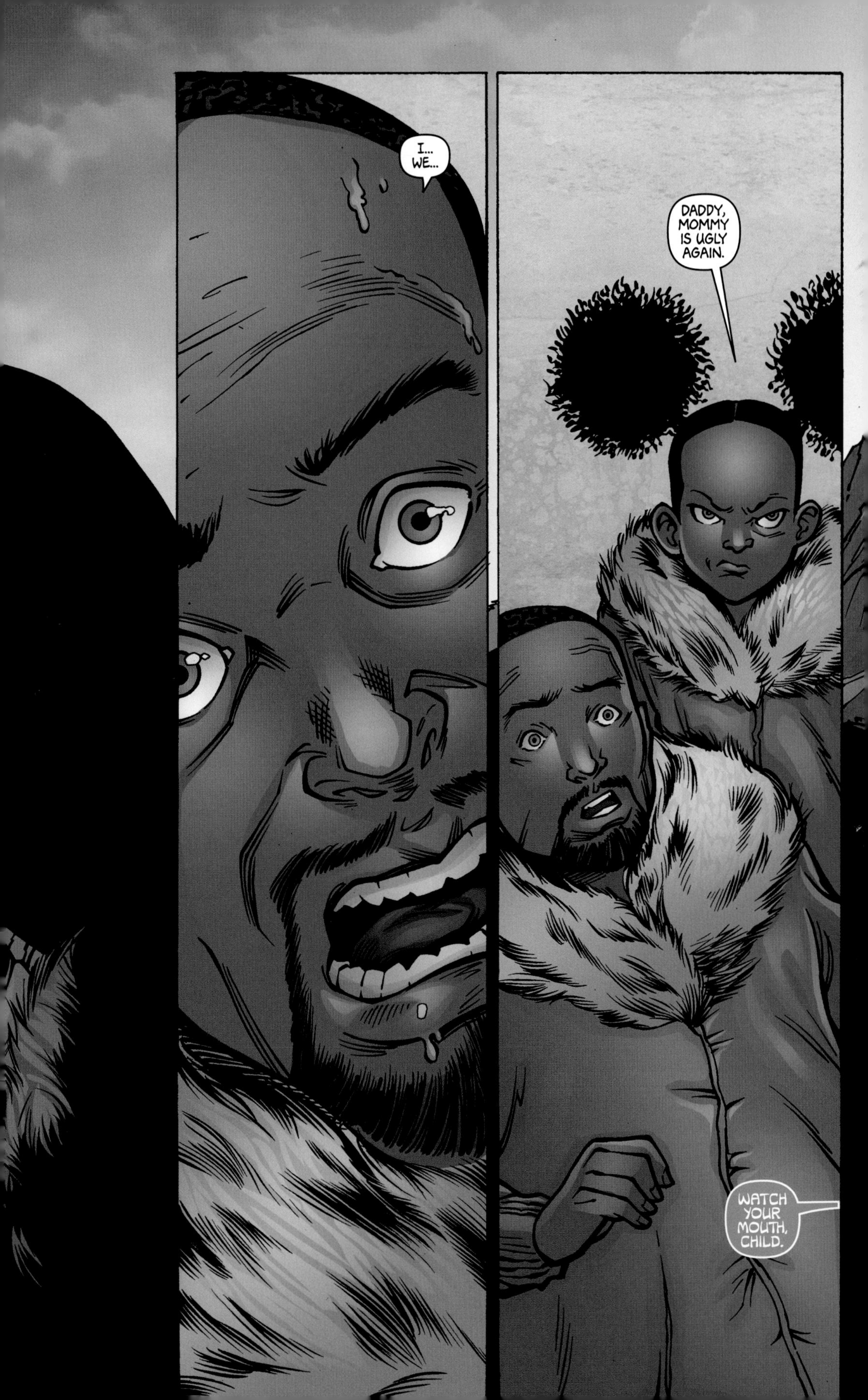
I... WE...
DADDY, MOMMY IS UGLY AGAIN.
WATCH YOUR MOUTH, CHILD.

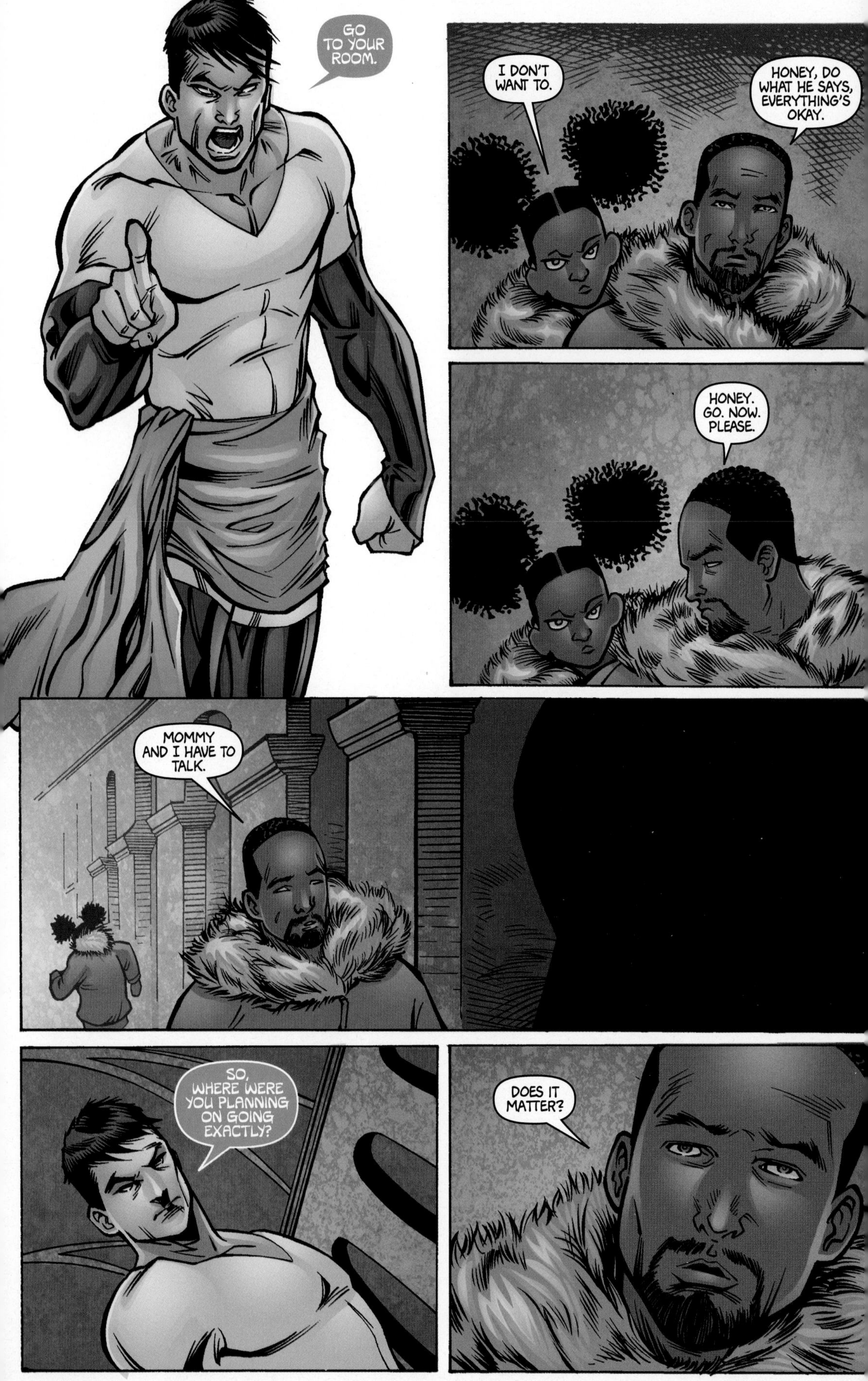
GO TO YOUR ROOM.
I DON'T WANT TO.
HONEY, DO WHAT HE SAYS, EVERYTHING'S OKAY.
HONEY. GO. NOW. PLEASE.
MOMMY AND I HAVE TO TALK.
SO, WHERE WERE YOU PLANNING ON GOING EXACTLY?
DOES IT MATTER?

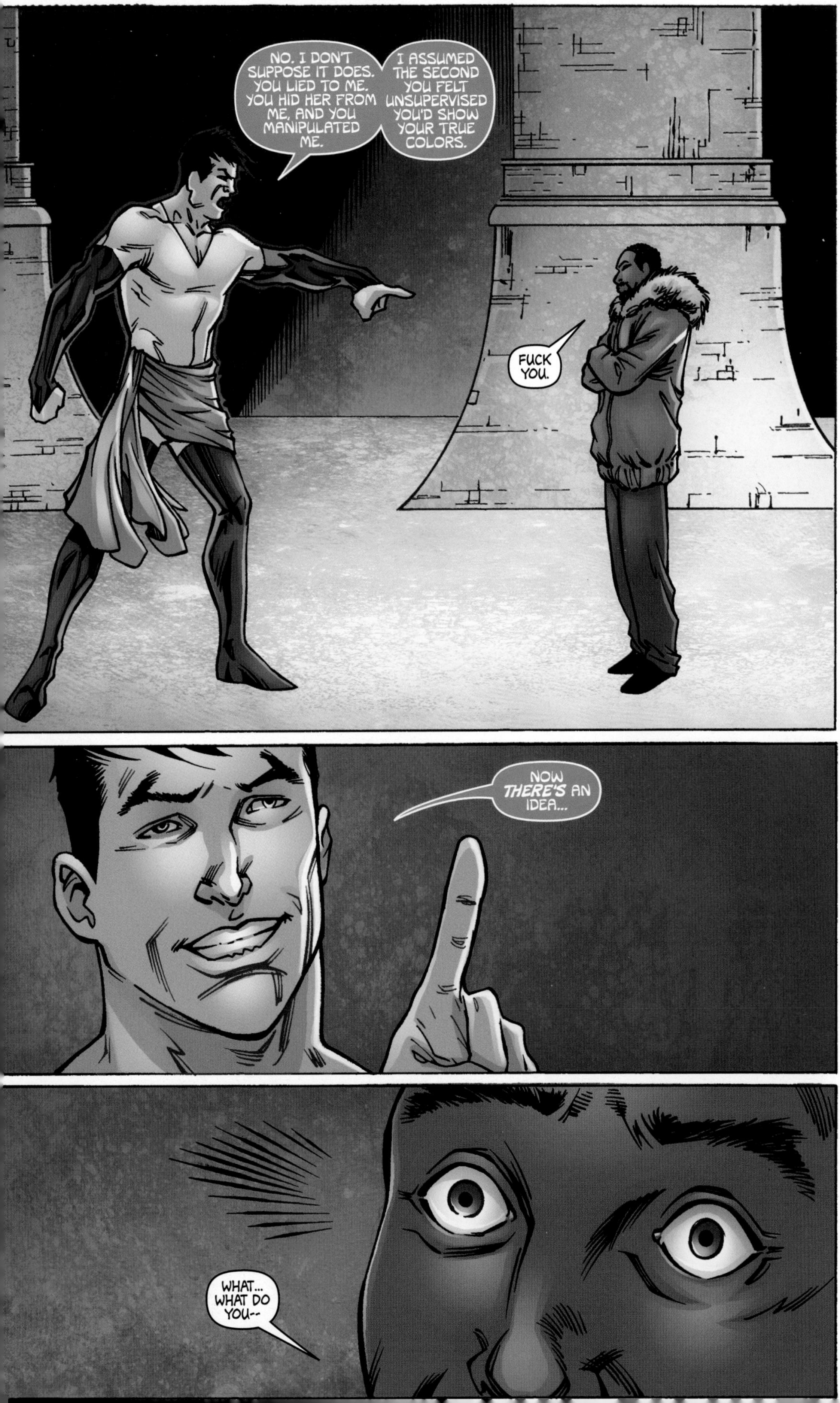
NO. I DON'T SUPPOSE IT DOES. YOU LIED TO ME. YOU HID HER FROM ME, AND YOU MANIPULATED ME.
I ASSUMED THE SECOND YOU FELT UNSUPERVISED YOU'D SHOW YOUR TRUE COLORS.
FUCK YOU.
NOW *THERE'S* AN IDEA...
WHAT... WHAT DO YOU--

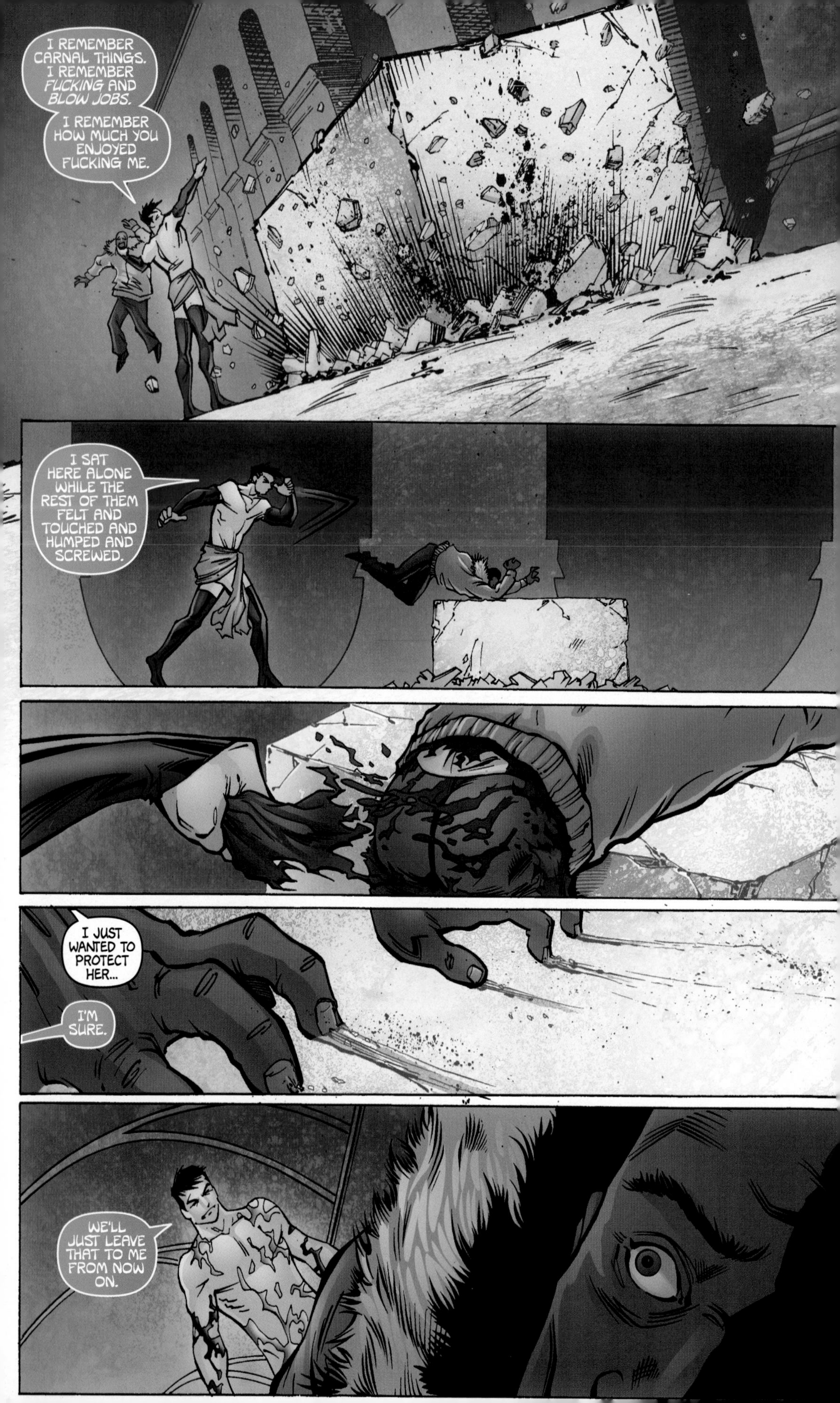

I REMEMBER CARNAL THINGS. I REMEMBER *FUCKING* AND *BLOW JOBS.*
I REMEMBER HOW MUCH YOU ENJOYED FUCKING ME.
I SAT HERE ALONE WHILE THE REST OF THEM FELT AND TOUCHED AND HUMPED AND SCREWED.
I JUST WANTED TO PROTECT HER...
I'M SURE.
WE'LL JUST LEAVE THAT TO ME FROM NOW ON.

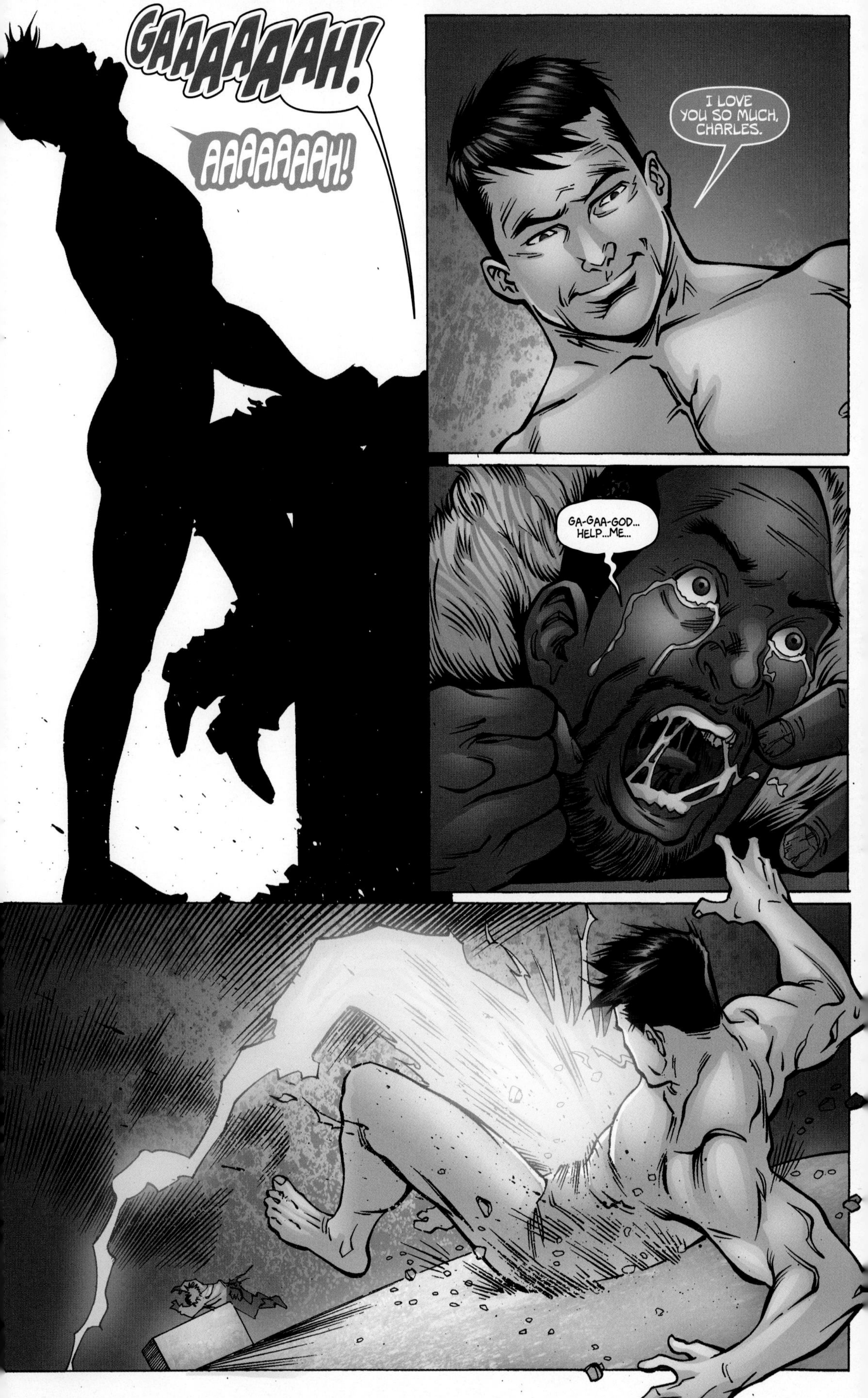
GAAAAAAH!
AAAAAAAH!
I LOVE YOU SO MUCH, CHARLES.
GA-GAA-GOD... HELP...ME...

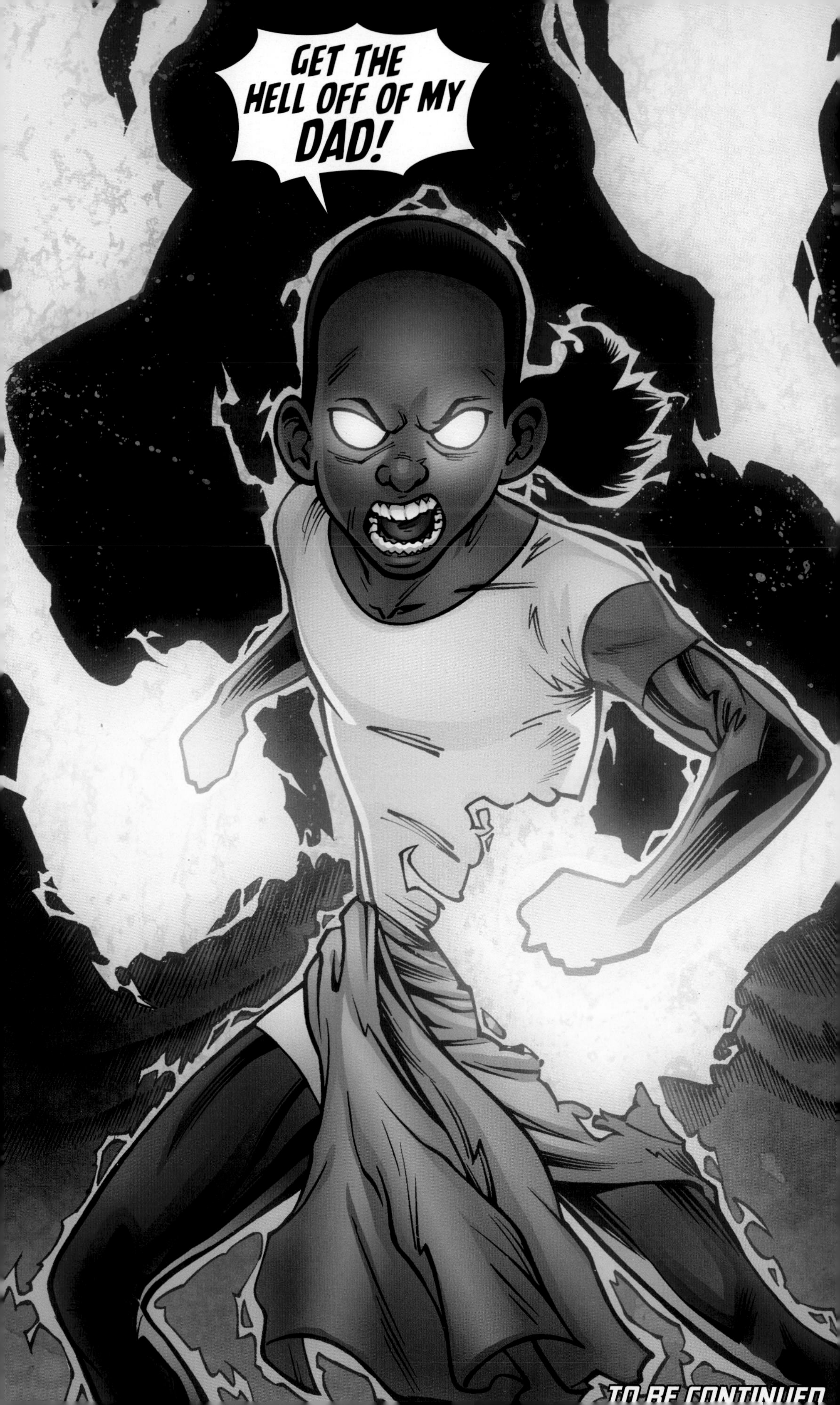
GET THE HELL OFF OF MY DAD!
TO BE CONTINUED

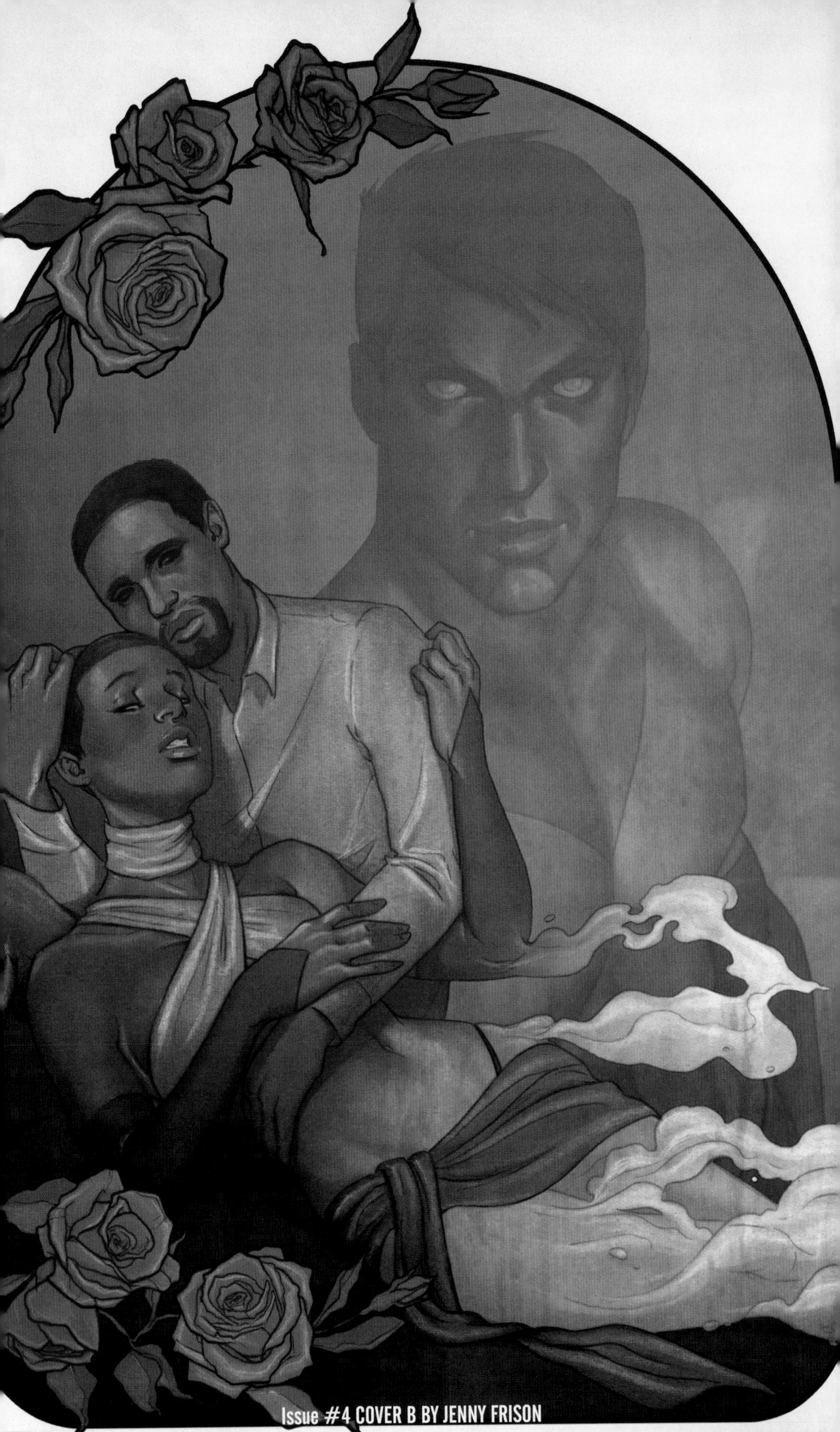

Issue #4 COVER B BY JENNY FRISON

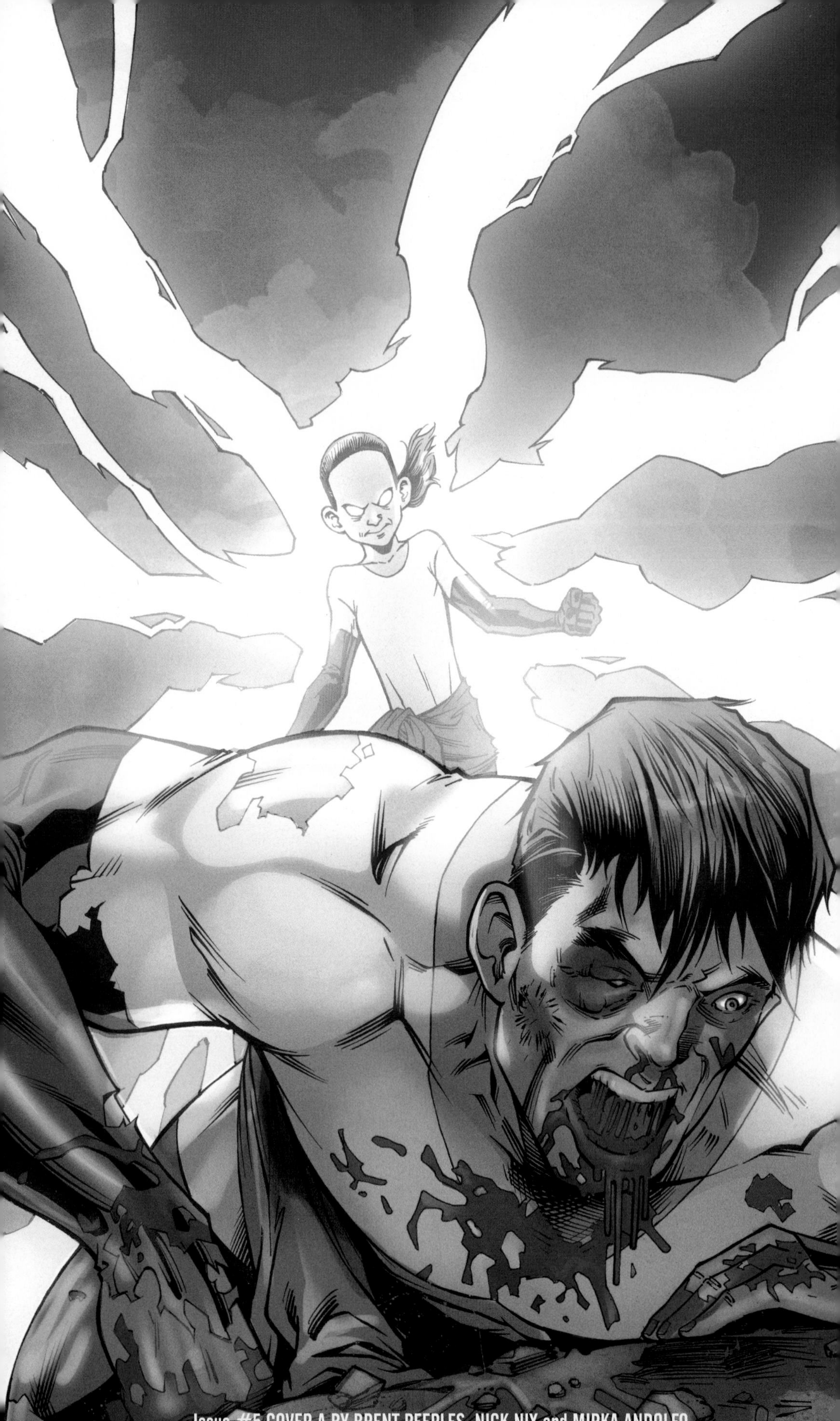

Issue #5 COVER A BY BRENT PEEPLES, NICK NIX and MIRKA ANDOLFO

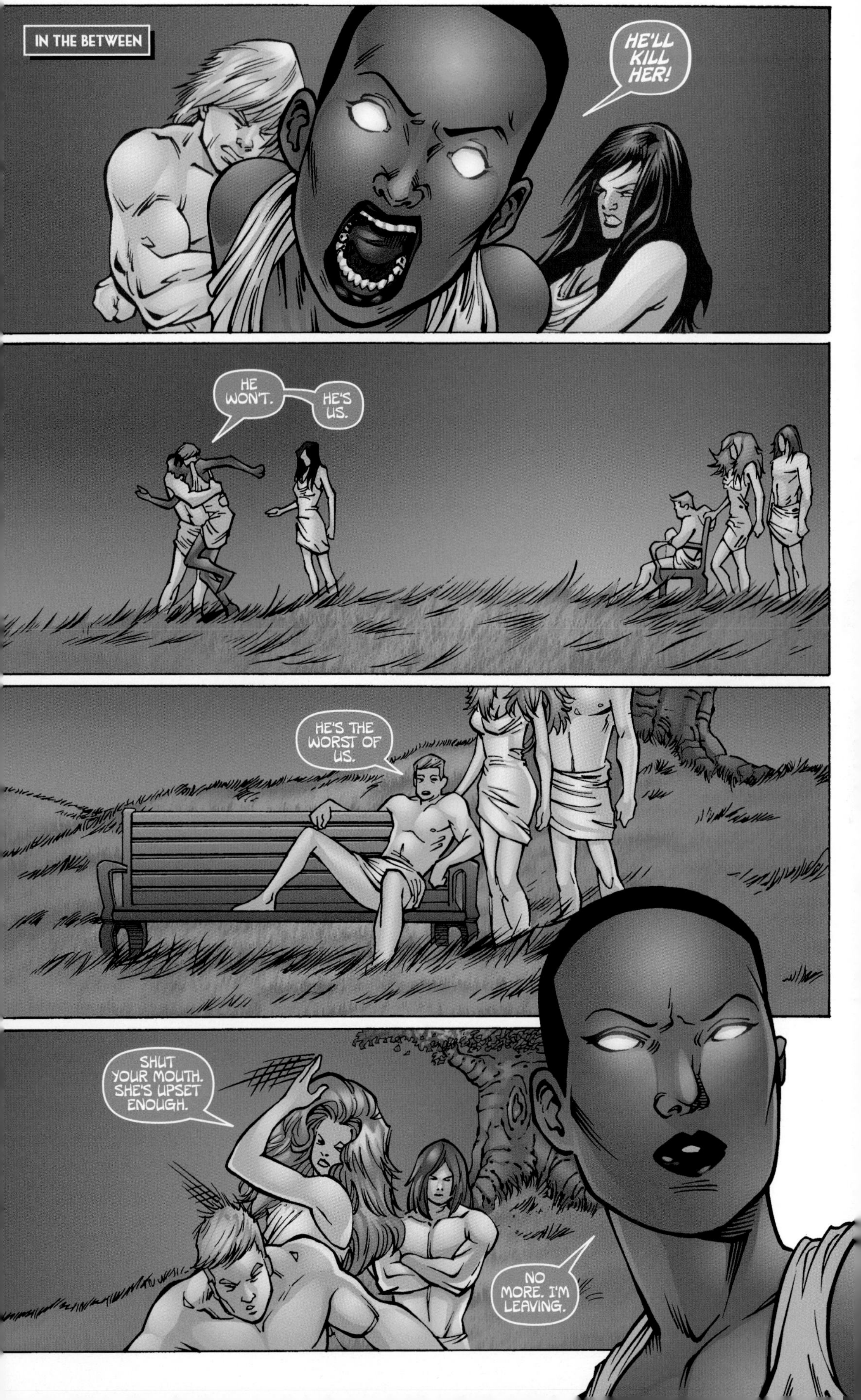
IN THE BETWEEN
HE'LL KILL HER!
HE WON'T.
HE'S US.
HE'S THE WORST OF US.
SHUT YOUR MOUTH. SHE'S UPSET ENOUGH.
NO MORE. I'M LEAVING.

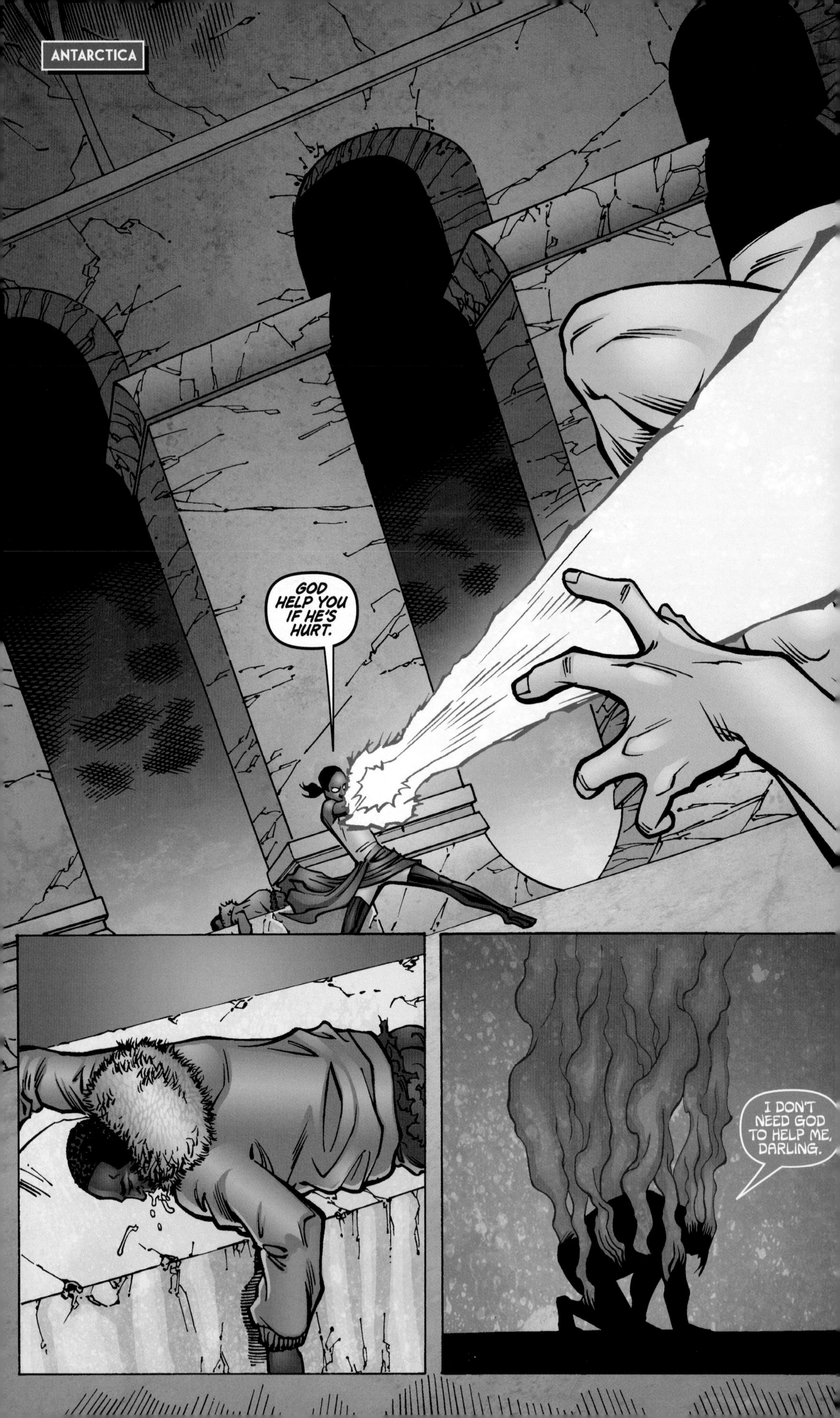
ANTARCTICA
GOD HELP YOU IF HE'S HURT.
I DON'T NEED GOD TO HELP ME, DARLING.

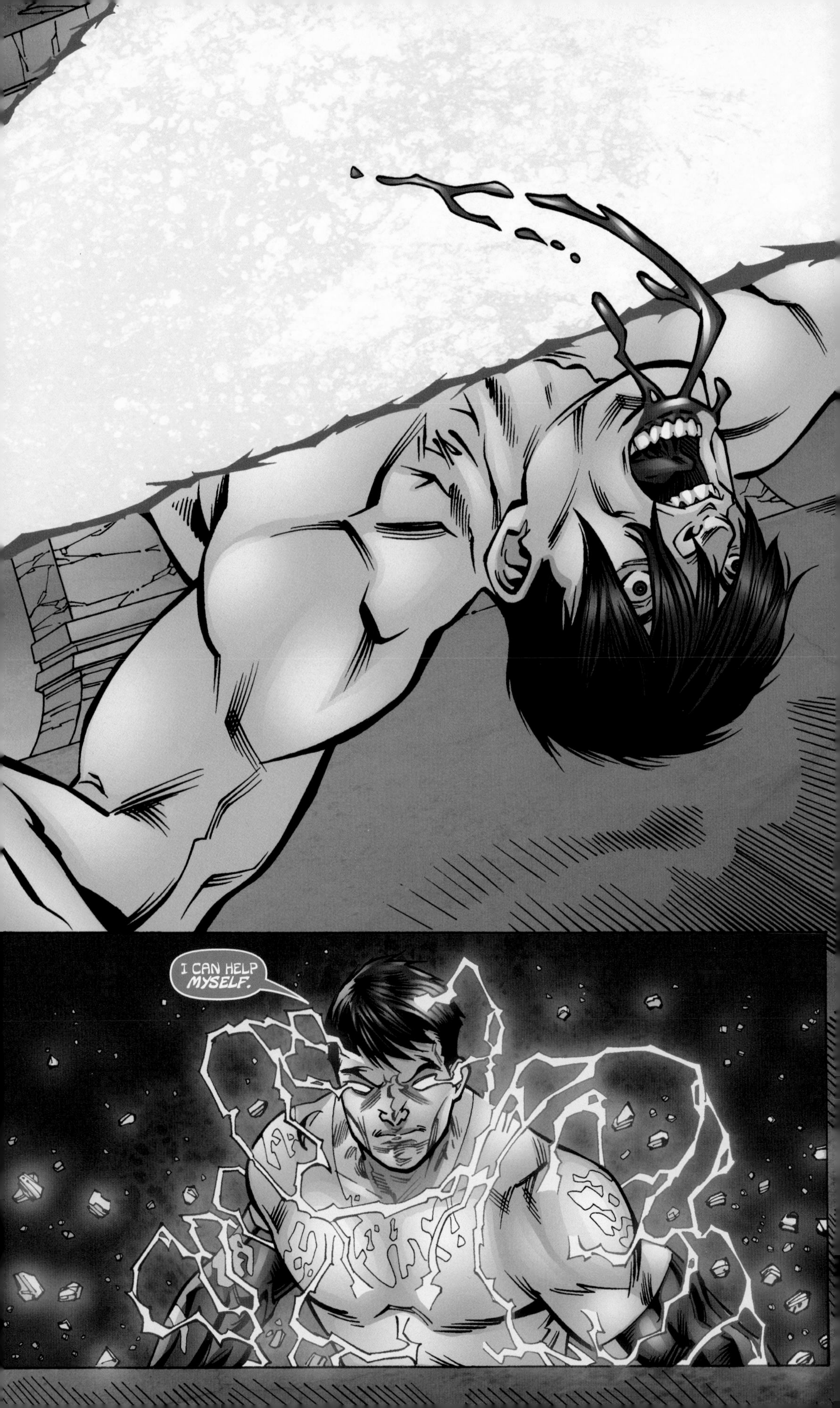
I CAN HELP MYSELF.

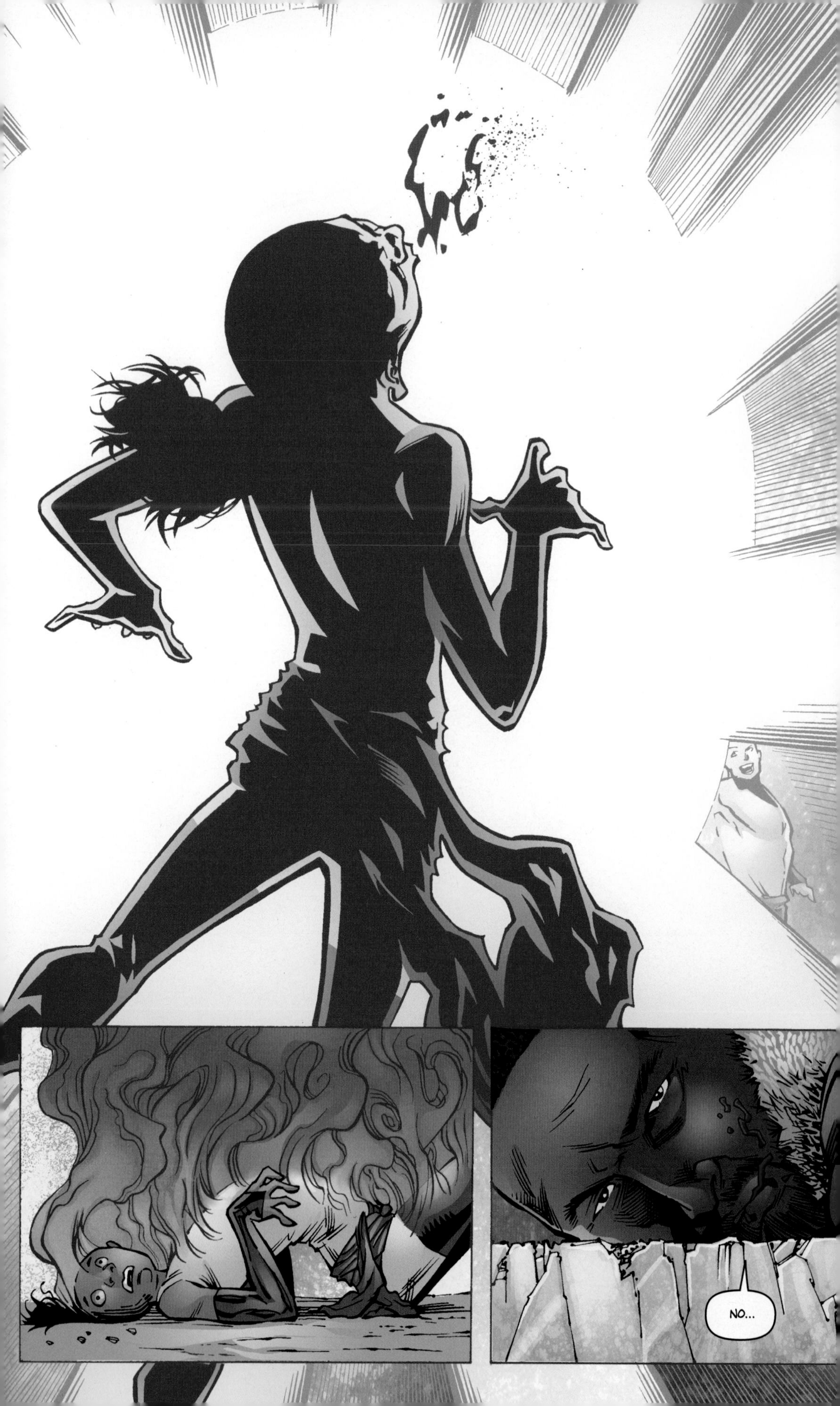
NO...

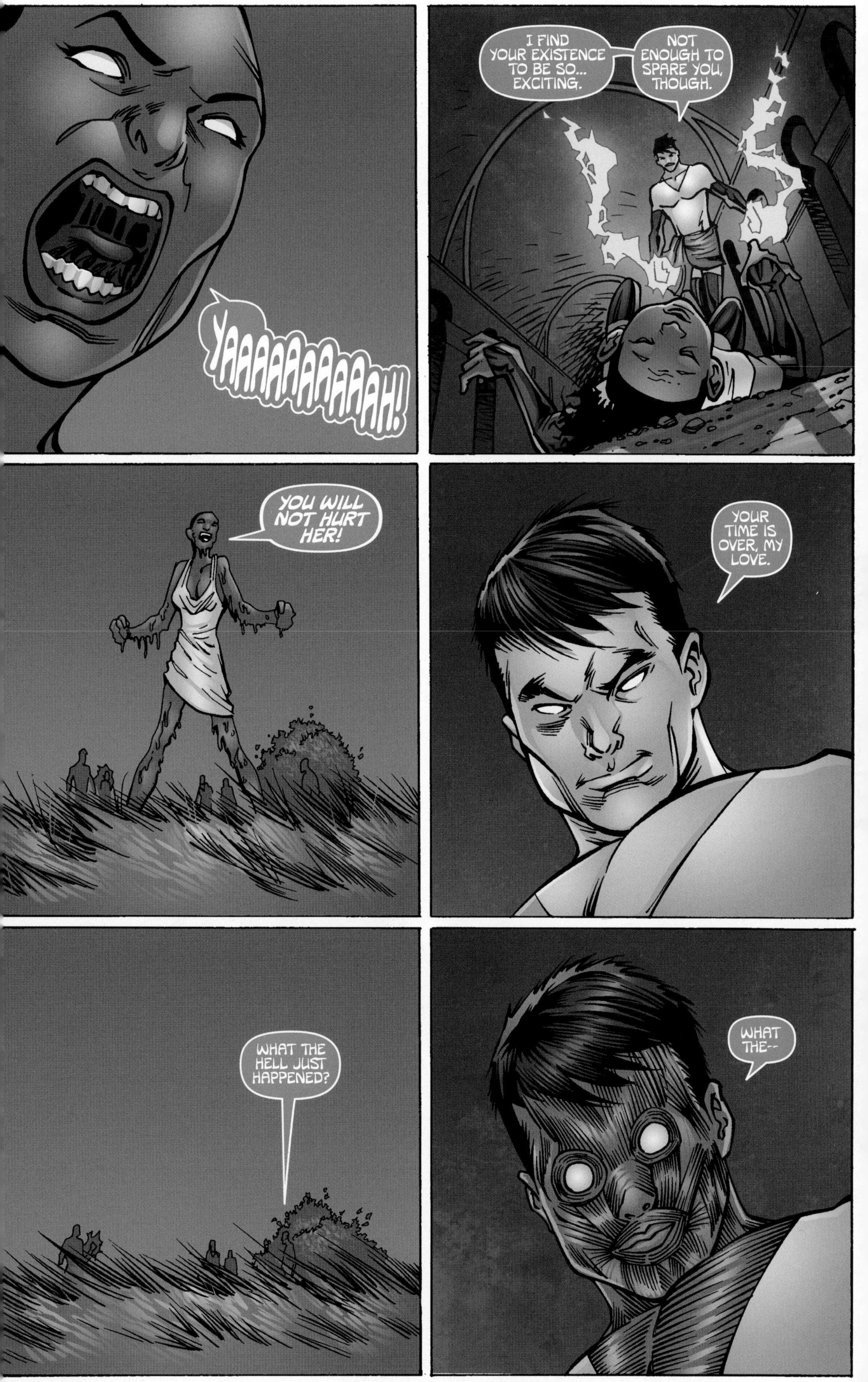
YAAAAAAAAAAAH!
I FIND YOUR EXISTENCE TO BE SO... EXCITING.
NOT ENOUGH TO SPARE YOU, THOUGH.
YOU WILL NOT HURT HER!
YOUR TIME IS OVER, MY LOVE.
WHAT THE HELL JUST HAPPENED?
WHAT THE--

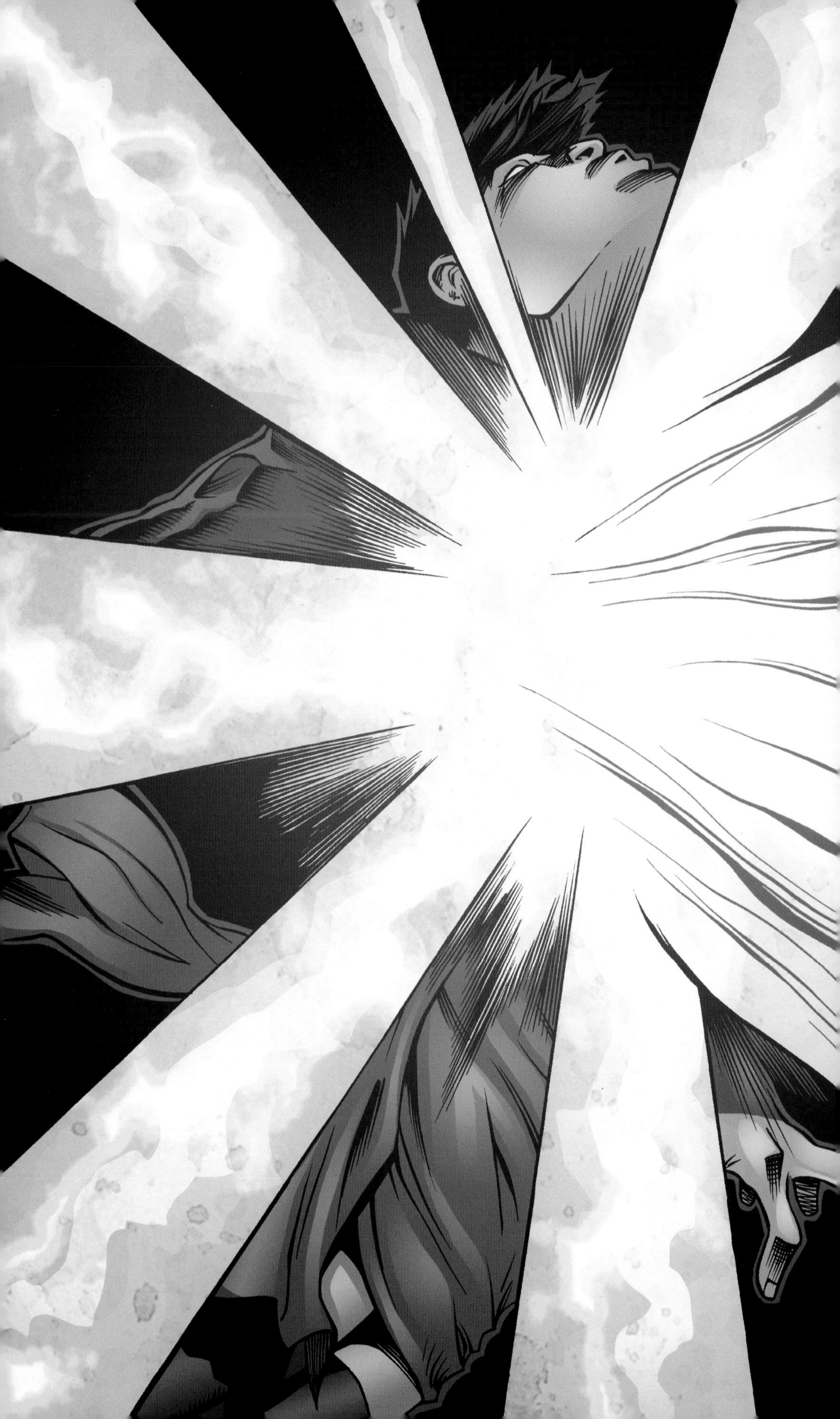

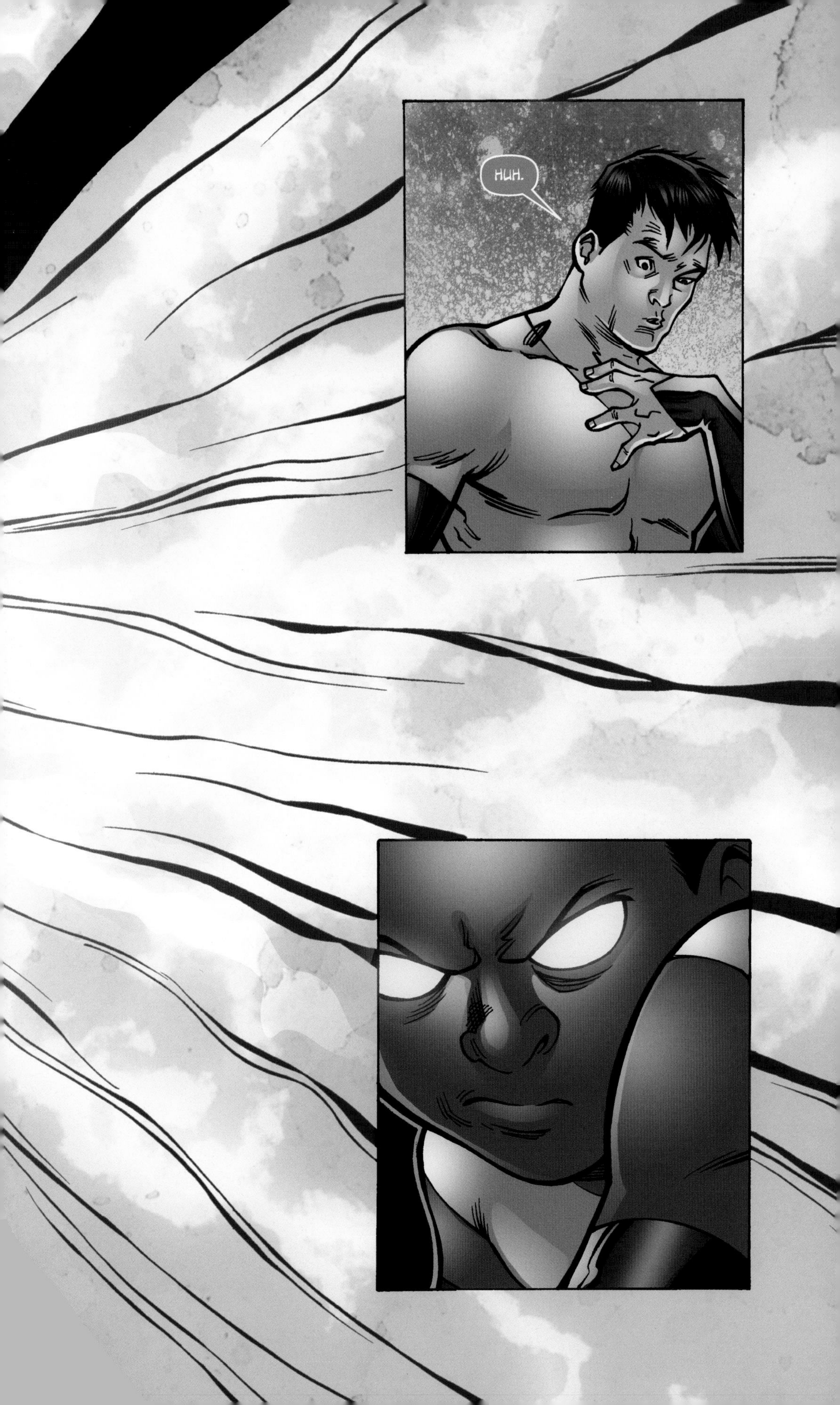
HUH.

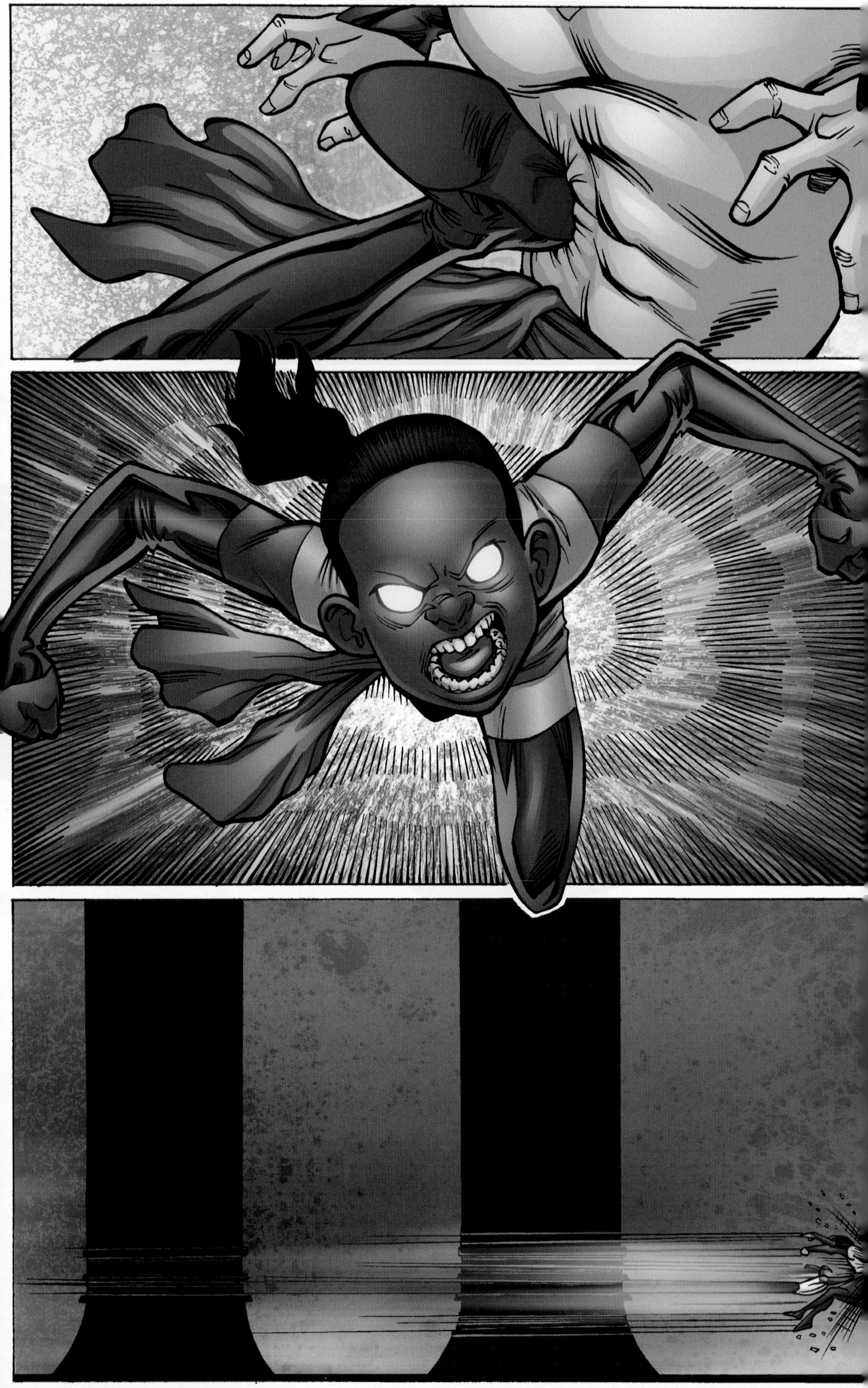

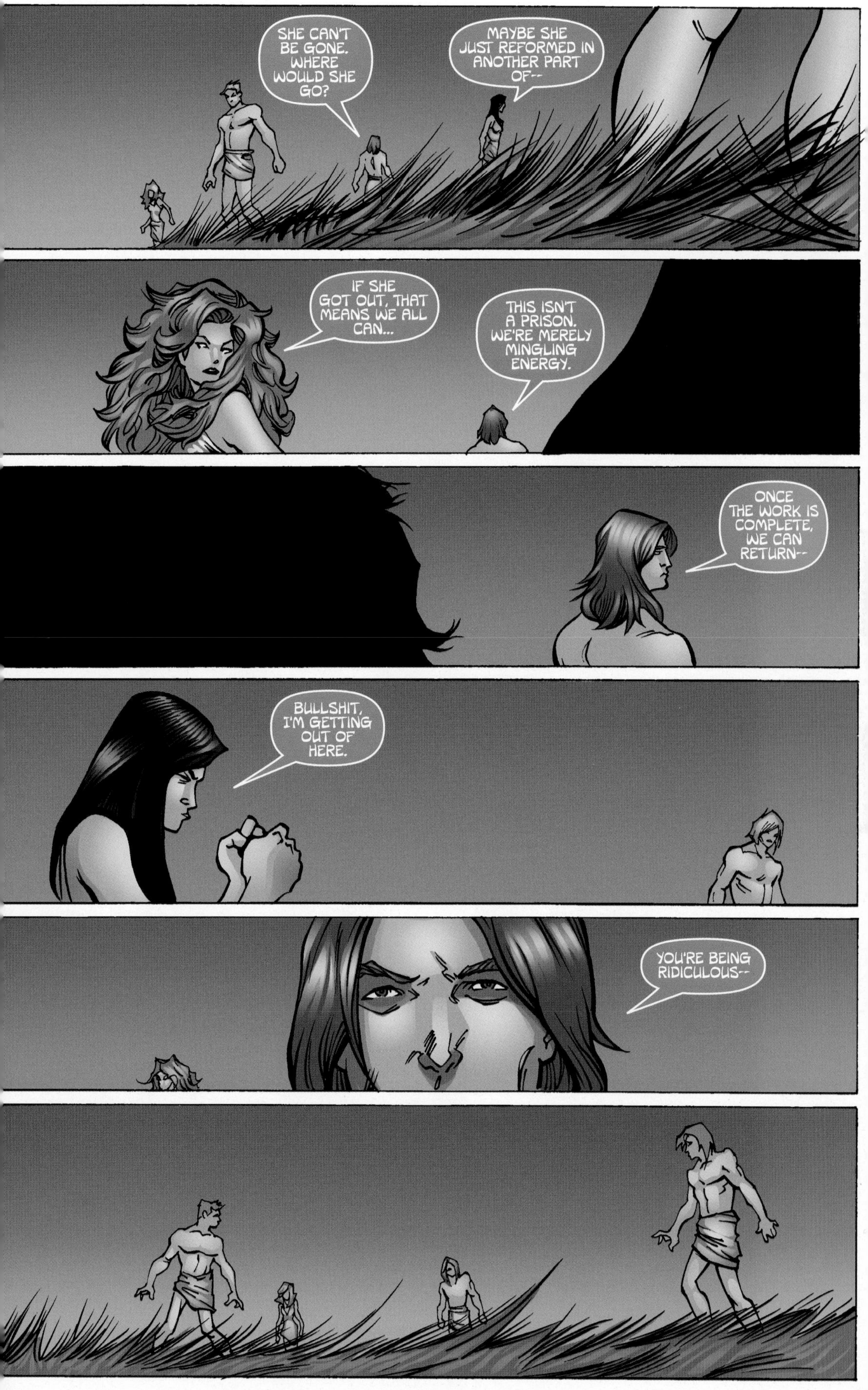
SHE CAN'T BE GONE. WHERE WOULD SHE GO?
MAYBE SHE JUST REFORMED IN ANOTHER PART OF--
IF SHE GOT OUT, THAT MEANS WE ALL CAN...
THIS ISN'T A PRISON. WE'RE MERELY MINGLING ENERGY.
ONCE THE WORK IS COMPLETE, WE CAN RETURN--
BULLSHIT, I'M GETTING OUT OF HERE.
YOU'RE BEING RIDICULOUS--

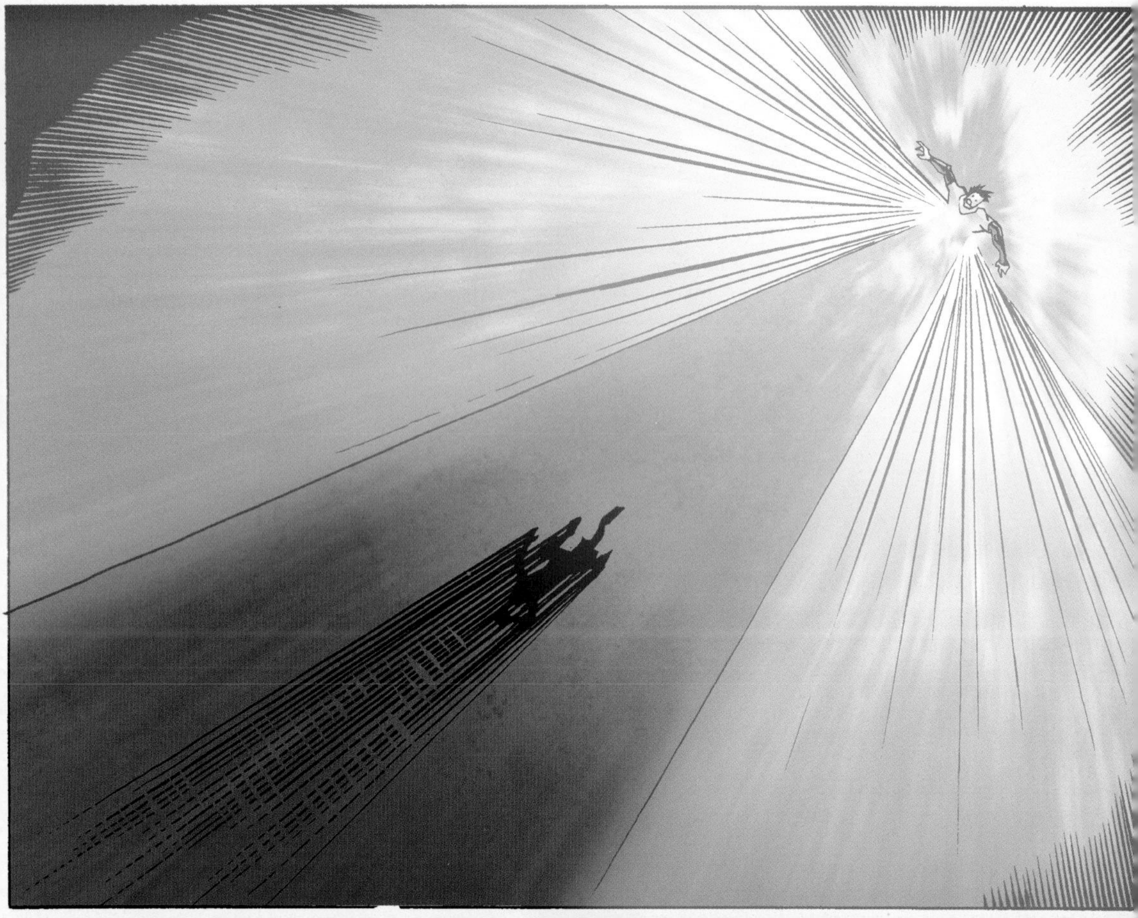
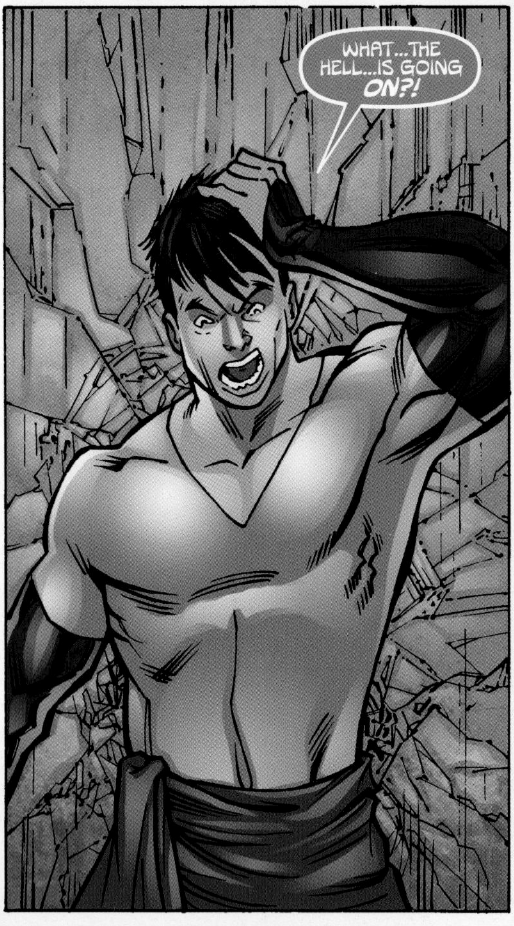
WHAT...THE HELL...IS GOING ON?!
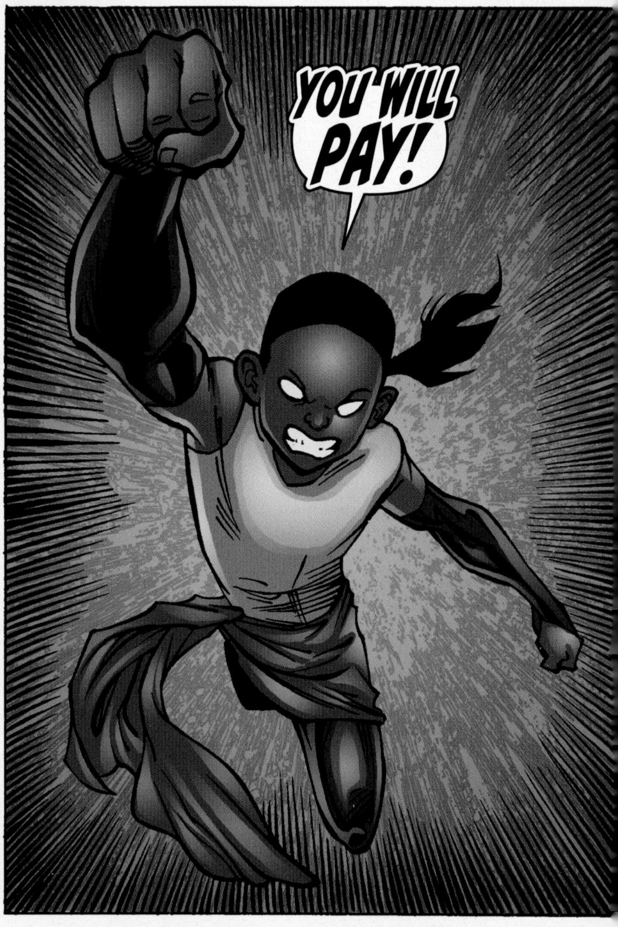
YOU WILL PAY!

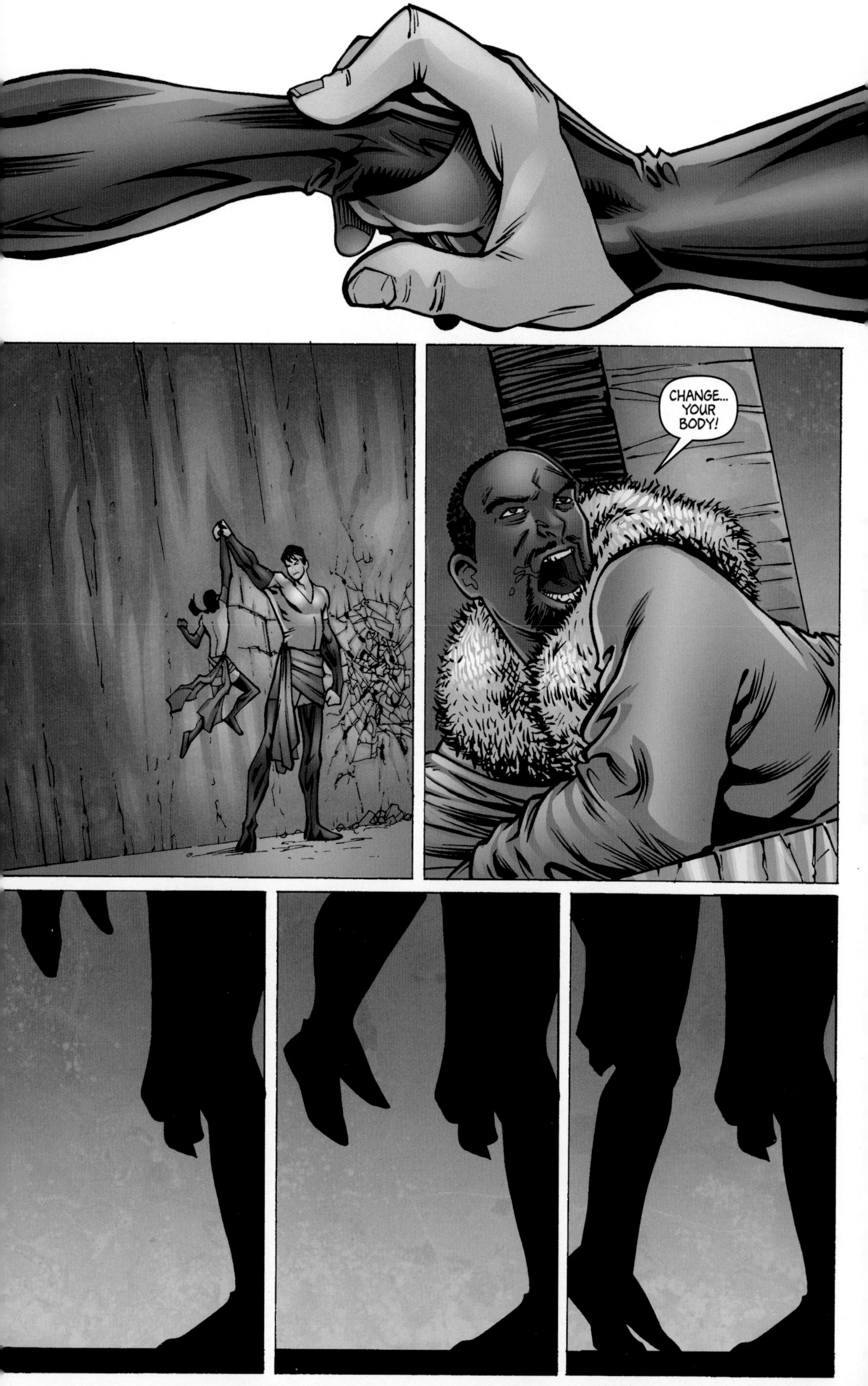
CHANGE... YOUR BODY!

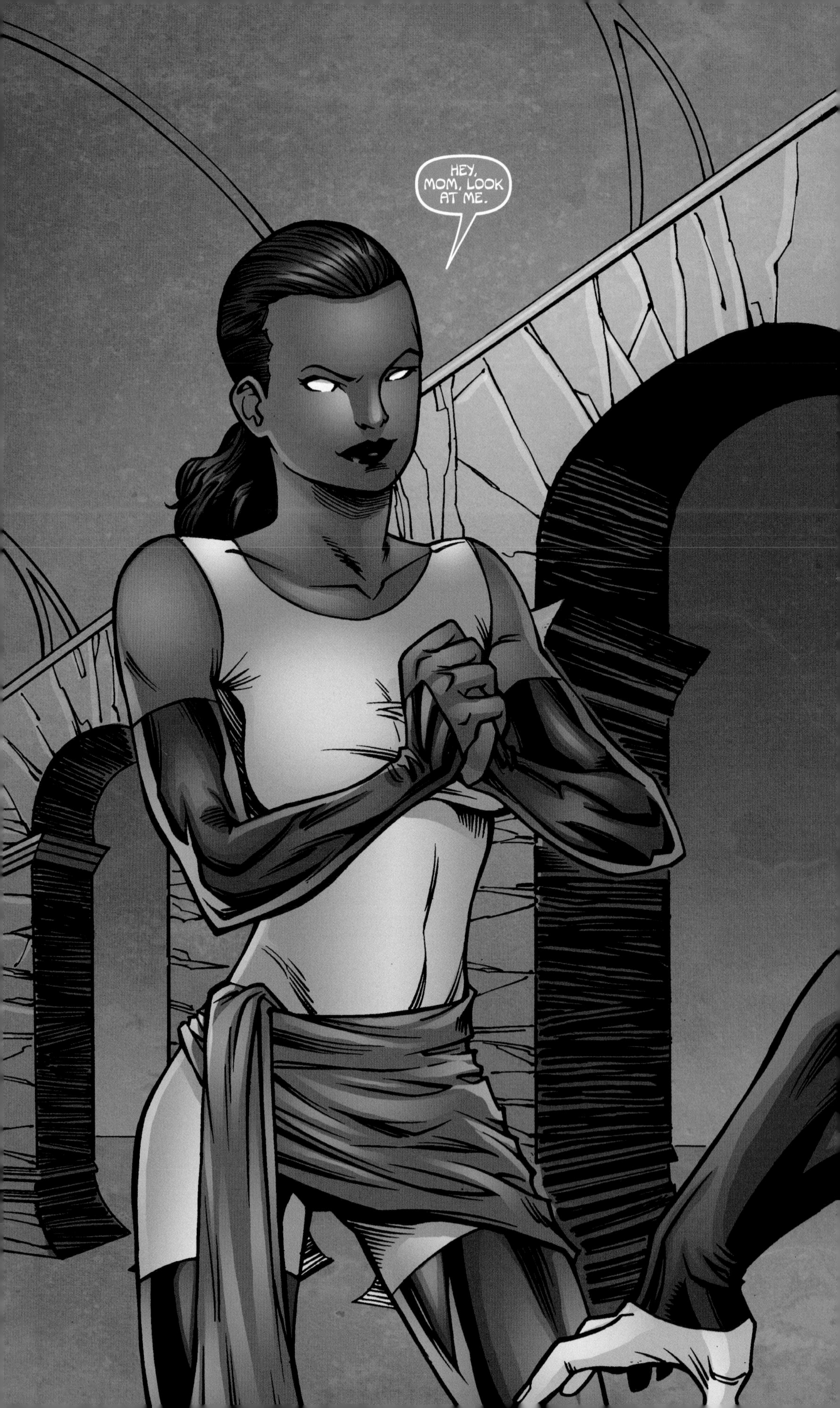
HEY, MOM, LOOK AT ME.

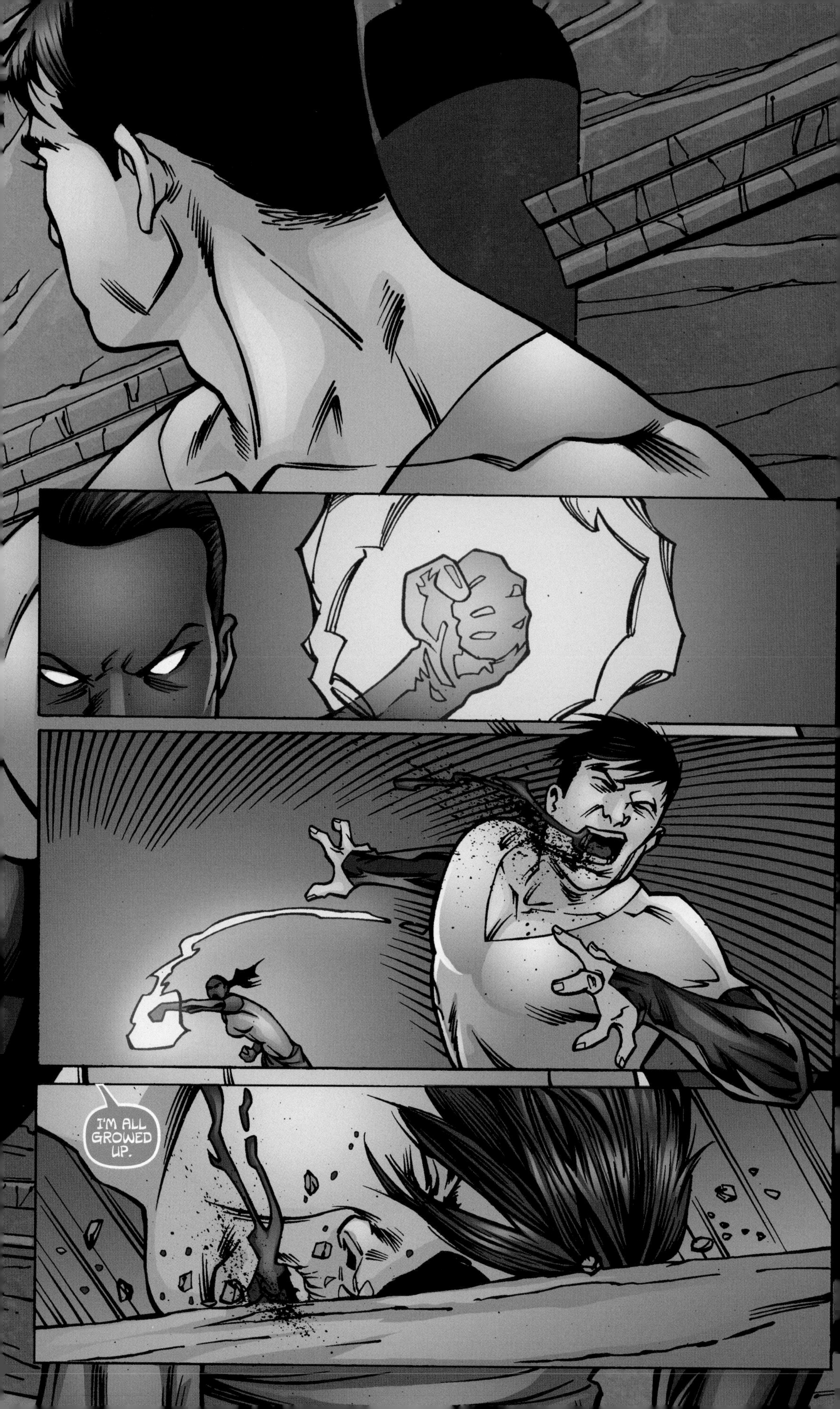
I'M ALL GROWED UP.

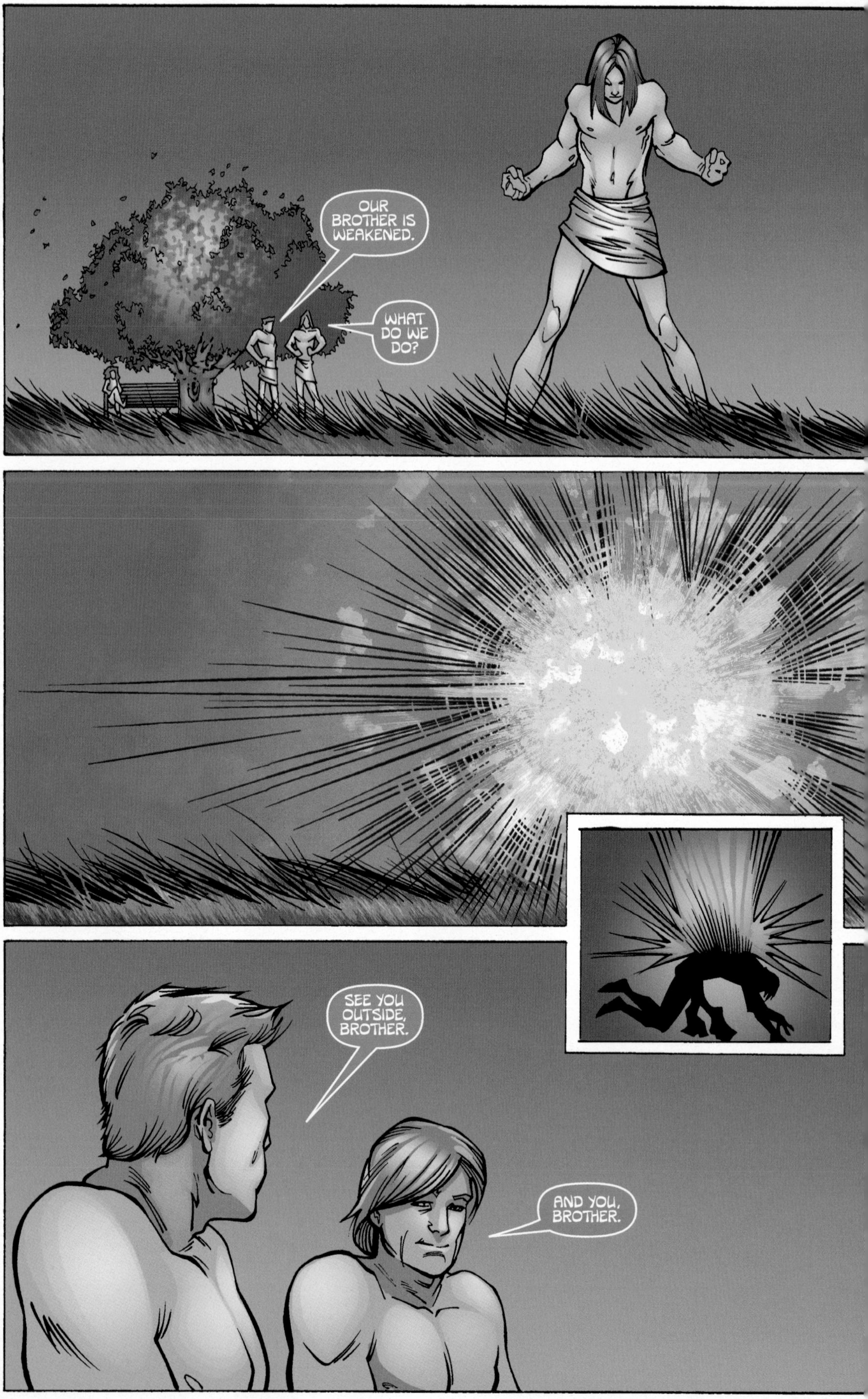
OUR BROTHER IS WEAKENED.
WHAT DO WE DO?
SEE YOU OUTSIDE, BROTHER.
AND YOU, BROTHER.

I WANT TO GET YOU TO SAFETY, AND THEN--

YOU...YOU HAVE TO KILL HIM.

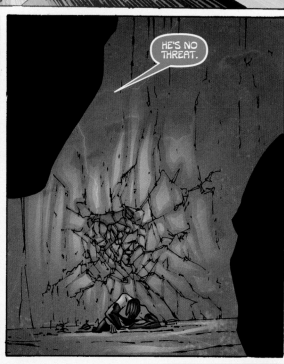

HE'S NO THREAT.

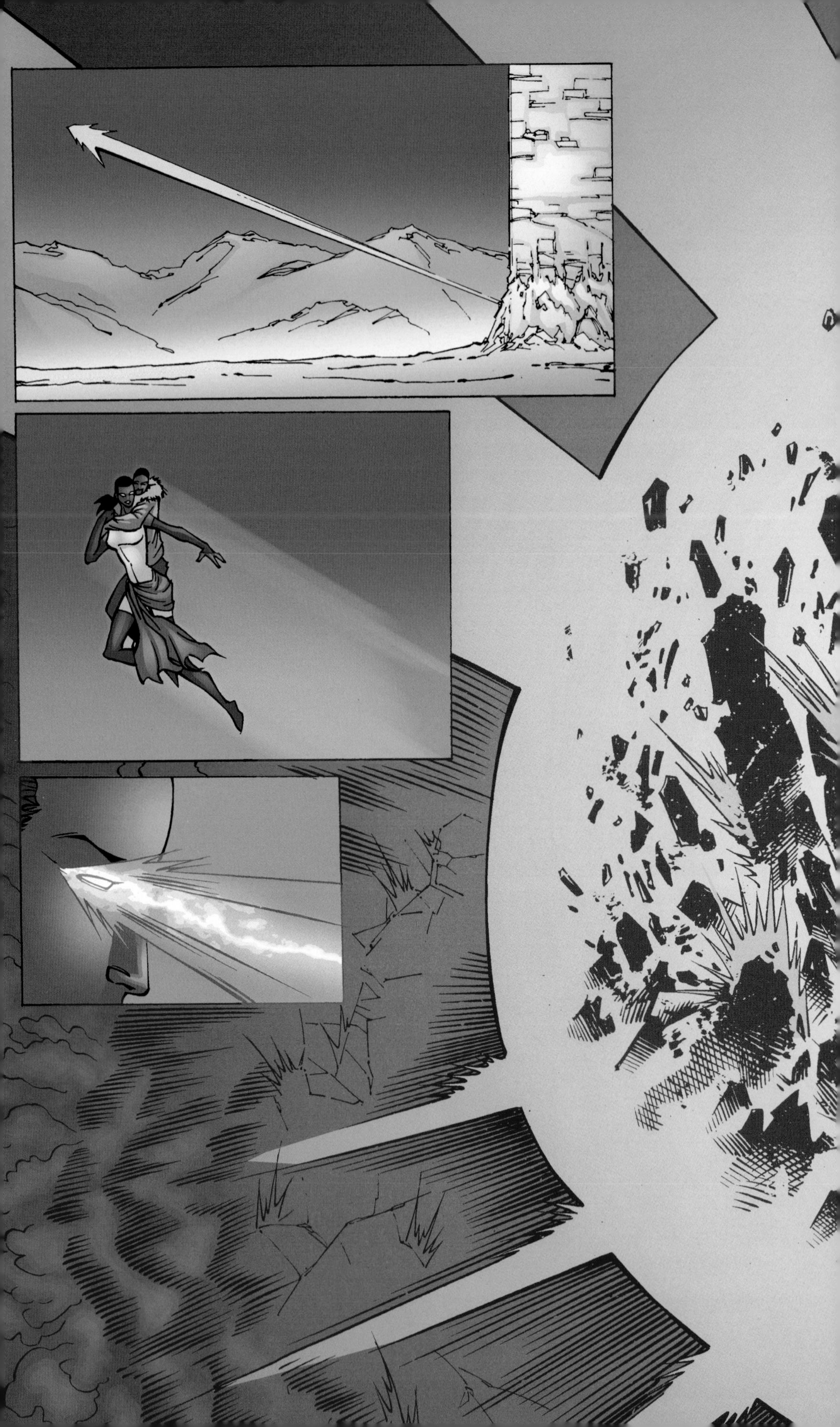

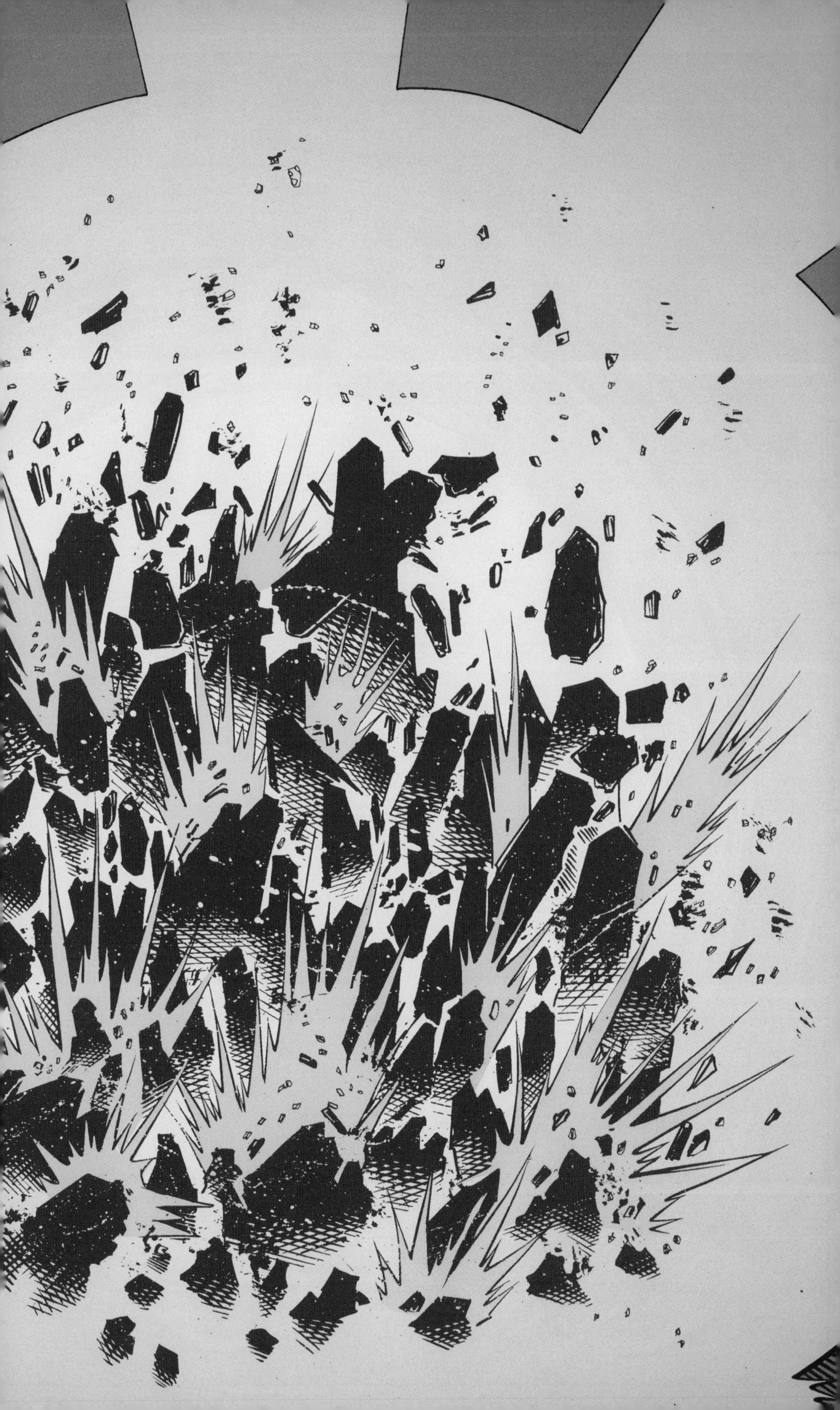

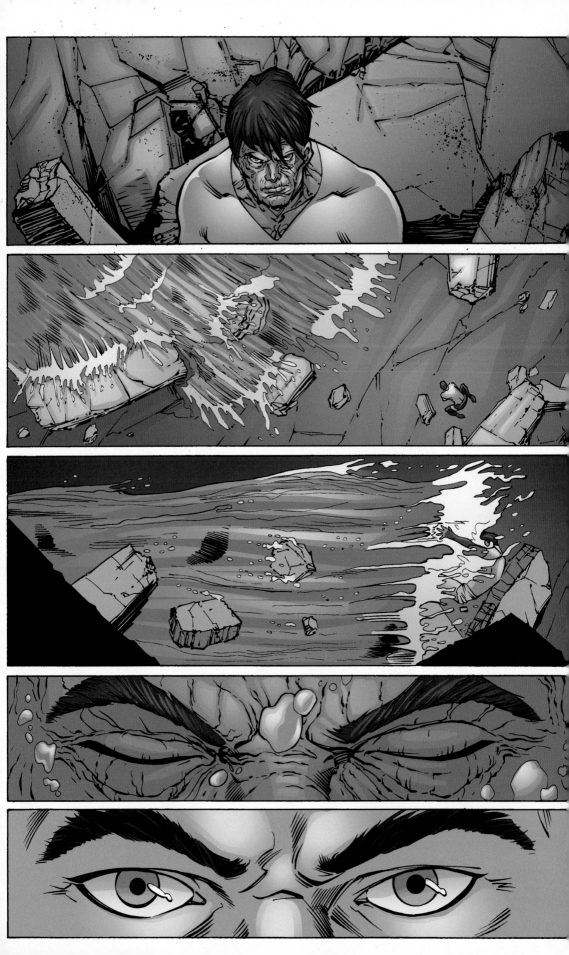

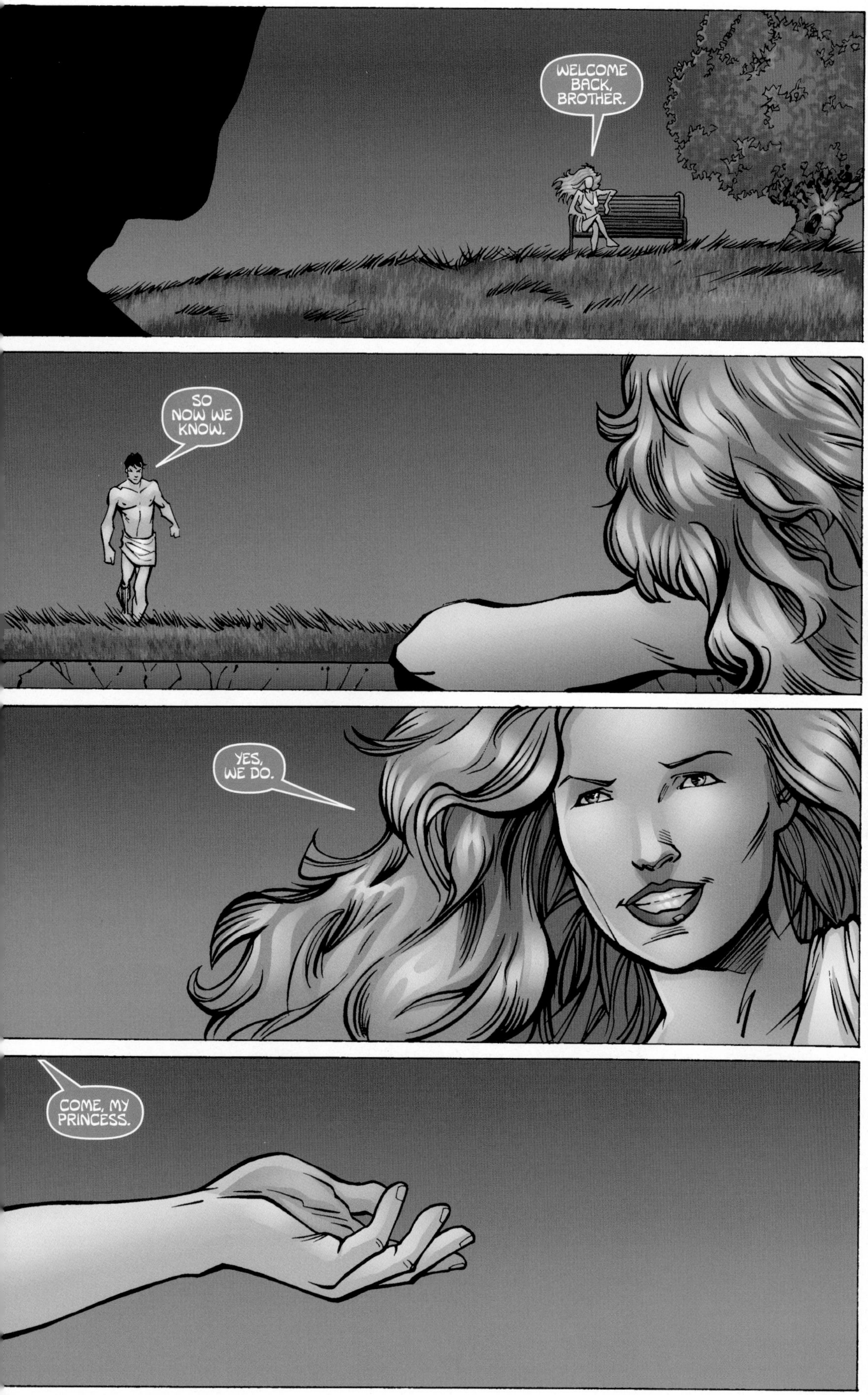

WELCOME BACK, BROTHER.
SO NOW WE KNOW.
YES, WE DO.
COME, MY PRINCESS.

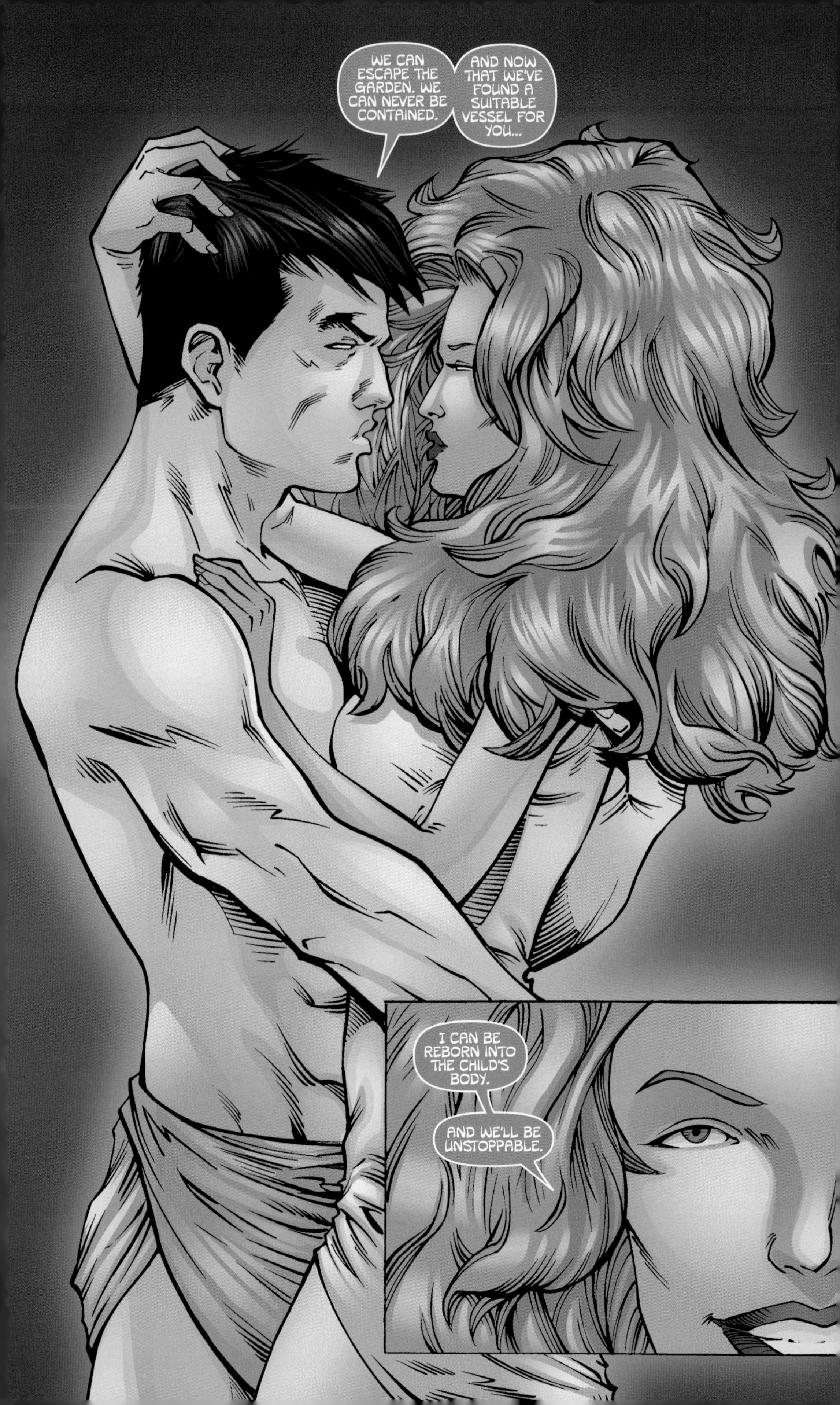
WE CAN ESCAPE THE GARDEN. WE CAN NEVER BE CONTAINED.
AND NOW THAT WE'VE FOUND A SUITABLE VESSEL FOR YOU...
I CAN BE REBORN INTO THE CHILD'S BODY.
AND WE'LL BE UNSTOPPABLE.

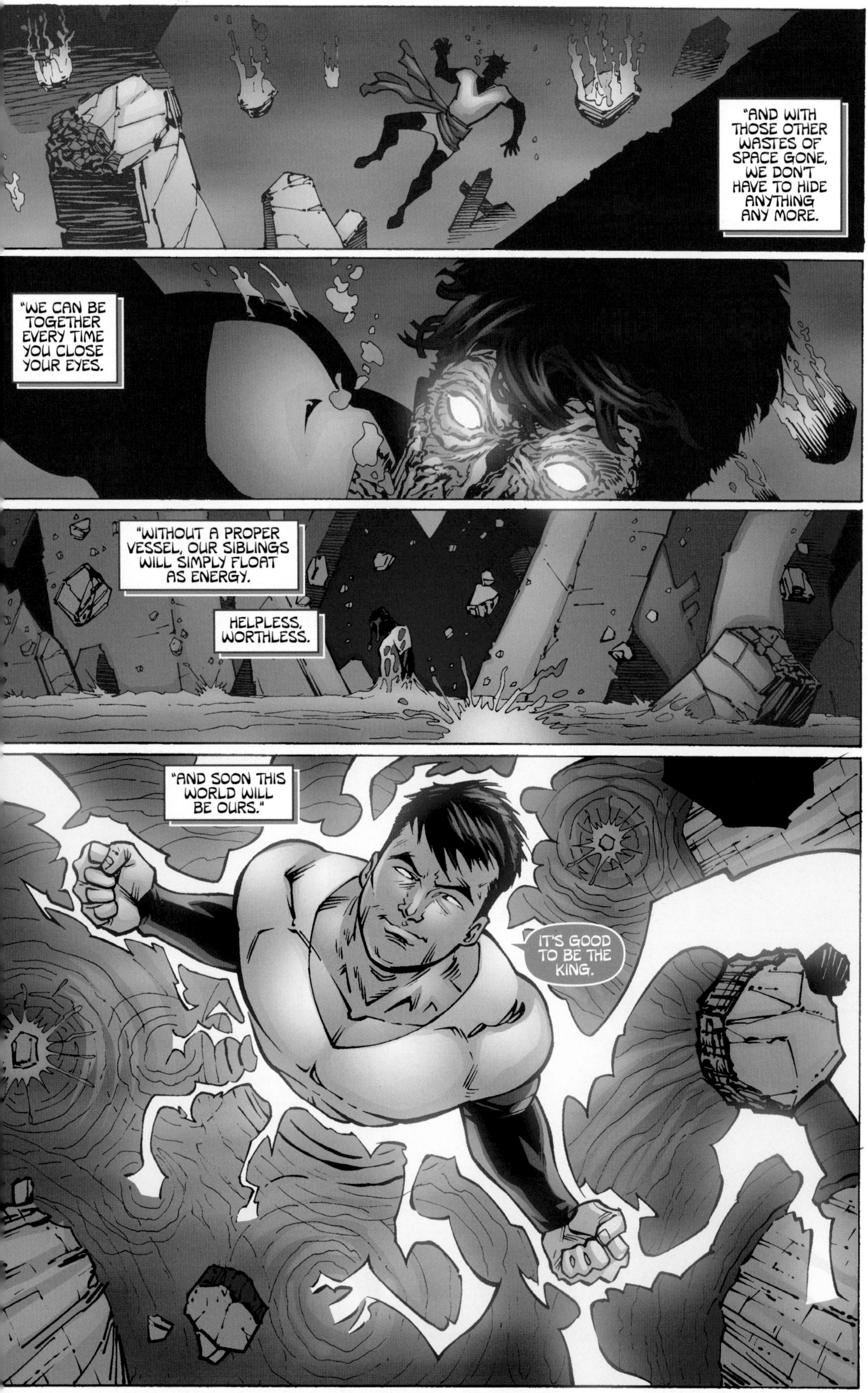
"AND WITH THOSE OTHER WASTES OF SPACE GONE, WE DON'T HAVE TO HIDE ANYTHING ANY MORE.
"WE CAN BE TOGETHER EVERY TIME YOU CLOSE YOUR EYES.
"WITHOUT A PROPER VESSEL, OUR SIBLINGS WILL SIMPLY FLOAT AS ENERGY.
HELPLESS, WORTHLESS.
"AND SOON THIS WORLD WILL BE OURS."
IT'S GOOD TO BE THE KING.

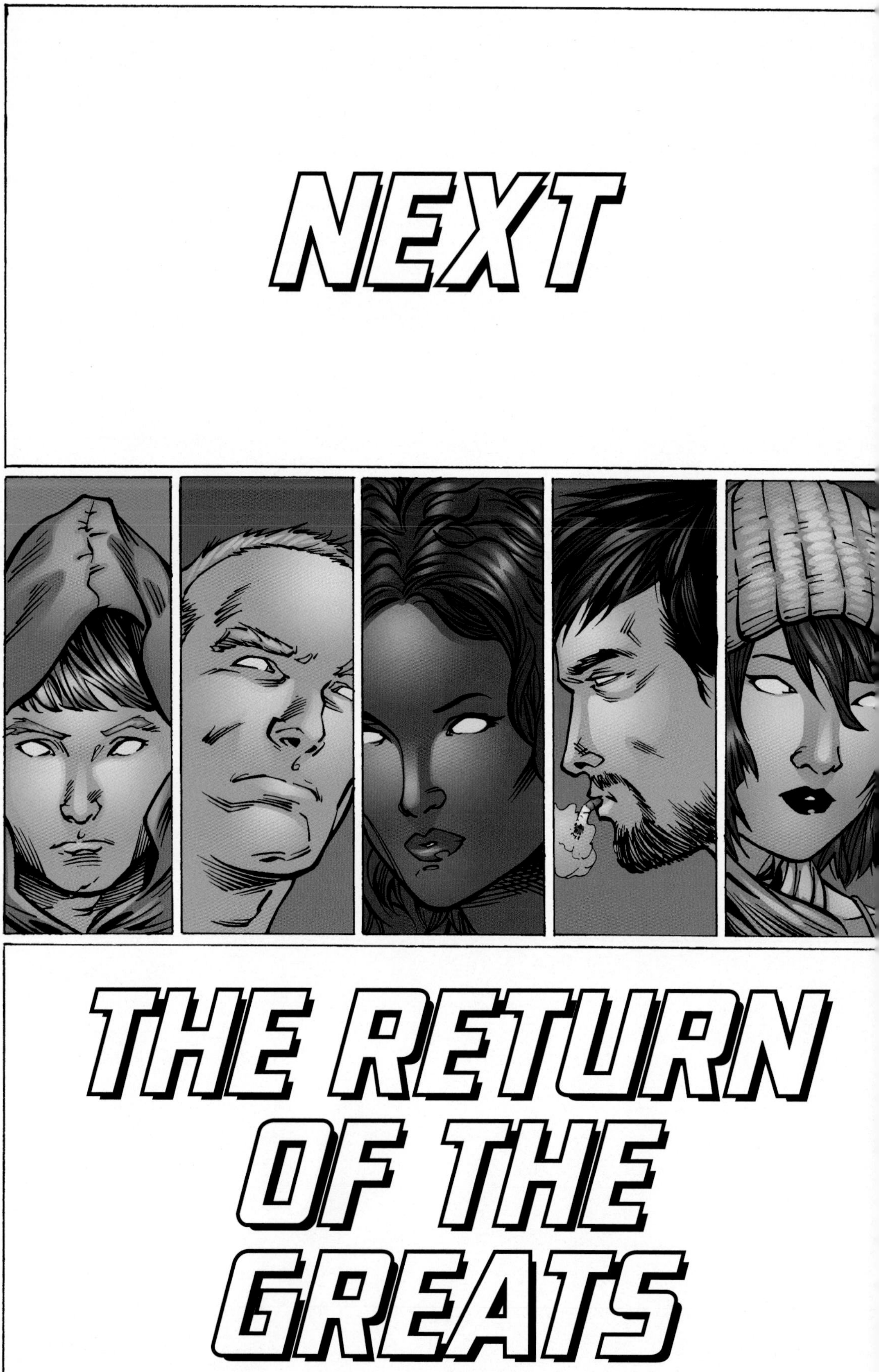
NEXT
THE RETURN OF THE GREATS

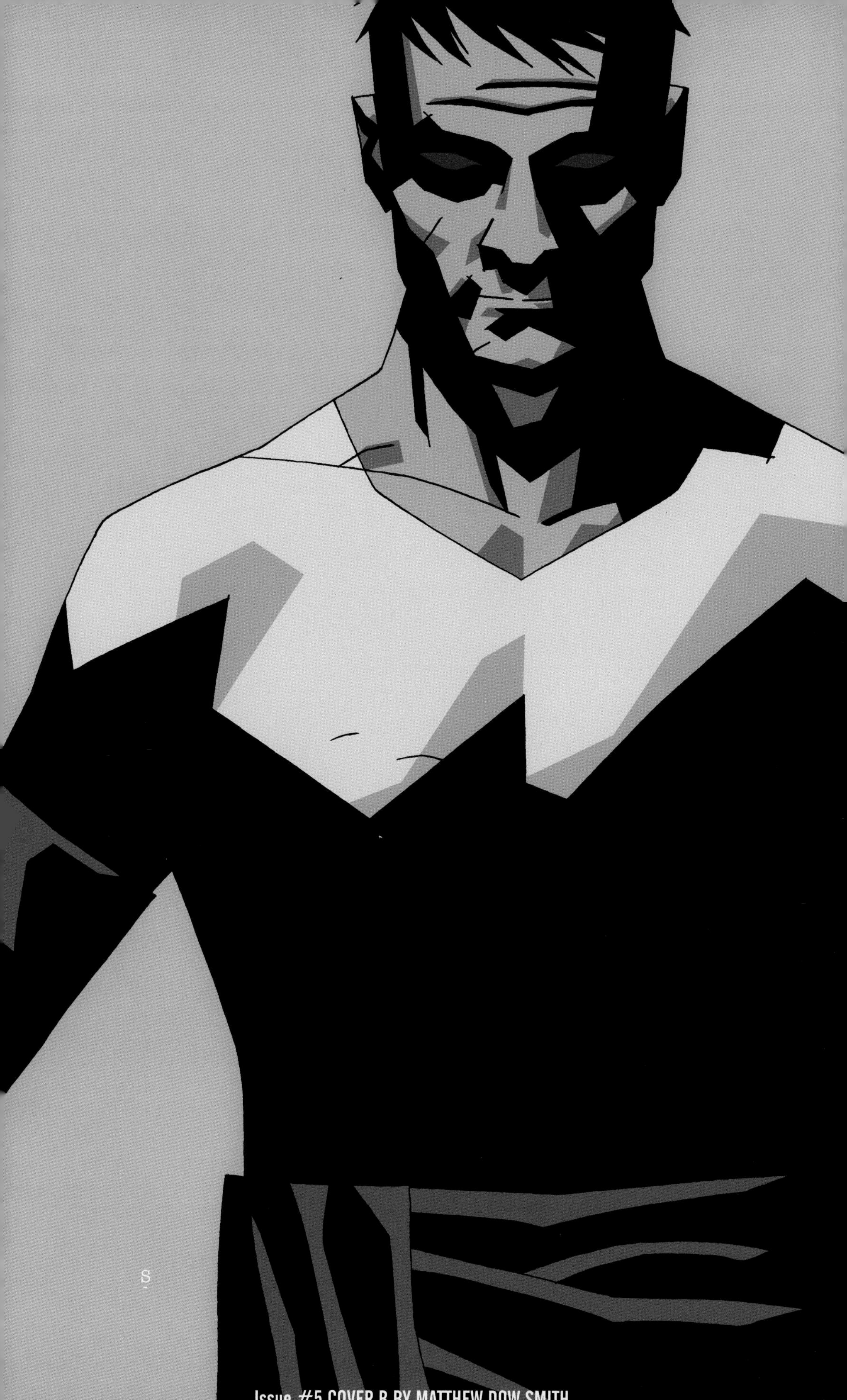

Issue #5 COVER B BY MATTHEW DOW SMITH

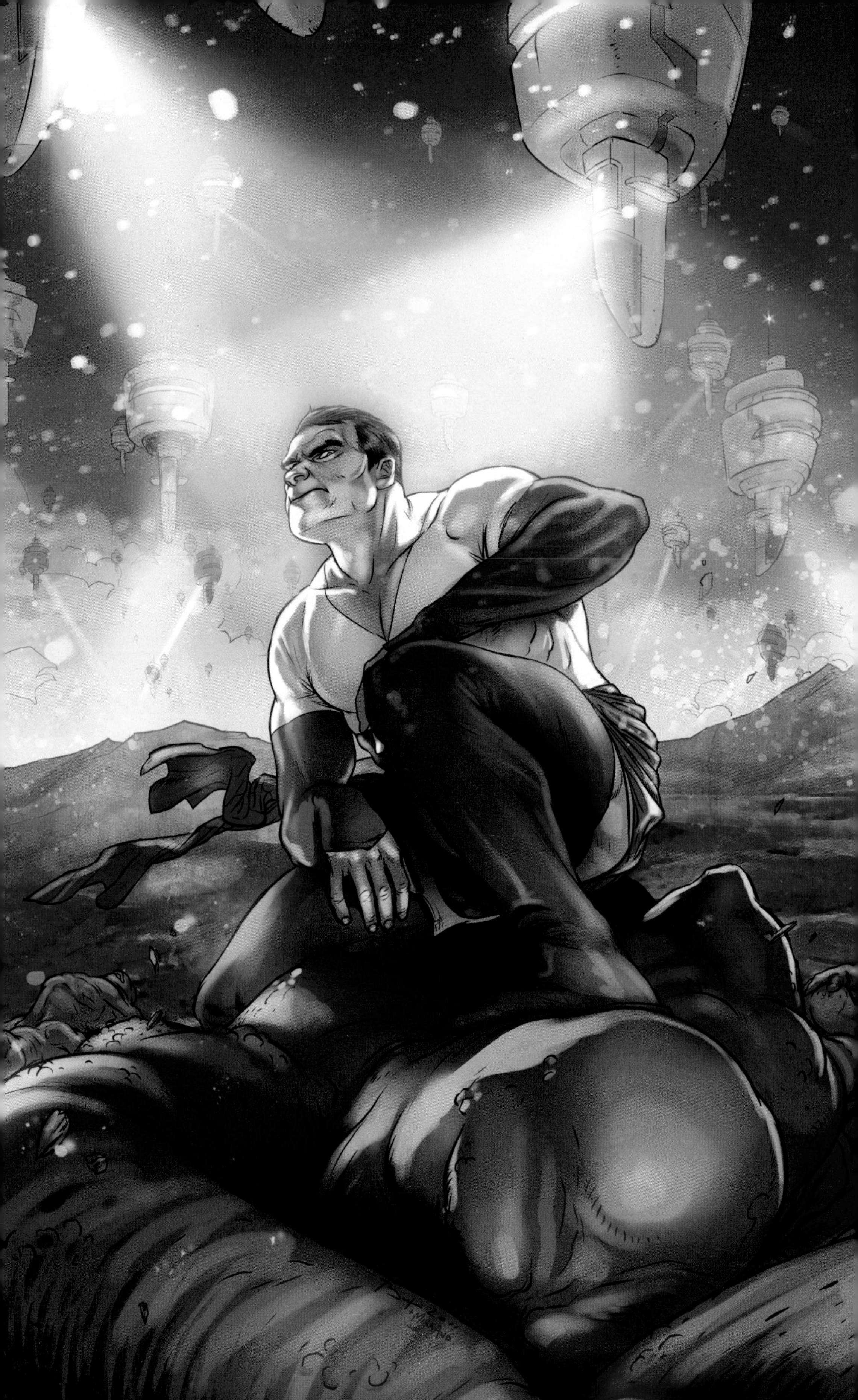

ALT. COVER BY ENNIO BUFI and MIRKA ANDOLFO

ALT. COVER BY ROB DAKAR MELI and MIRKA ANDOLFO

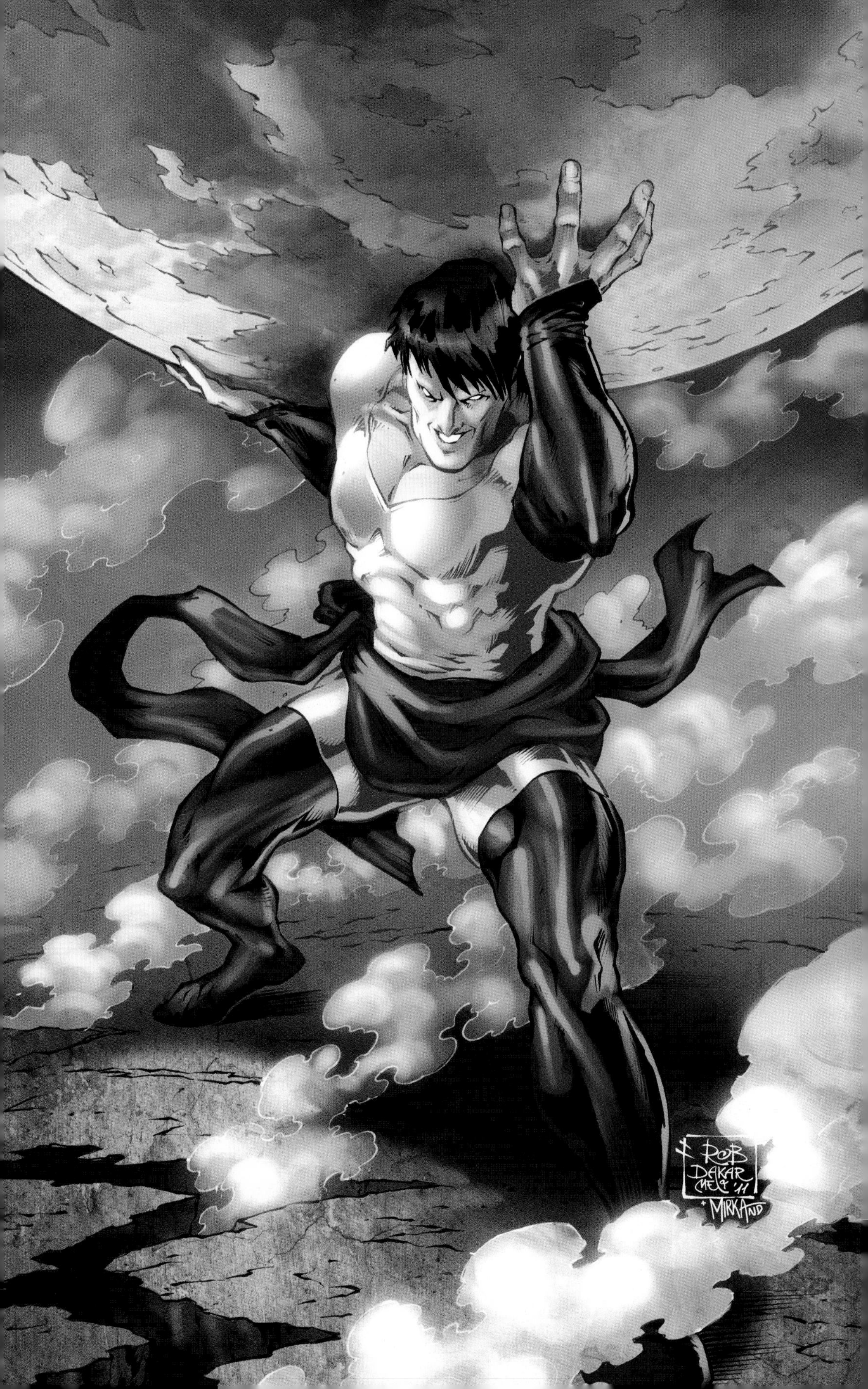

ALT. COVER BY MIRKA ANDOLFO

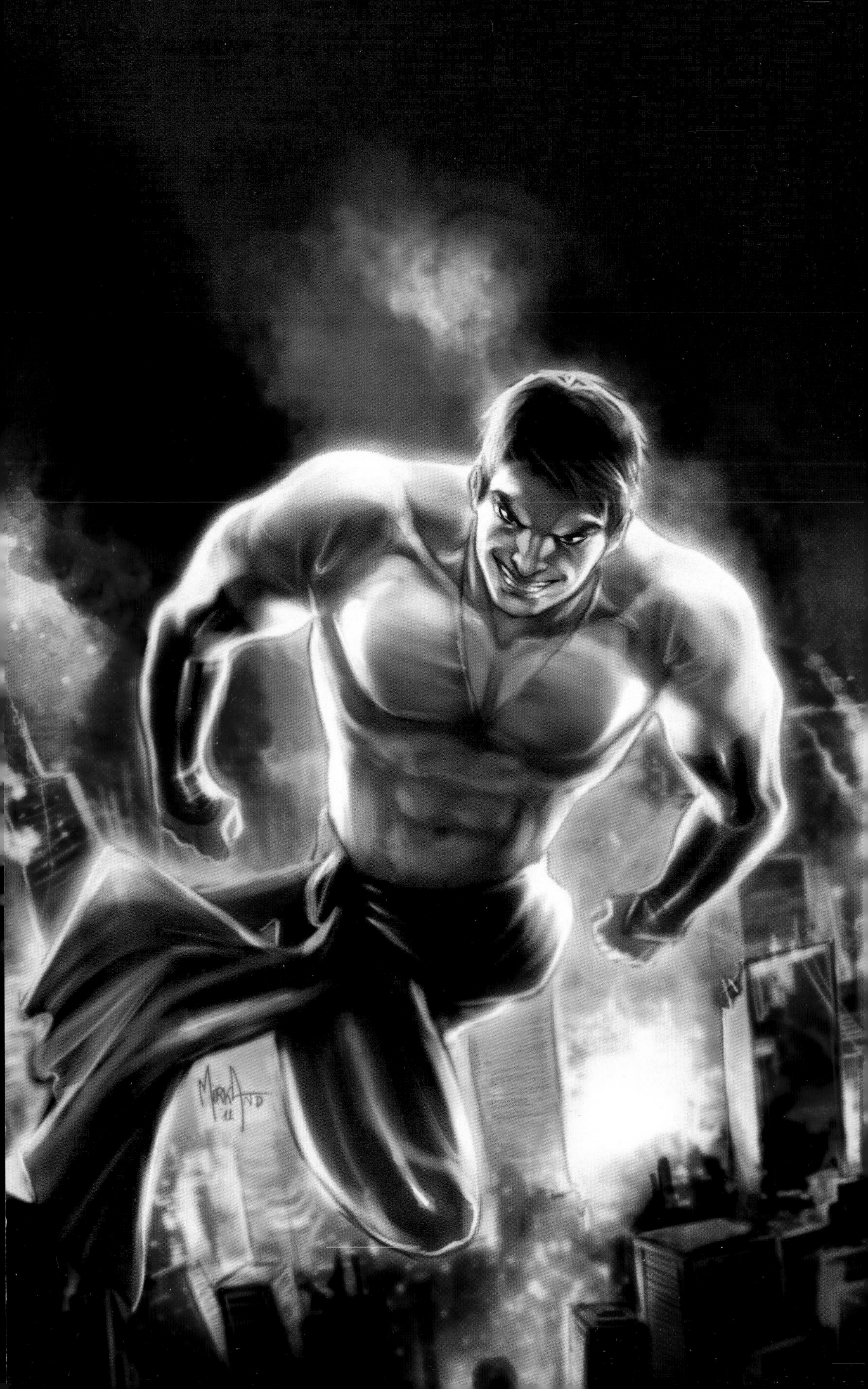